PENGUIN BOOKS

THE ACTOR'S BOOK OF CLASSICAL MONOLOGUES

STEFAN RUDNICKI was born in Krakow, Poland, and lived in Stockholm, Sweden, and Montreal, Canada, before arriving in the United States—where he was educated principally at Columbia University and the Yale School of Drama.

In addition to having directed more than one hundred and twenty theatrical productions in New York, regional theatre, and abroad (more than a quarter of them classics and fifteen by Shakespeare), he is also an actor, producer, award-winning playwright, photographer, and film and video director.

He has taught at the University of Rochester, the Eastman School of Music, New York University, Dartmouth College, and Long Island University's C. W. Post Campus, where for six years he chaired the Department of Theatre and Film.

He has been Artistic Director of Skyboat Road Company since 1979, and with his wife, Judith, lives in New York City, developing new media projects, teaching privately, and evolving his "Interactive Matrix Process" for performers.

THE
ACTOR'S BOOK
OF
CLASSICAL
MONOLOGUES

COLLECTED AND INTRODUCED BY
Stefan Rudnicki

PENGUIN BOOKS

PENGUIN BOOKS
Published by the Penguin Group
Viking Penguin Inc., 40 West 23rd Street,
New York, New York 10010, U.S.A.
Penguin Books Ltd, 27 Wrights Lane,
London W8 5TZ, England
Penguin Books Australia Ltd, Ringwood,
Victoria, Australia
Penguin Books Canada Ltd, 2801 John Street,
Markham, Ontario, Canada L3R 1B4
Penguin Books (N.Z.) Ltd, 182–190 Wairau Road,
Auckland 10, New Zealand

Penguin Books Ltd, Registered Offices:
Harmondsworth, Middlesex, England

First published in Penguin Books 1988
Published simultaneously in Canada

1 3 5 7 9 10 8 6 4 2

Portions of this book first appeared in the author's earlier publications,
Classical Monologues 1: Shakespeare and *Classical Monologues 2: Shakespeare
and Friends*. Copyright © Stefan Rudnicki, 1979, 1980.

Page 317 constitutes an extension of this copyright page.

LIBRARY OF CONGRESS CATALOGING IN PUBLICATION DATA
The Actor's book of classical monologues / edited by Stefan Rudnicki.
p. cm.
1. Monologues. 2. Acting. 3. Greek drama. 4. English drama.
I. Rudnicki, Stefan, 1945–
PN2080.A283   1988
882'.01'08—dc19   88-1378
ISBN 0 14 01.0676 6

Printed in the United States of America by
R. R. Donnelley & Sons Company, Harrisonburg, Virginia
Set in Caledonia
Designed by Robert Bull

ACKNOWLEDGMENTS

I wish to thank Will Nixon and Laura Ross of Viking Penguin for their conceptual and editorial contributions respectively; Ralph Pine of Drama Book Publishers, who published and nurtured the original Classical Monologues series; the translators of the Greek material—in particular Kenneth Cavander and William Arrowsmith, whose work I have performed and staged and admired for many years; my wife, Judith Cummings, who has been involved in every phase of this enterprise and whose commitment to the magic of the spoken word has been a continuing inspiration to me; and finally the actors, all of them, who persist in drawing life from the obscurity of centuries past.

It is to the actors, with their unique ability to compress all history into a single present moment, that this volume is dedicated.

Stefan Rudnicki
New York City, 1988

CONTENTS

Other Tragedies
Introduction 53

Choruses, Comics, and Messengers
Introduction 74

THE AGE OF SHAKESPEARE
Sixteenth- and Seventeenth-Century English Monologues
Introduction 95

WILLIAM SHAKESPEARE

Heroic
Introduction 97

Romance and Comedy
Introduction 128

MONOLOGUES FOR WOMEN

King Lear
Introduction 166

SHAKESPEARE'S FRIENDS

Sermons, Prayers, Tales, and Dreams
Introduction 173

Arguments and Entertainments
Introduction 206

THE AGE OF STYLE
Restoration and Eighteenth-Century
English Monologues
Introduction 233

Comedy of Wit
Introduction 235

Comedy of Character and Situation
Introduction 252

Tragedy
Introduction 276

Romance
Introduction 291

Parodies
Introduction 305

T H E
ACTOR'S BOOK
O F
CLASSICAL
MONOLOGUES

General Introduction

Preparing a classical monologue need not be the chore or the terror many actors seem to find it. This collection is conceived as a tool for actor and student, a guide to the preparation of classical material without benefit of director, production concept, or acting ensemble.

It is not my intention to provide a substitute for an intelligent reading of the complete text of any play; indeed the actor is urged to see each monologue as much as possible in the context of the role. Neither am I interested in imposing exclusively scholarly interpretations on the material. Rather, I offer a simple interpretive focus for each piece that is addressed to an actor's problems exclusively.

I have chosen material that makes dramatic sense even when removed from the plot and thematic support of a full play. Where a speech does not naturally have a beginning, a middle, and an end, I have sometimes interpolated other material to supply the missing component. In other cases, I have taken portions of several speeches (sometimes from different scenes) and devised a composite in order to give an actor something worth wrestling with.

I am also concerned that each monologue have the potential to involve the actor in an active, positive manner with his external surroundings, so I have avoided those pieces that are for the most part introspective in focus or passive in tone.

None of the Shakespeare monologues has received exposure so excessive as to render it tiresomely common, and many of the other selections are unknown outside of a small circle of specialists. Greek drama in particular has long been ignored by actors, and it is my hope that this book will encourage a revival of interest in this valuable resource. I believe that the less familiar an audition speech, the more likely that it will be heard with attention.

The monologues are generally two to three minutes in length.

It is better to proceed slowly, rather than racing through to the finish, and it is always wiser to choose a shorter scene than one that is too long. For those pieces that might run over three minutes, I have indicated cuts for briefer versions.

To aid the actor in structuring his work, I have placed beats where there may be natural pauses, decisions, or transitions. These are meant to provide a map of the scene, and are not meant to be followed slavishly. I have tried to indicate a plausible resting place within the first three lines of each scene, to allow the actor a chance to pause, evaluate his opening, and change focus or calm nerves as necessary. The pattern of beats is less consistent in the Greek section, where I have tried to remain as faithful as possible to the punctuation and structure of each translator.

Although I address the reader as "actor," I hope that this book will be useful to other theatre professionals and to students in a variety of disciplines as well. I do, however, assume an active involvement with the text.

Acting

It is my assumption that a good actor's work is essentially the same whether he is preparing an entire role, a scene for class, or an audition piece, and that this preparation begins with a careful and detailed development of the relationships implicit in the material and in the situation in which the work is to be performed or shown. Each positive choice the actor makes places him in a new relationship to others (imaginary persons, other actors, or audience), his environment (including costumes, props, and the very space he occupies), his own physical being, and the words he is to speak. The more detailed the choices and the fuller the actor's involvement, the richer the matrix of relationships becomes. It is that matrix, rather than some vague mental image derived from preconceptions and the imitation of others, that defines characterization at its best.

Most often bypassed by an actor in search of emotional truth is his relationship to his text. In classical material, especially verse, the specifics of that relationship are crucial. I asked a class once why King Lear spoke in verse, and was told that it was because people spoke like that in those days. Perhaps some future generation of students will come to a similar conclusion about why *La Bohème* was written to be sung.

Verse speech and song are similar in that they are extensions beyond "normal" forms of experience and expression. Whether the verse derives from heightened emotion, extreme public formality, or some other source, the actor must be prepared to make the text entirely his own, a direct manifestation of his own personal choices.

Classical verse must be rehearsed aloud. The way a word or phrase sounds when spoken, screamed, or whispered may often provide the key to a whole scene. An intensely honest and talented actor I knew, a week before opening as Vendice in *The Revenger's Tragedy*, was on the verge of going to a hypnotist for help in learning his lines—a last resort. None of his usual study techniques were of any use until another actor, with considerable classical experience, took him for an evening stroll. After a couple of hours of shouting lines to the moon and tall trees, the problem was solved and Vendice was on his way to a brilliant portrayal. Whether the playwright is Shakespeare or Tourneur, much of the actor's work has been done in the writing: it lives in the sounds and rhythms of the words themselves.

Choosing a Monologue

I have tried to suggest in many instances the sort of actor who should or should not attempt a particular monologue, but mostly with reference to fairly traditional interpretations. I do not wish to discourage innovative work. Women especially should look carefully at the men's selections. Considering the relative dearth of good and appropriate material for women, they should perhaps consider all classical roles fair game.

THE
GOLDEN
AGE

Monologues from Greek Drama

Introduction

> It would not be too much to say that myth is the secret opening through which the inexhaustible energies of the cosmos pour into human cultural manifestation. Religions, philosophies, arts, the social forms of primitive and historic man, prime discoveries in science and technology, the very dreams that blister sleep, boil up from the basic, magic ring of myth.
> —Joseph Campbell,
> *The Hero with a Thousand Faces*

Although often dismissed as too distant or too difficult, the extant Greek drama can provide a wellspring of source material for the serious actor or student. Closely bound to the myths through which we view ourselves, each other, and our relationships, the tragedies in particular of the Athenian Golden Age (written between 475 and 400 B.C.) supply a wealth of characters that define our most basic archetypes. Even to someone unfamiliar with the stories, the names Electra, Oedipus, Antigone, and Prometheus are rich in meaning and associations. A working familiarity with Greek drama gives the actor a kind of character vocabulary as useful for approaching Shakespeare or O'Neill or Pinter as it is for acting Aeschylus.

Central to performing the Greeks, and what seems most to scare actors away, is the question of scale or size. In an age when a great deal of actor training emphasizes the "private moment," it is easy to understand why the very public and heroic scale of the plays can make them appear alien and obscure. And yet it is this specific element which speaks most directly to the media explosion that daily places each of us in closer contact with the most remote places imaginable and serves to render true privacy impossible. What we perceive as the immediacy of global communication, the Greeks saw as a network of experience made manifest principally by the actor, who could tell stories to audiences of seventeen thousand or more at a time. These stories not only united the community in common purpose and celebration but also wove together its past, present, and future.

Preparing the Monologue

Mythologist Joseph Campbell and others have pointed out that Western mythology, as it comes to us via the Greek experience of the world, is about external relationships: between Man and God, Man and Nature, Man and Man; and that religious, political, and social systems are attempts to organize and define those relationships. Hence the Greek preoccupation with proportion and physical structure. So, in order to create his own special performance space, the actor becomes an architect. Here is a simple exercise to help the actor/architect build on a large scale.

1. As you study your chosen monologue, make a list of places, objects, and persons, either specifically mentioned or implied, that could be significant. A list for the Watchman's monologue from *Agamemnon*, for example, might include: the gods (collective or individual), roofs (also other parts of the palace), stars (several constellations, most likely), Troy, the signal-fire, Clytemnestra, his bed, dreams, terror, the streets, Agamemnon, old stones (reference to the past), and the audience.

2. Look around the room (rehearsal hall, classroom, performance or audition space) and quickly locate at least a half-dozen landmarks or points of focus. These might include other persons, pieces of furniture, cracks in the ceiling, etc. Make sure that the points you've chosen are sufficiently scattered about the room to fill the space.

3. Identify each landmark as a place, object, or person from your list.

4. Imagine strings attaching you to each of the landmarks. You've just constructed a matrix, a map of history and associations unique to your monologue, the moment, and the space in which you are working. Explore the pattern, feel the pull of one string over another as priorities arrange and rearrange

themselves for you. When you begin to speak, you will be initiating a public event made larger and more important by the multiple focus you've created.

With practice the process should become easier, and steps two through four can eventually be accomplished within a few seconds of entering a room, even for the first time. The exercise is especially useful in giving a monologue (or scene, for that matter) a vitality and immediacy which helps you avoid the pretentious mannerisms of size without substance. Greek heroes are more powerful than we generally view ourselves and are usually in the throes of some violent catastrophe. They are each portraying a myth, usually aware that their actions will affect not only their contemporaries but generations to come; each is also taking responsibility in some way for a whole nation or a generation or all the members of one sex. To connect with myth in this manner, the actor/architect must now become an archaeologist, excavating the myths by which we live. If Iphigenia's sacrifice leaves the actor cold, substitutions are permissible, but only of myth for myth, so that the scale of the event remains large. The media access we have to modern events and situations is awesome, and the emotional associations we experience are often as real and as powerful as if we had participated ourselves. From Hitler to Kennedy, from Kirsten Flagstad to Michael Jackson, from *Gone With the Wind* to *Star Wars*, the actor is bombarded by role models whose mythic scale is a function of the millions who are touched by them. If the actor recognizes the myths, ancient or modern, that are truest to his experience, he will be closing in on the awareness that was central to the Greek view of life, and the size of his portrayal will never be in question.

The Texts

Whatever else we say, the Greek drama makes for excellent theatre, and some of the best minds of our time have been occupied in rendering the material viable in modern English to an audience unused to listening for nuance and subtlety. I am proud to include texts prepared by a number of distinguished translators and adapters, and to retain the tone of each, I have made virtually no editorial concessions to consistency. Consequently, there are significant variations in style, line format, and even the spelling of common names and places. In order to aid the actor in achieving size, I have usually chosen verse translations, but certain prose versions, notably W. B. Yeats's and Robert Lowell's, could not be omitted, and they do have a grandeur of their own. Some selections are more theatrical than others, and to a certain extent this reflects characteristics typical of each playwright, his voice still unobscured by the translator's style. At the risk of oversimplifying, I shall state that Aeschylus usually provides a strong narrative line but little humor. His language is dense, full of multiple meanings rarely apparent in translation, but which make his dialogue sound spare and economical. Sophocles' situations are based on strong dramatic conflict. His characters are often engaged in rational argument, and he is generally fair, giving both sides of an issue a good case. Euripides tends to be more lyrical and emotional than the other two, and he can be very funny in a dark, ironic way. Aristophanes is characterized by broad humor and sharp satire. He is especially fond of attacking other artists, and whole sections of his plays are direct parodies of others' work.

In the interest of brevity, I have only included as much of the story of each character as is required to perform the monologue. I encourage the actor not only to read the entire play but to place each character in the larger context of the appropriate myth by going to a good reference work. Robert Graves's *The Greek Myths* (in two volumes) and *Mythology* by Edith Hamilton are both available in inexpensive paperback editions, and make fascinating reading in their own right.

THE TROJAN WAR

The story of the Trojan War, as told by Homer in *The Iliad* and learned verbatim by generations of Greeks, served as the largest single source of material for the tragedies. Except for the sacrifice of Iphigenia at the start of the war and a couple of crises centering mostly around Achilles and his cohorts, the dramatists seem to have been most interested in the aftermath, concentrating on the fall of the House of Atreus (the story of Agamemnon, Clytemnestra, Electra, and Orestes) and the fate of the women of Troy who were enslaved and brought home by the victorious Greeks. As preparation for any of these monologues, I suggest reading all the selections in this section. They are all related.

The Watchman's monologue from *Agamemnon* takes place on the most important day of his life, the day Troy falls and he sees the particular signal-fire he's been waiting for. He compares Queen Clytemnestra with King Agamemnon (away at Troy but soon to return) and finds her wanting. The political references are oblique, but the immediacy of the moment carries the speech nicely.

Ajax and Philoctetes are both Greek heroes of the war, the former for his strength, the latter for his bow—without which Troy cannot be captured. Passed over by the Greek leaders for a tribute he felt he deserved, Ajax vowed revenge but was struck mad by the goddess Athene. Thinking they were Agamemnon, Menelaus, Odysseus, and their men, Ajax attacked a field of sheep and cattle. Now sane again and mortified by the experience, he prepares for suicide, making his farewells to his wife Tecmessa, his son Eurysaces, and a chorus of mariners, his countrymen. Both the gentleness and formality of the speech are uncharacteristic of Ajax, a function of his preparation for death. By contrast, the Philoctetes monologue is all momentum, as he tries every way he can to be taken off the island where he has been an outcast for ten years because of a festering wound that will not heal (the "ugly cargo" to which he refers). He is speaking to Neoptolemos and a crew of sailors, and there is a wonderful low cunning about the way he changes tactics.

Orestes, with the help of his sister Electra, has killed his mother Clytemnestra to avenge his father Agamemnon's murder. In return, he is being hounded by the Furies. There are some wonderful transitions in this monologue, from dream to waking, from violence to tenderness; and the intimacy of brother and sister at the end is a special moment. A real prop need not be used for the bow.

On the way to begin the Trojan War, the Greek leader Agamemnon, his navy becalmed, has been told that only the sacrifice of his daughter Iphigenia will raise the winds necessary to get to Troy. In *Iphigenia in Aulis*, his wife, Clytemnestra, protests and, with great simplicity and dignity, tells the story of their "courtship" and her loyalty. By contrast, Iphigenia accepts her fate and prepares for death as for a wedding. Casting off Aphrodite, goddess of passion, she dedicates herself to chaste Artemis, enlisting the chorus—a group of sightseers fron nearby Chalcis—to be her bridesmaids. There is a nearly fanatic passion about Iphigenia's acquiescence that makes this a particularly rich monologue for an ingenue.

Clytemnestra's next monologue is a public welcome to her husband Agamemnon on his return from Troy. What makes it both fascinating and difficult is that the subtext is not only to lure him to his death, but also to justify his murder. The crimson tapestries laid out for Agamemnon are a luxury the Greeks associated with the excesses of the Persian Empire, and so an invitation to the sin of pride. For a shorter version, omit lines 41 through half of line 57. In the scene from Sophocles, Clytemnestra is excusing Agamemnon's murder to their daughter Electra by citing his sacrifice of Iphigenia and the flaunting of his captive "Virgin Priestess," Cassandra. There is an especially strong public dimension to the last section of this speech that suggests Clytemnestra is speaking not just for herself but for all wives, perhaps all women.

In *Orestes*, Electra does something similar, identifying with her homeland and, by extension, with all mankind. Her monologue is low-key, yet rhythmically compelling.

From the power struggles of Agamemnon's household we move to a story of power enslaved. Hecuba, Queen of Troy and mother to Hector, the city's chief champion, is placed in bondage to Odysseus. In a simple but moving speech, her daughter Polyxena agrees to be sacrificed on Achilles' funeral pyre rather than live a slave. Then Hecuba must beg Odysseus for the most basic rites of burial to be performed for her son, Polydorus, who was murdered by an ally, the Thracian king Polymestor, into whose keeping the boy had been sent. In addition to Hecuba's passion, two striking images dominate the monologue: her injunction to Odysseus to "Be like a painter" and the vision of becoming "all speech." With equal vividness, Hecuba's other daughter, Cassandra, tells the story of her encounter with Apollo. In the Aeschylus speech, Cassandra, seeing Agamemnon's death and her own, tries to cast aside the skill that is her curse, her second sight, by stripping off the garments that identify her as a priestess of Apollo.

Agamemnon
by Aeschylus
Translated by Robert Fagles

WATCHMAN

Dear gods, set me free from all the pain,
the long watch I keep, one whole year awake . . .
propped on my arms, crouched on the roofs of Atreus
like a dog.
    I know the stars by heart,
the armies of the night, and there in the lead
the ones that bring us snow or the crops of summer,
bring us all we have—
our great blazing kings of the sky,
I know them, when they rise and when they fall . . .
and now I watch for the light, the signal-fire   10
breaking out of Troy, shouting Troy is taken.
So she commands, full of her high hopes.

That woman—she manoeuvres like a man.

And when I keep to my bed, soaked in dew,
and the thoughts go groping through the night
and the good dreams that used to guard my sleep . . .
not here, it's the old comrade, terror, at my neck.
I mustn't sleep, no—
      Look alive, sentry.

And I try to pick out tunes, I hum a little,
a good cure for sleep, and the tears start,   20
I cry for the hard times come to the house,
no longer run like the great place of old.

———

Oh for a blessed end to all our pain,
some godsend burning through the dark—
                                    I salute you!
You dawn of the darkness, you turn night to day—
I see the light at last.
They'll be dancing in the streets of Argos
thanks to you, thanks to this new stroke of—
                                    Aieeeeee!
There's your signal clear and true, my queen!
Rise up from bed—hurry, lift a cry of triumph   30
through the house, praise the gods for the beacon,
if they've taken Troy . . .
                    But there it burns,
fire all the way. I'm for the morning dances.
Master's luck is mine. A throw of the torch
has brought us triple-sixes—we have won!
My move now—
                    Just bring him home. My king,
I'll take your loving hand in mine and then . . .
the rest is silence. The ox is on my tongue.
Aye, but the house and these old stones,
give them a voice and what a tale they'd tell.   40
And so would I, gladly . . .
I speak to those who know; to those who don't
my mind's a blank. I never say a word.

24. some godsend burning through the dark—: *(Light appears slowly in the east; he struggles to his feet and scans it)*, translator's stage direction.
36. My move now—: *(Beginning to dance, then breaking off, lost in thought)*, translator's stage direction.
40. tale: the reference is to Clytemnestra's infidelity and perhaps other dark doings during Agamemnon's absence. The Watchman has clearly been watching in as well as out, and these last subdued lines suggest a shift in focus.

Ajax
by Sophocles
Translated by John Moore

AJAX

Strangely the long and countless drift of time
Brings all things forth from darkness into light,
Then covers them once more. Nothing so marvelous
That man can say it surely will not be—
Strong oath and iron intent come crashing down.

My mood, which just before was strong and rigid,
No dipped sword more so, now has lost its edge—
My speech is womanish for this woman's sake;
And pity touches me for wife and child,
Widowed and lost among my enemies.   10

But now I'm going to the bathing place
And meadows by the sea, to cleanse my stains,
In hope the goddess' wrath may pass from me.
And when I've found a place that's quite deserted,
I'll dig in the ground, and hide this sword of mine,
Hatefulest of weapons, out of sight. May Darkness
And Hades, God of Death, hold it in their safe keeping.
For never, since I took it as a gift
Which Hector, my great enemy, gave to me,
Have I known any kindness from the Greeks.   20
I think the ancient proverb speaks the truth:
An enemy's gift is ruinous and no gift.

Well, then,
From now on this will be my rule: Give way
To Heaven, and bow before the sons of Atreus.
They are our rulers, they must be obeyed.
I must give way, as all dread strengths give way,

In turn and deference. Winter's hard-packed snow
Cedes to the fruitful summer; stubborn night
At last removes, for day's white steeds to shine.　　　30
The dread blast of the gale slackens and gives
Peace to the sounding sea: and Sleep, strong jailer,
In time yields up his captive. Shall not I
Learn place and wisdom? Have I not learned this,
Only so much to hate my enemy
As though he might again become my friend,
And so much good to wish to do my friend,
As knowing he may yet become my foe?
Most men have found friendship a treacherous harbor.
Enough: this will be well.

　　　　　　　　　　　You, my wife, go in　　　40
And fervently and continually pray the gods
To grant fulfilment of my soul's desire.

And you, my friends, heed my instructions too,
And when he comes, deliver this to Teucer:
Let him take care for me and thought for you.
Now I am going where my way must go;
Do as I bid you, and you yet may hear
That I, though wretched now, have found my safety.

25. sons of Atreus: Agamemnon and Menelaus.
44. Teucer: Ajax's half brother, absent during these events. Ajax is sending him
a message appointing him guardian of his son Eurysaces.

Philoctetes
by Sophocles
Translated by Kenneth Cavander

PHILOCTETES
Boy—listen—I'm giving you the power of life and
death over me! I'm asking you, in the name of your father
and your mother, in the name of everything you hold

dear at home—don't leave me behind! Don't leave me
here alone, in this prison, this hell . . .

You've heard what it's like, you've seen it. Give me a
corner in your ship, anywhere! It's an ugly sight, I know,
an ugly cargo, but try, *try* to bear that. You're a king's
son—honor has a good sound to you, shame appalls
you . . . leave me here and you earn nothing but dis-   10
grace. But just do what I ask and you'll have honor, honor
everywhere, if I reach my home in Oeta alive. Come,
the cost is . . . what? One day's work—no, not that. Brave
it out. You can take me and throw me where you like—
in the prow, in the stern, in the bilge—wherever I'll be
least trouble to your crew . . . Say yes, boy! In the name
of Zeus who pities people in distress, can't I persuade
you? . . . Look . . . this is what I do, broken in heart
and body, lame! Don't abandon me to this desert, this
utter loneliness. Save me, take me to your home—no,   20
as far as the plains of Chalkedon in Euboea—from there
the journey to my country is nothing. I'll get back somehow to Trachis and the Spercheios, and because of you
I'll see my father again . . . and yet, it's ten years and I
am afraid for him. Is he dead by now? When travelers
came I sent him messages, time and time again I begged
him to launch a ship, come himself, and save me. But
either he's dead or . . . I don't know, more likely those
messengers had no time for my petty business and hurried on to their homes. But now you are my messenger   30
and my rescuer all in one. I come to you—be the one
to save me, the one to pity me, seeing that man walks
in the midst of danger all his life, threatened with sorrow
when he is most happy . . .

If you are free from suffering, then watch. When your
life goes well, then is the time to be on guard. You may
never know the day of your destruction.

12. Oeta: Philoctetes' home is in southern Thessaly, near Thermopylae, a district dominated by Mount Oeta (pronounced "eat'a"). Other places mentioned in the speech include: Trachis (pronounced "tray'kiss"), a city at the foot of the mountain; Spercheios ("spare ky'us), a nearby river; and Euboea ("you be'a"), the largest island of the Greek archipelago, and clearly on the way from Troy to just about anywhere in Greece.

18. Look—: (PHILOCTETES *kneels at* NEOPTOLEMOS' *feet*), translator's stage direction.

Orestes
by Euripides

Translated by William Arrowsmith

ORESTES

Get me my horn-tipped bow,
the bow Apollo gave me to scare these bitches off
if they threatened me with madness.

                      Vanish, demons!
Goddesses you may be, but unless you go,
this human hand shall draw your blood.

                        Damn it, go!
Ignore me, do you?

               Do you see this bow
already drawn, this arrow notched and ready?
What? Still here?

             Vanish, spread your wings!
Skim the air, will you! Go hound Apollo,
accuse his oracle. But go! Go!   10

What was I saying?

            And why am I panting so?
What am I doing here, out of bed?

                 But wait—
I remember now—a great storm, the waves crashing—
but now this calm—this peace . . .

             Why are you crying?

Why do you hide your face?
　　　　　　　　　　Oh, my poor sister,
how wrong it is that what I have to suffer,
this sickness, this madness, should hurt you too
and cause you shame.
　　　　　　　　Please, please don't cry,
not on my account.
　　　　　　　　Let me bear the shame.
I know, you consented to the murder too,　　　　　　20
but I killed, not you.
　　　　　　　　No—
I accuse Apollo. The god is the guilty one.
It was he who drove me to this dreadful crime,
he and his words, egging me, encouraging me,
all words, no action.
　　　　　　　　I think now
if I had asked my dead father at the time
if I should kill her, he would have begged me,
gone down on his knees before me, and pleaded,
implored me not to take my mother's life.
What had we to gain by murdering her?　　　　　　30
Her death could never bring him back to life
and I, by killing her, would have to suffer
as I suffer now.
　　　　　　　　It seems so hopeless, dear,
I know.
　　　　　　But lift your head; do not cry.
And sometimes when you see me morbid and depressed,
comfort me and calm me, and I in turn,
when you despair, will comfort you with love.
For love is all we have, the only way
that each can help the other.
　　　　　　　　　　Now go inside.
Bathe and eat and give those tired eyes　　　　　　40
their needed sleep. If you should leave me now,
if you fall ill yourself from nursing me,

then I am dead. You are all my help;
you are my hope.

3. they threatened me with madness: (ELECTRA *hands him the bow and quiver.* ORESTES *notches an arrow and draws the bow*), translator's stage direction.

10. But go! Go!: (*He suddenly stumbles, dropping his bow, and sanity returns*), translator's stage direction.

14. this calm—this peace: (*He catches sight of* ELECTRA, *her face hidden in her robes, sobbing softly by the bed*), translator's stage direction.

Iphigenia in Aulis
by Euripides

Adapted by John Barton and Kenneth Cavander
Translated by Kenneth Cavander

CLYTEMNESTRA

Then listen, Agamemnon.
Let us have truth between us:

Let's have the fierce truth.
You took me as your bride
Although I did not want you.
You were a barbarian.
Our wedding was an act
Of violence. You had killed
My first husband and my child,
The baby at my breast,   10
And smashed its living body
Brutally on the earth.
But when my brothers came
To fight with you, you ran
Abjectly to my father
And begged to him for mercy.
When he protected you
I had to become
Your wife, your property.

Then you said to me,   20
"The history of my house
Is full of hate and bloodshed
But I want to be civilised.
Please help me." So I did.
I learned to forget my hatred,
I helped your palace grow

In wealth and influence,
And so in time I came
To look to you for love.
Your palace of itself   30
Is dark and cold and grim
But now the rooms are all
Light and fair and friendly
With things from across the sea,
Libya, Phrygia, Egypt.
And so I have appeased
The old ghosts of your house
By my gentleness and kindness.

I have been a rare wife.
I have borne you four children,   40
Three daughters, and a son:
Iphigenia,
Chrysothemis,
Electra
And Orestes . . .
O are you made of stone?
What will you say if someone
Asks "Why are you murdering her?"
How will you answer? Tell me:
Because you want to be famous?   50
Menelaus has a daughter,
So let him slaughter her
If he wants her mother back,
Or else draw lots to decide
Whose child will have to die.
But no, it must be me
Who has to lose her child
While the guilty one, the cheating one,
Keeps her own daughter safe.
Think: if you do it   60
What will be in my heart
As I sit home and stare

At my daughter's empty chair?
What shall I pray to the gods?
If they exist at all
They will punish you.
And how do you think that I
Will greet your coming home?
With the welcome you deserve . . . ?
No. I do not want that!   70
Please do not turn me
Into an evil woman.
I love you now:
Do not let my love
Be turned into hatred.
It is so easy. Help me.
If I am wrong then show me
But if you think I'm right
Then change your mind . . . change it.
O be clear, think clearly,   80
And so be whole again.

51. daughter: Hermione, daughter of Menelaus and Helen (whose defection with
    Paris caused the Trojan War in the first place).

Iphigenia in Aulis
by Euripides
Adapted by John Barton and Kenneth Cavander
Translated by Kenneth Cavander

IPHIGENIA

Listen, mother, listen.
You know nothing can change
What is going to happen.
I must die. And I want it.

My father was right: on me depends
The sailing of the ships

And the defeat of Troy.
What is so precious
About this life of mine?
I give my mortal self 10
To Greece for sacrifice
To destroy our enemies.
This will be my monument
In times to come. This
Will be my children. This
Will be my marriage. This,
This will be my fame.

Remember what they say:
Men, and women too,
Must endure. I say 20
An old, worn, ancient thing
And yet it is a true thing.
Nothing's new or changes
But each of us must learn
To discover it anew.
You must not weep.
I am happy, dying.
Life is brief and brutish.
By how we live we make it
Have a little meaning 30
And have a little brightness,
As light braves the darkness . . .
O I love you very much.

Take from me a lock of hair
And let's have no more weeping.
Fetch me my wedding veil
And give me wreaths to wind
Around my head. Bring them.

You are now my women.
You shall come with me and dance 40

Around Artemis' altar.
Let us praise and honour her
And dance the wedding dance.
I give myself to her.
If Achilles had married me
I should have been given
To hot Aphrodite
As other women are.
But I will worship Artemis
And so I will be free   50
Clean and bright and strong.
I am the bride now
Of Greece. I love you. Take me.
Take me. I am conqueror
Of Troy, of Ilion.
Come women, sing,
Sing to Artemis,
Protector of travellers
And of the army waiting.

Now sing of my country's earth   60
And of my home, Mycenae.

55. Ilion: another name for the city of Troy, after its founder, Ilus.

Agamemnon
by Aeschylus
Translated by Robert Fagles

CLYTEMNESTRA

Old nobility of Argos
gathered here, I am not ashamed to tell you
how I love the man. I am older,
and the fear dies away . . . I am human.
Nothing I say was learned from others.

This is my life, my ordeal, long as the siege
he laid at Troy and more demanding.
                                        First,
when a woman sits at home and the man is gone,
the loneliness is terrible,
unconscionable . . .   10
and the rumors spread and fester,
a runner comes with something dreadful,
close on his heels the next and his news worse,
and they shout it out and the whole house can hear;
and wounds—if he took one wound for each report
to penetrate these walls, he's gashed like a dragnet,
more, if he had only died . . .
for each death that swelled his record, he could boast
like a triple-bodied Geryon risen from the grave,
"Three shrouds I dug from the earth, one for every body 20
that went down!"
                        The rumors broke like fever,
broke and then rose higher. There were times
they cut me down and eased my throat from the noose.
I wavered between the living and the dead.
                                                And so
our child is gone, not standing by our side,
the bond of our dearest pledges, mine and yours;
by all rights our child should be here . . .
Orestes. You seem startled.
You needn't be. Our loyal brother-in-arms
will take good care of him, Strophios the Phocian.   30
He warned from the start we court two griefs in one.
You risk all on wars—and what if the people
rise up howling for the king, and anarchy
should dash our plans?
                        Men, it is their nature,
trampling on the fighter once he's down.
Our child is gone. That is my self-defence
and it is true.
                        For me, the tears that welled

like springs are dry. I have no tears to spare.
I'd watch till late at night, my eyes still burn,
I sobbed by the torch I lit for you alone.   40

I never let it die . . . but in my dreams
the high thin wail of a gnat would rouse me,
piercing like a trumpet—I could see you
suffer more than all
the hours that slept with me could ever bear.

I endured it all. And now, free of grief,
I would salute that man the watchdog of the fold,
the mainroyal, saving stay of the vessel,
rooted oak that thrusts the roof sky-high,
the father's one true heir.   50
Land at dawn to the shipwrecked past all hope,
light of the morning burning off the night of storm,
the cold clear spring to the parched horseman—
O the ecstasy, to flee the yoke of Fate!
It is right to use the titles he deserves.
Let envy keep her distance. We have suffered
long enough.
                    Come to me now, my dearest,
down from the car of war, but never set foot
that stamped out Troy on earth again, my great one.

Women, why delay? You have your orders.   60
Pave his way with tapestries.
                              Quickly.
Let the red stream flow and bear him home
to the home he never hoped to see—Justice,
lead him in!
            Leave all the rest to me.
The spirit within me never yields to sleep.
We will set things right, with the god's help.
We will do whatever Fate requires.

19. Geryon: a fabled three-bodied, or alternately three-headed, monster of the Gorgon family and a grandchild of Medusa.
57. long enough: (*Reaching towards* AGAMEMNON), translator's stage direction.
61. Pave his way with tapestries: (*They* [The WOMEN] *begin to spread the crimson tapestries between the king and the palace doors*), translator's stage direction.

Electra
by Sophocles
Adapted by John Barton and Kenneth Cavander
Translated by Kenneth Cavander

CLYTEMNESTRA

So you are out loose again.

You only do it because
Aegisthus is away.
You harangue everyone
With tales of my cruelty.
You are all malice and venom
But I am not an evil woman.
Before people pass judgement
They should first check their facts.

Your father, I killed him: 10
It is true and I do not deny it
But it was not me alone.
There was another with me:
Justice, Justice did it.
I will say it once again:
Your precious father
Was brutal enough to murder
Iphigenia, your sister.
Her throat was cut
In front of the whole army.   20
Why did he kill her?
For the Greeks or for Menelaus?

I don't know what the truth was
But one thing is certain:
He was cruel and a coward.

Yet for all of that
I would not have killed him
But he had to bring home
A mad girl, a prophetess,
Flaunting her before me.   30
Two brides. One bed. He did that.
You would not still love him
If you really had known him.
He was a self-deceiver
Who always blamed the gods
For his own mistakes. He talked
Of doing what is right
But he never did it. No,
He always did the wrong things,
The selfish, the mean, the easy.   40
He thought he could steal from Apollo
His so-called "Virgin Priestess";
He thought he could bring her home
And be sweet with her in front of me.

O can't you understand?
Nothing in the world
Hurts a woman more
Than to love and to be hurt.
When a husband looks for love
Outside his marriage   50
Shall we not do as he does?
Why are women blamed for it
But never our guilty husbands?
I have no regrets,
And if you think me evil
Look into your own hearts
Before you judge another.

Orestes
by Euripides
Adapted by John Barton and Kenneth Cavander
Translated by Kenneth Cavander

ELECTRA

O land of my fathers,
I cry and lead the dirge
For myself and my brother.

Now with my nails
I tear at both my cheeks
And beat at my breast.
Now the cry of pain
Gathers at my throat
Like a jet of blood,
Black grief pulsing,   10
Drum beats of anguish
On my head, a marching song
For the Queen of Death.
Mourn now, mourn,
You land of my fathers;
Tear your hair, women,
And cry out for pity
On those that have to die.

My house is destroyed,
My family is gone.   20
We that were once
The envy of the world
Are broken by the hatred
Of men and of the gods.
Weep for it, weep,
All of you that are human.
Your lives are so brief:

Look at them. Yes, look
At your own hopes and failures:
They all end in death.   30
Look, the long procession
Of generations passes:
Look at all the changes
And see behind them all
How the suffering is constant.
Decay, sorrow, pain
Make up the life of man.

Take me, you gods in heaven,
Heave me up to the rock
Which hangs between heaven and earth.   40
I want to cry my grief out
And my anger and despair
To the founder of my house,
Tantalus, who began
The curse which has destroyed us.
Cry, women, cry.
The curse's stain has spread
With murder upon murder,
And now it falls and feeds
On my brother and myself.   50

17. cry out for pity: *(The* CHORUS *start to weep)*, adapters' stage direction.
44. Tantalus: in punishment for a sin against the gods, he was placed, as various
    versions have it, in a pool of water from which he could not drink, beneath
    fruit trees he could not reach to satisfy his hunger, or under a giant boulder
    threatening to fall on him.

Hecuba
by Euripides

Adapted by John Barton and Kenneth Cavander
Translated by Kenneth Cavander

POLYXENA

Odysseus, I see
That you have tucked your hand
In the folds of your cloak.

Afraid I'll try to touch you?
Do not be afraid.
I am not going to beg:
I will not grovel to you.
I shall go with you
Because I must. You see,
I want to die, Odysseus.   10
My city, Troy, is gone
Which was the greatest city
In all the world of men,
So why should I want to live?
My father was a king,
I was a royal princess,
And fine men, noble men,
Came to woo me once.

Now I am a slave
And it is that word, "slave,"   20
That makes me glad to die.
Shall I become a drudge
And knead bread
And scrub floors
And sleep in the brutal bed
Of some Greek far off in Greece?
I will not do that:

No, now while I am free
I do renounce the light
And I embrace my death.   30
Cut my throat. I want that:
I want to go under the earth,
I want to see my father
And my dear brother Hector
Who was the noblest man
That there ever has been.
Don't try to stop me, mother.

Try to be patient, Odysseus,
And you, mother, listen.
Do you want to be thrown down   40
And kicked and dragged along
On your back by Greek thugs?
That's what they will do
If you try to stop them.
You must accept it, mother.
Give me your hand, so,
And your cheek to kiss, that's right.
I am going now.

38. In the beat preceding, Odysseus and Hecuba argue, she offering to die in
    Polyxena's place.
46,47. If the physicality of the farewell feels awkward, these two lines can simply
    be cut.

Hecuba
by Euripides

Translated by William Arrowsmith

HECUBA

But let me tell you why I kneel
at your feet. And if my sufferings seem just,

then I must be content.
               But if otherwise,
give me my revenge on that treacherous friend
who flouted every god in heaven and in hell
to do this brutal murder.
               At our table
he was our frequent guest; was counted first
among our friends, respected, honored by me,
receiving every kindness that a man could meet—
and then, in cold deliberation, killed   10
my son.
       Murder may have its reasons, its motives,
but this—to refuse my son a grave, to throw him
to the sea, unburied!
             I am a slave, I know,
and slaves are weak. But the gods are strong, and over them
there stands some absolute, some moral order
or principle of law more final still.
Upon this moral law the world depends;
through it the gods exist; by it we live,
defining good and evil.
             Apply that law
to me. For if you flout it now, and those   20
who murder in cold blood or defy the gods
go unpunished, then human justice withers,
corrupted at its source.
            Honor my request,
Agamemnon.
        Punish this murder.
               Pity me.
Be like a painter. Stand back, see me
in perspective,
        see me whole, observe
my wretchedness—
          once a queen, and now
a slave; blessed with children, happy once,

now old, childless, utterly alone,
homeless, lost, unhappiest of women   30
on this earth . . .

                    O gods, you turn away—
what can I do? My only hope is lost.

It may be futile now
to urge the claims of love, but let me urge them
anyway. At your side sleeps my daughter
Cassandra, once the priestess of Apollo.
What will you give, my lord, for those nights of love?
What thanks for all her tenderness in bed
does she receive from you, and I, in turn,
from her?
                    Look now at this dead boy,   40
Cassandra's brother. Revenge him. Be kind to her
by being kind to him.
                              One word more.
If by some magic, some gift of the gods,
I could become all speech—tongues in my arms,
hands that talked, voices speaking, crying
from my hair and feet—then, all together,
as one voice, I would fall and touch your knees,
crying, begging, imploring with a thousand tongues—
O master, greatest light of Hellas,
hear me,
              help an old woman,
                              avenge her!   50
She is nothing at all, but hear her, help her
even so. Do your duty as a man of honor;
see justice done. Punish this murder.

---

1. To give the opening a bit more punch, omit "But" and begin with "Let me
   tell you why I kneel."

Hecuba
by Euripides
Adapted by John Barton and Kenneth Cavander
Translated by Kenneth Cavander

CASSANDRA

The sun . . . I dreamed that the sun
Came alive in my brain.

I felt light pour in
To my skull and I *knew*.
I saw a landscape
Of time spread out before me—
My kingdom—and I saw
All things that are to come.
Then he said, "Now pay me.
Give yourself now. Let me own you   10
And I will give you time to rule
Forever" . . . I was frightened.
I said I would but I could not.
My mind was riddled, scorched
With too much seeing and brightness.
I longed for shadows . . . caverns . . .
Dim sea-beds . . . all I wanted
Was to hide from him, from seeing.
I hid. I shut my eyes.
I wanted so much to be   20
Alone in the dark.

Whiteness . . . his heat is white
And despair is white and madness
And the thoughts which race in my skull.
Please, Apollo, I cannot
Give you myself. I'm frightened.
Then he said, "So be it,"

And he grew quiet and gentle.
He begged one kiss of me.
I gave my lips to him.   30
And he spat into my mouth
And said, "Keep my gifts.
Keep my brightness in you.
See it all, the truth
About the war and all things
But since you lied to me
When you tell that truth
It will seem to those you tell it
Toys, baubles, babble,
And they will laugh at you."   40

40. In this version, Agamemnon laughs at the end of Cassandra's speech, which
    suggests a moment of stillness as reaction before dropping character.

Agamemnon
by Aeschylus
Adapted by John Barton and Kenneth Cavander
Translated by Kenneth Cavander

CASSANDRA

O, O it hurts:
The truth, true prophecy,
It hurts inside my head.

See, there above the house
Children like dreams, dead children,
Their flesh served up as meat
Which their own father ate.
One plots revenge for this
And O my lord, my lord,
Female shall murder male.   10

You heard her cry out
But you still do not believe it.
It is going to happen . . .

You are going to look on Agamemnon dead.

O lord Apollo,
Why do I wear this?
This dress? This wreath? It mocks me.
Before I die I'll spoil you,
Yes, curse, destroy you
As you've destroyed me.   20
Make some other woman
As miserable as I was.
Look how Apollo
Is stripping me himself.

Look, look . . . Apollo . . .
He watched me in this dress
And saw how I was laughed at
By friends and enemies
And how they hated me
And he enjoyed it all.   30
They said that I was mad
Or a witch or a fortune-teller:
That's what I've endured,
And now my Apollo
Has finished with his priestess
And brought me here to die.
Yes, my lord and I must die
But the god will avenge us.
One will come to kill
His mother to atone   40
For his murdered father.
No tears then, no, none.
Don't pity me, don't pity.
My turn has come.

The doors of this house
Are the doors of death for me.

It reeks of blood inside.
It smells, it reeks like a grave.
I am going in.

Strangers, I am not   50
Some little bird that's scared
By some branch the wind blows.
I mourn for myself
And for my Agamemnon.
I will say one more thing:
No dirge about myself
But in the sun's last light
I pray that it may shine
On those that are to come
Who will avenge my death,   60
A common slave, a woman,
So easy to destroy.
Poor men and women . . .
Human Happiness . . .
A shadow can destroy us.

THE THEBANS

The history of Thebes is dominated by the conflict between worldly power and reverence for the gods. Dionysos, a relative newcomer to Greek mythology, is a complex figure representing variously the cultivation of the vine, drunkenness, the law, sexual abandon, and the tragic drama. In the first selection he returns to his birthplace to make himself known to the people of Greece. The monologue is particularly rich with a sense of history made immediate and accessible through place. Dionysos's great power is suggested by an attitude of absolute divine arrogance that actually serves to make the character endearing. Shorter versions might omit lines 6 through 29 and/or lines 72 through 91.

Another kind of arrogance leads Oedipus to pursue an investigation that must reveal himself to be his father's murderer and his mother's lover. In his single-minded determination he alienates everyone around him, in this case his brother-in-law/uncle Creon, who defends his loyalty with clear, logical precision. In case we ever doubted that power corrupts, it is this same Creon who, when king himself, forgets about humility and reverence. When Oedipus abdicates, his sons Eteocles and Polyneices are killed in a brief civil war that leaves Creon in charge. His first action is to refuse burial rites to Polyneices, the attacker. It is now Creon's son Haemon who argues a rational path. His approach is interestingly oblique, and the speech has humor and gentleness. Then Tiresias, in a much more flamboyant fashion, tries to put the fear of the gods into Creon by graphically depicting the chaos that results when the traditional rituals are not observed. Tiresias is an immensely powerful priest and seer, but he is blind and requires the assistance of a boy guide to get around. Rather than play blind, the actor should choose a single strong visual focus and perhaps use a stick or some other object through which to draw strength and power. I have, incidentally, twice seen Tiresias played very effectively by women.

As portrayed by Sophocles, Oedipus's daughter Antigone— chief champion for her brother Polyneices' burial—seems to me too rhetorical, so I have chosen instead to include a selection from Euripides' version of the story, *The Phoenician Women*. The piece is a tour de force of sustained momentum, ritual formality, and carefully controlled passion. Euripides raises the level of horror and poignancy by including both brothers' corpses as well as the body of Jocasta, their mother, and the imminent arrival of Oedipus himself.

The Bacchae
by Euripides
Translated by Kenneth Cavander

DIONYSOS

Dionysos has come.

Here, in Thebes, Zeus came swooping down and took
A woman of the earth. Lightning made
Her labour quick, and out of her burning thighs
I was born.

Today I walk on the piece of land enclosed
By two rivers—Dirce and Ismenos—
The land they call . . . Thebes.
Today I look like a man, but I am more.

Here was the lightning blast that killed my mother,   10
Semele, here was her room and . . .
There's something alive! Smoke in the rubble, the fire
Of Zeus . . . still. So, something alive
Still . . .

Yes, Kadmos has said: "On this ground
No man walks!" to remind Thebes
Of Semele, his daughter, to keep her alive in the heart
Of Thebes. I am glad. He was right.
The vines that cover that wall are mine. They flush.
And cluster . . .   20
And swell . . .

Behind me—Lebanon and its golden plains,
Iraq, the sun-struck steppes of Persia,
The fortresses of Syria, the harsh country
Where the Afghans live, Arabia drugged,

And all the eastern coasts, where Greece and Asia
Merge, and towers fringe the teeming cities;
Behind me—dance swaying bodies, intoxication,
Life.

Here—Greece. And first in Greece—Thebes.   30
My own country, where I will be known,
Where I must be known.
There is a reason why Thebes comes first.
I made this city wild with women shrilling
My name, I slung hide on their backs, I stuck
Branches in their hands, spears tipped
With ivy—for a reason.
Because my mother's sisters denied I was
The son of Zeus; because they said Semele
Lost her virginity to a man here in Thebes,   40
Then blamed the result on Zeus; because they swore
Kadmos invented it all; because they claimed
Zeus killed Semele for lying about
Her husband.

They shouldn't have said that. They,
Particularly, should not have said all that.
Because now, they hurtle out of their homes, possessed,
Scatter to the hills, and they all wear my uniform,
They all know how to bring me to life . . .

I willed it, and they must.   50
Every woman in this city is mine,
Totally.
They have abandoned Thebes, and now they have joined
My mother's sisters in the green pine shades,
Among the cliffs and hollows. Mad. Bacchae.
This place must find out what it means
To be half-born, to have no
Dionysos, never to have tried me or tasted me,
This place must take account of my birth

In Semele, my descent from Zeus, my presence here,   60
And my power over man. This place
May wish it did not have to, but it must learn.

Kadmos has given way to Pentheus, his grandson.
Authority, decision, are now all Pentheus,
Who resists me and my power, keeps me
Clear out of thought. When he looks outside
Himself for help, he never looks to me.
I am despised, pushed aside, stamped upon.
And therefore I'll turn him round to face me. Show
Myself in Thebes, show them they are small   70
And I am great.

This one matter set to rights I pack up
And move on, to make myself known
Elsewhere.
If Thebes recklessly tries to bring the women
Back from the hills and their madness by *force*, you
Will see a fight—the army versus Bacchae—
Arranged by me.

And so I have dressed myself in flesh today.
I have the body and blood of a man, but   80
My real nature is . . . still my own.

Friends, you have been loyal, you have followed me
From countries far across the sea, travelled
Beside me, never deserted me. Lift your drums
Now. Let these proud walls of Pentheus,
The king, hear the sound of the east, the creation
Of Earth, my mother, and myself. The beat!
The beat! Let the city open its eyes.
I will go to the heights of Kithairon where
The women are dancing on the slopes, and join   90
The Bacchae.
——

12–13. the fire/Of Zeus: reference is most likely to the altar, a standard part of the orkestra or principal downstage acting area of the Greek amphitheatre, in this case alight and smoking.

36–37. spears tipped/With ivy: the thyrsus, a phallic wand carried by Dionysos's followers.

82. Friends: he speaks to the Chorus.

King Oedipus
by Sophocles
Translated by William Butler Yeats

CREON

Not so;

     reason this out as I reason it, and first weigh this:
who would prefer to lie awake amid terrors rather than
to sleep in peace, granting that his power is equal in
both cases?

     Neither I nor any sober-minded man. You
give me what I ask and let me do what I want, but were
I King I would have to do things I did not want to do.
Is not influence and no trouble with it better than any
throne, am I such a fool as to hunger after unprofitable
honours? Now all are glad to see me, every one wishes
me well, all that want a favour from you ask speech of   10
me—finding in that their hope. Why should I give up
these things and take those? No wise mind is treacherous.
I am no contriver of plots, and if another took to them
he would not come to me for help. And in proof of this
go to the Pythian Oracle, and ask if I have truly told
what the Gods said: and after that, if you have found that
I have plotted with the Soothsayer, take me and kill me;
not by the sentence of one mouth only—but of two mouths,
yours and my own. But do not condemn me in a corner,
upon some fancy and without proof. What right have you   20
to declare a good man bad or a bad good? It is as bad a
thing to cast off a true friend as it is for a man to cast

away his own life—but you will learn these things with
certainty when the time comes; for time alone shows a
just man; though a day can show a knave.

1. Not so: Oedipus has just called Creon a false friend. Cutting the phrase will
   make the opening of the monologue quieter and more reflective.
15. Pythian Oracle: Apollo's oracle at Delphi, named for Pythia, its priestess.
   Creon has just returned from the oracle, where he was sent by Oedipus to
   seek a cure for the plague ravaging Thebes.
17. Soothsayer: Tiresias, whom Oedipus has also accused of lying and of con-
   spiring against him for money.

Antigone
by Sophocles
Translated by Robert Fagles

HAEMON

Father, only the gods endow a man with reason,
the finest of all their gifts, a treasure.

Far be it from me—I haven't the skill,
and certainly no desire, to tell you when,
if ever, you make a slip in speech . . . though
someone else might have a good suggestion.

Of course it's not for you,
in the normal run of things, to watch
whatever men say or do, or find to criticize.

The man in the street, you know, dreads your glance,   10
he'd never say anything displeasing to your face.
But it's for me to catch the murmurs in the dark,
the way the city mourns for this young girl.
"No woman," they say, "ever deserved death less,
and such a brutal death for such a glorious action.
She, with her own dear brother lying in his blood—

she couldn't bear to leave him dead, unburied,
food for the wild dogs or wheeling vultures.
Death? She deserves a glowing crown of gold!"
So they say, and the rumor spreads in secret,   20
darkly . . .
                    I rejoice in your success, father—
nothing more precious to me in the world.
What medal of honor brighter to his children
than a father's growing glory? Or a child's
to his proud father? Now don't, please,
be quite so single-minded, self-involved,
or assume the world is wrong and you are right.
Whoever thinks that he alone possesses intelligence,
the gift of eloquence, he and no one else,
and character too . . . such men, I tell you,   30
spread them open—you will find them empty.
                                        No,
it's no disgrace for a man, even a wise man,
to learn many things and not to be too rigid.
You've seen trees by a raging winter torrent,
how many sway with the flood and salvage every twig,
but not the stubborn—they're ripped out, roots and all.
Bend or break. The same when a man is sailing:
haul your sheets too taut, never give an inch,
you'll capsize, and go the rest of the voyage
keel up and the rowing-benches under.   40

Oh give way. Relax your anger—change!
I'm young, I know, but let me offer this:
it would be best by far, I admit,
if a man were born infallible, right by nature.
If not—and things don't often go that way,
it's best to learn from those with good advice.

Antigone
by Sophocles
Translated by Robert Fagles

TIRESIAS

You will learn
when you listen to the warnings of my craft.

As I sat on the ancient seat of augury,
in the sanctuary where every bird I know
will hover at my hands—suddenly I heard it,
a strange voice in the wingbeats, unintelligible,
barbaric, a mad scream! Talons flashing, ripping,
they were killing each other—that much I knew—
the murderous fury whirring in those wings
made that much clear!
           I was afraid,   10
I turned quickly, tested the burnt-sacrifice,
ignited the altar at all points—but no fire,
the god in the fire never blazed.
Not from those offerings . . . over the embers
slid a heavy ooze from the long thighbones,
smoking, sputtering out, and the bladder
puffed and burst—spraying gall into the air—
and the fat wrapping the bones slithered off
and left them glistening white. No fire!
The rites had failed that might have blazed the future   20
with a sign. So I learned from the boy here:
he is my guide, as I am guide to others.
                And it is you—
your high resolve that sets this plague on Thebes.
The public altars and sacred hearths are fouled,
one and all, by the birds and dogs with carrion
torn from the corpse, the doomstruck son of Oedipus!
And so the gods are deaf to our prayers, they spurn

the offerings in our hands, the flame of holy flesh.
No birds cry out an omen clear and true—
they're gorged with the murdered victim's blood and fat.   30

Take these things to heart, my son, I warn you.
All men make mistakes, it is only human.
But once the wrong is done, a man
can turn his back on folly, misfortune too,
if he tries to make amends, however low he's fallen,
and stops his bullnecked ways. Stubbornness
brands you for stupidity—pride is a crime.
No, yield to the dead!
Never stab the fighter when he's down.
Where's the glory, killing the dead twice over?   40

I mean you well. I give you sound advice.
It's best to learn from a good adviser
when he speaks for your own good:
it's pure gain.

The Phoenician Women
by Euripides
Translated by Philip Vellacott

ANTIGONE

No seemly veil covers
The curling hair and soft cheek;
No maidenly reserve hides
The flush under the eyes, the hot forehead,
As I come, a Bacchant of the dead,
Tearing loose the band that held my hair,
Flinging free my saffron robe of silk,
To lead the march of mourning for these dead.
Wail aloud, weep and cry!
Polyneices, Man of Strife, so truly named   10
(Alas unhappy Thebes!),
Yours was the quarrel—and yet
No quarrel, but murder matched with murder—
Which, accomplished in a horror of blood,
In an anguish of blood,
Has overwhelmed the house of Oedipus.
What music, what chorus of tears,
What song of weeping shall I summon
To mourn for you, my home, my home?
Here I bring three killed with the sword,   20
Of one family, a mother and her sons,
A welcome sight to the spirit of vengeance
Which doomed our house to utter ruin
On that day when the wisdom of Oedipus
Found easy the hard riddle of the cruel Sphinx
And destroyed her life.

Father, dear father, I cry aloud your sufferings!
What other man of our mortal race,
Hellene or barbarian, or hero of ancient royalty,

Endured before all men's gaze   30
The torment of such disasters?
What bird, hidden aloft
In the leafy boughs of oak or pine,
Mourning for a mother dead,
Will sing in tune with my sorrow,
With my dirge of despair
For the long life of solitary days that awaits me,
And the tears that will not cease?
On which body shall I cast first
The offering of hair torn from my head?   40
On the two breasts of my mother
Where once I was fed?
Or on the piteous wounds of my dead brothers?

Father, father! Leave your room,
Blind as you are, and old,
Come, Oedipus, show your unhappy self,
Drawing the slow breath of a long life,
You who once in this palace
Plunged your eyes in misty darkness,
And now grope your feeble way along the walls,   50
Or rest on a bed of pain;
Do you hear me? Come!

5. Bacchant of the dead: she compares herself to the followers of Dionysos, as
   she indulges in an orgy of grief.
25. Sphinx: it was by correctly answering the riddle of the Sphinx, a creature
    half lion and half woman, that Oedipus, an apparent stranger, became King
    of Thebes.
29. Hellene: Greek.

OTHER TRAGEDIES

Robert Lowell's *Prometheus Bound* is a long way from Aeschylus, but both in the deceptive simplicity of his prose and in the ironic interplay of images his version comes closest to suggesting a truly Promethean scale. Punished by Zeus for being mankind's great benefactor, Prometheus was chained to a rock on Mt. Caucasus, his liver the perpetual food for a ravenous eagle. Subject to intense pain, isolation, and near eternal boredom, Lowell's Prometheus seems to derive his principal satisfaction from the memory of his glory days and his gifts to humans. A later distraction comes in the form of Io, and her horror story is gratifying because of its indictment of the gods' cruelty. Her speech, with its overblown sensuality and underlying terror, is best handled with utmost simplicity. I recall Jonathan Miller's original production of the play, in which both Irene Worth as Io and Kenneth Haigh as Prometheus moved very little, but were always aware of the space, the emptiness around them above and below.

More domestic in scale but representative of forces and issues common to gods and mortals, *Hippolytus* is the story of Phaedra, wife of Theseus, who falls in love with her stepson Hippolytus, who rejects her. Spurned and humiliated, Phaedra tells Theseus that his son has attempted to dishonor her, and then kills herself. In their respective monologues, Theseus and Hippolytus speak powerfully and cogently for their generations, and their faults—the father's anger and the son's pride in his own virtue—tend to add credibility and fullness to the characters. There is the extra dimension of Hippolytus's dedication to Artemis, the virgin goddess of the hunt, a cultish association not only suspicious to his conservative father but also the cause of Aphrodite's anger. And, of course, it is Aphrodite, goddess of love, beauty, and fertility, slighted by Hippolytus, who ignites Phaedra's passion. Phaedra, ready to die, speaks with peace, complete composure, and a rare historical perspective on families and reputation.

There is an almost feminine gentleness, as well, in Admetus's monologue. *Alcestis*, it seems, was written not as a tragedy but as a satyr play, the short alternative piece commonly played as epilogue to each tragic trilogy. So this speech may originally have had comic overtones reflecting the thematic material of tragic plays now lost in obscurity. But in this translation and out of context it is a lyrical and loving pledge to a wife who has agreed to die so that her husband may live. By contrast, Medea's violence in reaction to being abandoned by her lover Jason is startlingly explosive. Robinson Jeffers's adaptation, with its uneven and disjointed line structure, is entirely suited to the sudden shifts of mood and focus. She speaks alternately to the Chorus, the audience, Jason, Hecate—the goddess of sorcery and witchcraft, and her two young sons whom she is planning to kill. Deianira also finds herself in a web of magic and poison, but as an unwilling victim. Jealous of her husband Heracles, she seeks to assure his fidelity by spreading on his robe a potion traitorously given to her by the centaur Nessus just before he died by Heracles' hand. With growing horror she realizes what she has done and is well on her way to suicide by the end of the speech.

Prometheus Bound
by Robert Lowell
Derived from Aeschylus

PROMETHEUS

That water is turning to ice, a fine dry snow. It dazzles me a moment, then bites my face. I pretend I can bear it; yet I begin to think of my enemies.
                                    Those gods! That innumerable jumble of upstarts, all screaming with one voice, all howling for power! Once they filled Zeus with the stupor of despair. And now? They are almost perfect. They spin about the head of Zeus—each as delicate and cold as a snowflake.

Enough. We know the gods. They watch us. I will tell you about the feverish miseries of man. Before he could 10
reason, he was an animal, perhaps the slowest and least graceful, a skull with less inside it than the shell of a turtle. I am not saying this in scorn of men, but to show the greatness of their change. Men had eyes and saw nothing: a shapeless presence, a threatening absence, nearness seeming so distant that it hit them in the eyes, distance seeming so near, they tried to duck their heads. No finer shades! They saw little in between the blinding yellow of the sun and the blank of night. They had ears and heard nothing: a splatter, a splash, fizzings, buzzings, 20
hissings, mazes of muddled vibration, sounds without the cutting edge of words. What did men know of houses built of brick, and turned to face the sun? They swarmed like ants, though with far less order, through a sunless underground of eroding holes. Leafless winter, flowering spring, and fruitful summer were all one season to them. The stars looked down on them like an aimless sprinkle of water drops running out into nothing.

I taught men the rising and the setting of the stars. From
the stars, I taught them numbers. I taught women to   30
count their children, and men to number their murders.
I gave them the alphabet. Before I made men talk and
write with words, knowledge dropped like a dry stick
into the fire of their memories, fed that fading blaze an
instant, then died without leaving an ash behind. Now
the brute forces of the earth obey man slavishly whenever
he thinks and speaks. I have put animals under his
thumb—dog, cat, and cow, horses to plow, horses to
saddle, horses to harness to the warrior's chariot. While
the animals drudge, man sits thinking so idly and so   40
profoundly that he can hardly be troubled to budge and
sort out the wealth and luxury that drops in his lap. Men
were set floating in boats, a pole to push, an oar to pull,
a sail to hoist. Those windy sails . . . men thought I'd
turned a block of wood into a bird!

All these inventions were given to men. Thousands more
followed. I could turn anything into anything.

Man's short life, when I first looked at it, short as it was,
was a long disease. Man was an animal without an animal's resolution for going on. If a man sickened, he would   50
usually die. No one mixed medicines, brought cooling
drinks, or knew what food to choose. I searched the
earth, and discovered it was a map of cures, covered up,
mislaid, rotting, but eagerly waiting. A cure was waiting
like a bride for every disease. But perhaps man couldn't
have faced living out his life, if death had abandoned him.

I stopped teaching cures. I taught men to see into the
future. What future they had was as close as death, but
not so certain. They had dreams, some true, some false,
some . . . I think I taught them which were true. They   60
heard voices in dreams, awake, anywhere. I made men

listen, then they understood what those modest seeping
sounds were trying to tell them. There were signs at
every step along man's way, yet he was trampling them
down, and hurting himself because he couldn't read their
message . . . Look, you cannot see it . . . a vulture is
swinging nearer to us from the distant sky. Crooked tal-
oned, fat, with an empty stomach—it seems to have
found us out. It might be our release. Man would know;
I taught him. I taught him the feuds, hungers, lusts of   70
birds, and why they gather. I made man stare into the
entrails of beasts, see their smoothness, roughness—each
had a meaning—see what kind of gall would please the
gods, see that the speckled symmetry of the liver lobe
had meaning, the thighbone swimming in fat, the long
spine jointed like these chains. Everything in animals,
even their excrement meant something. Their innards
would be correctly set on fire to appease the gods. I
made men look into the fire. Alone and bemused in the
slothful dark, they studied the fire's whirling and con-   80
suming colors, and believed they would some day taste
the breath of life. No one knows, I haven't told anyone,
the many wonders I have invented. I was out of my mind,
my hand was everywhere. Everything man knows . . .

29. A shorter version of the monologue might begin with this line, and perhaps
end with "It might be our release." on line 65.

Hippolytus
by Euripides
Translated by Kenneth Cavander

THESEUS
The human intellect saddens me. It marches
Onwards, always onwards, but where? Where
Will the end come to this reckless growth of confidence?

For suppose that, life in, life out, it swells and blooms,
And each generation dwarfs the crimes of the one
Before, heaven will have to build a second
Earth, another world, to hold the swarming
Breed of the wicked and the faithless.

Look at him! My son! My own son, who tried
To trail his filthy hands in my marriage, and now   10
Is convicted—see him!—convicted, by his dead
Accuser! . . . You fiend! Turn around, you creature, crawling
With your leprosy of guilt! Look your father in the eyes.
Here! . . . You were too good for this earth. You made
Your friends among the gods. Restrained and prudent,
A child in the matter of sin! I would not waste
A minute in believing your conceit; I would insult
Heaven's wisdom if I thought the gods could choose
Their friends so stupidly. Let me hear you boasting now!
"Orpheus is our master; we must not eat meat."   20
Oh, the theories you hawked about! Go back to your trances.
And your misty mumblings and your books. I know
You now, and I warn everyone to give you
And your kind a good distance. You hunt your victims
With pomposity and cant, you hellish spiders!
She is dead.
Will that save you? No, you are wrong, it is that
Decides your guilt, you murderer! This corpse has more
Voice than all your solemn oaths and your persuasion;
You will never persuade that accusing voice away.   30

You will say she hates you, that the bastard son is always
In conflict with the true born. But that would make her
Drive a wretched bargain—to trade her dearest
Possession, her life, out of hatred for you.
Or you will say that men have flawless morals,
That it is the fault of women. But I know youth;
When love meddles in a young man's heart, that man

Is more dangerous than any woman. His sex
Is like an urgent friend, furthering his love.
And so . . . But do I have to prove my case?   40
Here is a witness, this body, that cannot lie.

You are banished. Leave the country. Now! Now!
And do not dare go near Athens, my sacred
City, nor any country where my soldiers
Make me king.

Hippolytus
by Euripides
Translated by Kenneth Cavander

HIPPOLYTUS

Father, your battling temper, with its knots of fury,
Frightens me. Yet the facts, if you look between
Their folds, are not so fine and simple as you make
Them sound.
              I do not pride myself on expressing
My thoughts in public, although among my friends
And in small groups I can speak with point and purpose.
And the reverse is true. People who are dimmed
By brilliant company, will play like artists on the public . . .
But in this ruin of my life I must
Find words somewhere . . .
                        You attacked me where you thought   10
Attack would hurt me most, and I would have no reply.
I shall begin there—with my virtue. Look at these fields,
The sky above them. In all this, no one
Sees more sharply than I what his duty is
And does it so readily—well, you say not, but that
Is so. I am devout; my friends, too, would not

Even try to do wrong; they would blush to enroll anyone
Into sin or lend their efforts to dishonesty.
I do not jeer, father, at my neighbors;
I am the same man to my friends when they cannot hear
    me   20
As when they can.
                  There is one thing, and this
Is precisely what you hope to convict me of,
Which I have never known. Till this very moment
I have never slept with a woman, nor do I know
Anything of physical love except what others tell me
Or what I see in pictures—and even these
Never draw my mind to them; for my heart
Is pure . . . But I see my innocence does not convince you.

Very well.
Why should I fall in love with her? Tell me, why?   30
Because she was supremely beautiful? Or perhaps
I hoped to be master of your house one day
By marrying into property? Madness! The plan
Of an idiot! Perhaps I was in love with power? No one
Whose reason dictated to his desires would think of it.
Power is a pleasure that counts among the vices.
I would rather come first in a race in the games with all
Greece watching, and run second in politics
At home, where I would be happy with my noble friends.
It would be an active life—more pleasant than absolute   40
Power because it is less dangerous.

There is my defence, except for one last thing.
If I had a witness to my inner self
And Phaedra were alive to hear me plead my case,
You could have seen, by holding our actions to the light,
Where the wrong lay. But there is no witness,
And so I swear, by Zeus, who takes and tests
My oath, by this earth which gave me life, I have never
Laid a finger on your wife, never wished to, never

Conceived the thought;
                              if I am guilty, let me die,   50
Let my name be never heard of, never spoken,
Let my country and my home disown me, let neither
The sea nor the land give my body rest.

I do not know whether an anguish of fear made Phaedra
Take her life, and it would be wrong for me
To say more. In a way, her reason ruled her life
At the moment when its control was least, and my reason
Stood by, and could do nothing but harm.

———————————————

Alcestis
by Euripides
Translated by Philip Vellacott

ADMETUS

While you lived you were
My wife; and dying you alone will bear that name.
And no Thessalian bride shall ever take your place,
To call me husband;
                              there is none so royal in birth,
Of such rare beauty, that could win me. I am content
With these two children, and pray the gods to give me joy
In them, since I have lost the joy I had in you.

And not for one year only, Alcestis, but as long
As my life lasts, I shall endure my grief for you,
Counting my mother and my father as enemies,   10
Hating them; for they loved me in word but not in deed.
But you, by bartering your own precious life for mine,
Saved me. Shall I not mourn, when I am losing you—
So rare a wife? There shall be no more dancing here;
The crowded feasts, the merrymaking that filled this house,

The garlands, music—all that is finished. I could never
Finger my lyre again, or rouse my heart to sing
To the Libyan flute. My life's delights vanish with you.

I shall bid a cunning sculptor carve your image in stone,
And it shall lie stretched on our bed, and I shall kneel   20
Beside it, and throw my arms round it, and speak your name,
And vainly think I hold my dear wife in my arms—
Cold comfort, truly; none the less, a way to lighten
My heavy heart. Then in my dreams you'd come and go,
Making me glad; to see a loved face even in dreams
Brings pleasure, for as long as the illusion lasts.

Oh, if I had the songs that Orpheus had, his voice,
To enchant with music Pluto and Persephone,
I would go down to fetch you; and not Cerberus
Would stop me—no, nor Charon's ferry-load of ghosts,   30
Till I had brought you living to the light of day!—

It cannot be. Look for me there when I shall die;
And make a home ready, where you can be with me.
I shall command these children to entomb us both
In one coffin of cedar-wood, and to lay out
My body close to yours. I will not, even in death,
Be parted from you, who alone are true to me.

27. Orpheus: master musician, trained by the Muses in the playing of Apollo's
    lyre, known especially for having brought his wife, Eurydice, from the un-
    derworld. Admetus amplifies the image by naming several other principals
    from the story: Pluto (or Hades) and Persephone, reigning rulers of the dead;
    Cerberus, the netherworld's multiheaded guard dog; Charon, the boatman
    who ferries the souls of the dead across the river Styx.

Prometheus Bound
by Robert Lowell
Derived from Aeschylus

Io

The house of my father, Inachus, Prometheus . . . you must know it, it's the best house in Euboea, and has the largest herds.

There, a little before now . . . no, long before . . . just before my mother's death . . . I was born, another human lump, without shape or strength or the heart to crawl. The fields came close to me then, and cattle followed the fields, and the herdsmen seemed to lean on the shoulders of the cattle. And when men and animals changed places to look at me, I looked back at them with their own dazed, absent-minded stare—ribs   10
rising and falling together, one soothing sound of tooth and tongue and crunched stalk . . .

Then I learned to walk, and was allowed to follow the cattle. I went out with them at sunrise, came home with them at sunset. I could speak to the cattle. Later, I could speak to the herdsmen. Later, I could speak to my father . . . Animals, servants, and my father, their king— they went on looking at me with the same look of coarse, indifferent kindness. I might have been a boy, or a calf . . . Then one morning, I saw my father in a thun-   20
dercloud—no, not my father, but a face with splintered black eyebrows, a beard of black rope, and a smile, ob- scene and royal . . . the face of Zeus. Lightning flashed at me from the cloud, like the wink of a man, and I knew what the god desired. From then on, even in the clearest weather, the cloud would stand above the fields, and wait for me. My father's servants couldn't scare it from

the sky with their sticks. Then I began to scream at it.
I was led home, and shut in my room.

I was told the cloud still stood above the fields for days   30
and waited. Then at last, thundering and roaring and
whimpering to itself, it ran off like a wolf. That night, I
saw Zeus, still cloudy, but darker and made of flesh now.
I felt my breasts rise, and grow hard, I couldn't take my
eyes off the god. I pitied him too, because he was thin
and black, and looked scorched to the bone with his
despair. His hands smoothed and soothed me. His black,
swollen lips brushed my skin. His tongue slithered and
slimed in my mouth. My thighs unclenched. I heard the
voice of Zeus, saying "Io, your time has come. Our time   40
has come." Then a crash of thunder—God was gone. I
was unhappy. I felt a flatness. I missed my lover. When
I reached out for him, I saw Hermes, the messenger of
the gods, standing by my bed, and waving me back with
his wand. "Io," he said, "I have come to join you in
marriage with the highest power." Then I pitied Hermes,
because he seemed young and tense and unused to such
missions. His armor was like armor that had never been
worn, and not a feather on his wings was out of place.
Hermes said, "Zeus is on fire for you, Io. Don't you hear   50
the impatient grumbling of his thunder? Hurry. We must
leave this house, its molding would smother Zeus. Come
with me. The great pasture of your father will be the
marriage-bed of Zeus." . . . I remember that walk—hot
brown grass like an oven under my feet, excited cattle,
nudging against me, and rolling up their eyes. At every
step, I felt the slow swish and slap of a tasseled tail. The
air was thick and rich as hay. The whole pasture lay like
a huge panting body. Then I saw Zeus. He seemed to
say, "Take me. I must rest from my labors." Then I   60
looked at the cattle and thought to myself, "These creatures do not take life, or frighten anyone. I will be like
them. They have never resisted the gods." Then I be-

came like them, I became God's creature, and Zeus, for
a moment, had his rest in me.

No rest, no sleep. I hid in my room—no sleep there,
only drawn-out hours of half-sleep, soiled and ruffled by
my guilty visions. Tongues sticking to my tongue. Rough
hands chafing at my breasts like the sands of the desert.
At all hours, the bellowing of animals, their tails curling   70
between my legs, the watery, seductive gurgle of their
throats, their thick tongues saying, "Go to him. Go to
him." I was changing, I was growing larger, I was with
child. Each new swelling of my body was terrible and
painful to me, but I thought Zeus needed me, and I tried
to go to him. Then Hermes came again. His armor was
disheveled and comfortable on him now, and he spoke
with an easy arrogance, as he blocked the doorway like
a veteran soldier, and chewed the tip of his wand. "Io,"
he said, "stay where you are. Have pity on Zeus. He   80
will not be pleased when he sees how you have swollen."
Then I fell. When I woke, I saw a woman sitting by my
bed, and I thought she was my old nurse, because she
was brown and wrinkled and healthy, and because she
was soothing my head with a cold cloth. But it was Hera,
the wife of Zeus, and she was bending close to me and
singing, "Sleep, my child. I give you a day and a day,
and perhaps another day, to gather your strength. Then
I must never let you rest." My eyes had red splotches
on them, and the pain made Hera's face tremble a little   90
menacingly in the heat, but soon the room was still, and
I saw that Hera was doing her best to be gentle with
me, and was even trying to brush off two flies, as big as
her thumbs, that had crawled from my swollen stomach,
half-dead, and already beginning to mate. "Don't bother
with these flies," the wife of Zeus said. "When you see
them again, they will be a thousand. When women are
warm enough to make love, the gods send them flies.
The flies rise from your sticky flesh, are warmed by your

heat, and kept alive by the blood from your thighs or   100
the milk from your breasts."

I went to my father. He kept looking off in the distance,
and counting on his fingers, as if he were counting his
herds. I said, "I have been visited by Zeus." My father
didn't hear me. He went on counting on his fingers. Then
I said, "I am with child by Zeus." Then my father heard
me. In his madness, he struck me, and even sent out
men to beat the hills for the criminal. Then he sent
messengers to the oracles at Pytho and Dodona. They
answered darkly. "Give Io air. Let her breathe. Knock   110
holes in your walls. Tear the roof from your house." My
rooms were torn open. All day then, I was looked at by
the cattle and the herdsmen and my father and the gods
and the winds. The holes were like eye-holes in a skull,
and Zeus seemed to be watching me through the eye-
holes. Then the oracle spoke more clearly. "Give Io air.
Give her the world. She must leave her father's house,
and run across the earth and never stop running until
she dies. If you try to hold your daughter back, the fire
of God will destroy your house and your herds and your   120
kingdom."

Then I began running, and my mind grew small and
hard. Horns began to push through the side of my head.
They hurt at first, but the swelling of my stomach stopped,
as if my child had stopped growing. Then I thirsted, and
forgot my horns and my child, and the gods let me wade
in the slow sweet stream of Cerchnea, and drink from
its pools. No flies were pursuing me then, but the wife
of Zeus had already sent Argus, her herdsman with a
hundred eyes, to watch me. At each bend in the river,   130
I would see Argus sitting on the bank and dangling his
feet in the water. He would play pathetic tunes to me
on his shepherd's pipe. He never harmed me, and only
watched, but his eyes burned like the heat of a hundred

suns. Then Hermes came again. He said, "We can still
do you small favors, Io." Then he waved his wand over
Argus and lulled him asleep and cut off his head. Then
a swarm of flies swooped for the head as it floated down
river. Suddenly, the flies swerved and turned on me. I
see them always before me and behind me now, beautiful   140
and stinging . . . Oh Zeus, I am blinded by your splen-
dor spread out before me like a peacock's tail with a
hundred eyes! . . . I shall never stop running.

66. Prometheus prompts Io at this point, saying, "Zeus found his rest in you,
but you had none." An effective shorter version of this monologue might
begin here and run to the end, possibly leaving out lines 102–21.
109. Pytho: another name for Apollo's oracle at Delphi.
    Dodona: the most ancient oracle in Greece.

Hippolytus
by Euripides
Translated by Kenneth Cavander

PHAEDRA

Here, in Troezen, the Peloponnese ends, the traveler
Pauses and looks back . . .
                 I have looked back,
Women, as the nights have dragged their hours away,
And thought, idly, of people's broken lives.
I do not think we suffer for any flaw
Of intellect—most of us have a mind able
To see what is right. No, it is more like this:
We know what we ought to do, our reason is there
To tell us. We simply do not do it . . . a failure
Of will, perhaps, or perhaps we value some pleasure   10
More highly than our duty . . . any pleasure,
For life teems with them—the hours we spend in talking,
In doing nothing—all our useless amusements,

And silent longings to be high in another's thoughts.
And so we hold back; sometimes it does no harm,
At others, it is fatal;
                              this riddle always
Lies, unanswered, in the ambiguous present.
That is where my thoughts, like birds, have settled,
So that nothing can move them. There is no magic distilled
That can change me to what I was. I have traveled too far   20
With my thoughts—but let me show you the road we took.

I fell in love; it hurts; but at first I tried
To bear the pain, and keep my conscience whole.
And so I began with silence, to keep the wound concealed;
Oh, I could not trust my tongue, that clever critic
Of the world's mistakes, betraying the thousand faults.
It owns itself. Next, I thought I would calm
My frenzied heart, tame it by cold reason . . .
I tried, I tried hard, but could not defeat Aphrodite.
And at last I fixed on death, the most effective   30
Plan—oh, surely, it is? If I do good,
Let the world know. But if I sin, it must
Be hidden.
And I knew this desire that mastered me, this disease,
Would be talked of with horror; as a woman, I knew
It would revolt everyone. Oh, how I hate and curse
The wife who was the first unfaithful to her husband
With another man! The vile trick was begun
By women, and by women of distinction.
And if rich and great are placid toward evil,   40
The small and humble will see nothing wrong in it.
I hate those females with pious mouths, and secret
Lives of wickedness . . . Aphrodite,
Your power is high and your name great, how can they
Look in their husbands' eyes? Does not the night,
Their accomplice, bring cold terror with him, and when
They see the walls, do they not wait for them to speak?
It is this fear, the fear of discovery, of shaming

My husband, and my own children, that makes me turn
To death.
                    My children must be able to talk   50
Of me openly, happily, to live in Athens,
In a great city, where no one can insult their name
For what their mother was. Even a heart
As confident as a young soldier can be crushed
If the father or the mother leave memory
Of sin.
                Life is beautiful. Only one thing
Is nearly so beautiful—a conscience with no scar.
Time, as gently as a young girl, holds up
Her mirror, and you see the faces of those
Who have sinned. I must not be one of them.   60

1. Troezen: Theseus's birthplace, near the northern extremity of the Peloponnese, Greece's southern peninsula.

Medea
by Euripides
Adapted by Robinson Jeffers

MEDEA

Annihilation. The word is pure music: annihilation. To anni-
    hilate the past—
Is not possible: but its fruit in the present—
Can be nipped off.
                        Am I to look in my sons' eyes
And see Jason's forever? How could I endure the endless
    defilement, those lives
That mix Jason and me? Better to be clean
Bones on the shore. Bones have no eyes at all, how could they
    weep? White bones
On the Black Sea shore—

——

If I should go into the house with a sharp knife
To the man and his bride—
Or if I could fire the room they sleep in, and hear them   10
Wake in the white of the fire, and cry to each other, and howl
  like dogs.
And howl and die—

But I might fail; I might be cut down first;
The knife might turn in my hand, or the fire not burn, and
  my enemies could laugh at me.
No: I have subtler means, and more deadly cruel; I have my
  dark art
That fools call witchcraft. Not for nothing I have worshipped
  the wild gray goddess that walks in the dark, the wise one,
The terrible one, the sweet huntress, flower of the night,
  Hecate,
In my house at my hearth.

Ancient Goddess to whom I and my people
Make the sacrifice of black lambs and black female
  hounds,   20
Holy one, haunter of cross-roads, queen of night, Hecate,
Help me now: to remember in my mind the use of the venomous
  fire, the magic song
And the sharp gems.

Look at him: he loves them—ah? Therefore his dear children
Are not going to that city but a darker city, where no games
  are played, no music is heard. —Do you think
I am a cow lowing after the calf? Or a bitch with pups, licking
The hand that struck her? Watch and see. Watch this man,
  women: he is going to weep. I think
He is going to weep blood, and quite soon, and much more
Than I have wept. Watch and keep silence.
                                        Jason,
Are the boys dear to you? I think I am satisfied that you love
  them,   30

These two young heroes.
You shall take them to—Creon's daughter, your wife—and
make them kneel to her, and ask her
To ask her father to let them stay here in Corinth. He'll grant
it, he is growing old, he denies her nothing.
Even that hard king loves his only child.
What she asks is done.—You will go with the boys, Jason,
and speak for them,—they are not skillful yet
In supplication—and I'll send gifts. I'll put gifts in their hands.
People say that gifts
Will persuade even the gods.
With such jewels—and such a husband—ah? Her sun is rising,
mine is going down—I hope
To a red sunset. —The little gold wreath is pretty isn't it?
Vine leaves: the flashing   40
    Arrow-sharp leaves. They have weight, though.

Farewell, sweet boys: brave little trudging pilgrims from the
black wave
To the white desert: take the stuff in, be sure you lay it in her
own hands.
Come back and tell me what happens.
                                        Tell me what happens.

Rejoice, women, the gifts are given; the bait is laid.
The gods roll their great eyes over Creon's house and quietly
smile;
That robe of bright-flowing gold, that bride-veil, that fish-net
To catch a young slender salmon—not mute, she'll sing: her
delicate body writhes in the meshes,
The golden wreath binds her bright head with light: she'll
dance, she'll sing loudly:
Would I were there to hear it, that proud one howling. —
    Look, the sun's out again, the clouds are gone,   50
    All's gay and clear. Ai! I wish the deep earth would open
    and swallow us—
Before I do what comes next.

I wish all life would perish, and the holy gods in high heaven
  die, before my little ones
Come home to my hands.

The Women of Trachis
by Sophocles
Translated by Michael Jameson

DEIANIRA

O my friends, I am afraid! Can it be
I have gone too far in all I have just done?

Something has happened which, if I tell you, my friends,
will seem a marvel such as you never thought to hear.
Just now, when I anointed the robe I sent to be
my husband's vestment, I used a tuft of fleecy white wool.
This piece has disappeared, devoured by nothing in
the house but destroyed by itself, eaten away
and crumbled completely to dust. I want to tell you this
in detail, so you may know the whole story.   10

I neglected none of the instructions that beast
the centaur explained to me, lying in agony
with the sharp arrowhead in his side. I kept them
like an inscription on bronze that cannot be washed away.
And I only did what I was told to do—
I must keep this drug away from fire and always
deep in the house where no warm ray of light may touch it
until I should want to apply it freshly smeared.
And this is what I did. Now, when it had to do its work,
at home, inside the house, secretly I smeared it on   20
some wool, a scrap I pulled from one of the household sheep,
and then I folded my gift and put it in a chest
before the sun could shine on it, as you saw.

But when I go in again, I see something
unspeakable, incomprehensible to human reason.
Somehow I had happened to throw the ball of wool,
which I had used to smear the robe, into the full heat
of the sun's rays, and, as it became warm,
it all ran together, a confused mass, and crumbled
to bits on the ground, looking most like the dust one sees   30
eaten away in the cutting of a piece of wood.
Like this it lies where it fell. But from the earth
on which it rests, clotted foam boils up
like the rich liquid of the blue-green fruit
from the vines of Dionysus, poured on the earth.
And now I do not know what to think. I see
myself as someone who has done a terrible thing.
From what possible motive, in return for what,
could the dying beast have shown me kindness, when he
was dying because of me? No, he beguiled me,   40
only to destroy the man who shot him. But I
have come to understand now when it is too late.
I alone, unless my fears are fanciful,
I, his unhappy wife, shall destroy him.

I know that arrow which struck Nessus injured even
Chiron, who was a god, and all animals,
whatever it touches, it kills. This same poison which seeped,
black and bloody, from the wounds of Nessus, how can
it fail to kill Heracles too? At least, this is
my fear.
             And yet I have made a decision: if he goes down,   50
under the same blow I will die with him.
I could not bear to live and hear myself called evil
when my only wish is to be truly good.

46. Chiron: another centaur, the wisest of the lot and tutor to many Greek heroes.
    Although a friend to Heracles, he was severely injured when accidentally
    struck by one of Heracles' arrows, the tip poisoned by having been dipped
    into the blood of the monster, Hydra. This section of the monologue, be-
    ginning with line 45, may easily be omitted, to pick up again with "And yet
    I have made a decision . . . " on line 50.

CHORUSES, COMICS, AND MESSENGERS

I recommend specialty selections like these for the wide interpretive range to which they can be subjected, the opportunity for the actor to emphasize some special skill—movement or mime, for instance—and the great potential for offbeat character work. Further, most can be comfortably performed by either men or women, thus expanding the inadequate supply of women's classical monologues. Most choruses, I've found, when well translated, remain too musical and choreographic in feeling to function well as monologues. This selection from *The Trojan Women* is an exception in its clear attitude, direct storytelling, and highly personal punch line.

The choral interlude from *Thesmophoriazusae* (literally translatable as "The Women Who Worship at the Festival of Thesmophoria") is, of course, different because it's funny. To my mind, William Arrowsmith has an ear especially attuned not only to the explosive vulgarity demanded by that piece, but also to the affected self-conscious lyricism of Agathon's ode. Agathon, a friend of Euripides and Plato, was a tragic poet much respected by the Greeks, of whose work virtually nothing survives. He was responsible for the introduction of "New Music," an aesthetic that subordinated text to music. Aristophanes' parody of his work, Arrowsmith suggests, is respectful rather than comic. What is funny is the situation: a songwriter who doesn't know he is being observed playing both soloist and chorus. I concur with the translator's further suggestion that he be composing as he goes, so that we are witnessing a process rather than a finished performance, and that Agathon be good at what he does rather than a lame failure.

When the Greek dramatists presented their plays in festivals, a trilogy of tragedies would be followed by a satyr play, usually a humorous treatment of a myth. *The Cyclops* is the only complete such text surviving, and it deals with Odysseus's encounter with Polyphemus the Cyclops on his way home from the Trojan War. The monster, accused of impiety for holding Odysseus and his men captive, responds with more impiety. The actor has some delicious choices open to him regarding Odysseus's size relative to Polyphemus, another question of scale altogether.

Apparently Aeschylus himself fought in the battle of Salamis that is the subject of the Messenger's speech from *The Persians*, and there is a sense of authenticity about it that compensates for its relatively straightforward narrative—complicated only by being told from the Persian perspective. A shorter version might begin at line 24 and end at line 81. The brief personal note at the end is typical of such monologues, but Euripides takes it further, as in *The Bacchae*, where we sense the constant presence of the Herdsman's point of view, reacting, judging, and commenting. Here, as in other instances, Kenneth Cavander's translation is most effective in giving us a sense of a real, breathing person behind the event. Speaking to Pentheus, the disbelieving king, the Herdsman functions almost as an intermediary for Dionysos, using a sensual lyricism to seduce his audience into an appreciation of the horror to come.

The Trojan Women
by Euripides
Adapted by John Barton and Kenneth Cavander
Translated by Kenneth Cavander

CHORUS
Once upon a time
There was a Trojan shepherd.
His name was Ganymede,
And he spent his days on the hillsides
Guarding his sheep whom he loved

But he was so beautiful
That—how shall I say?—the gods
Wanted him with them for ever.
Zeus himself loved him,
So he sent down an eagle   10
And it carried Ganymede
To heaven between its talons.
And there he lives for ever:
He will never grow old,
He will always be happy,
He will have no cares or troubles
And he will pour the wine out
To the Father of us all.

We should still hold on to one thing:
When the gods walked on earth   20
They walked here in Troy.
There was nothing to rival Troy
In the whole of Asia.

The palaces were built of gold.
The streets were wide and lovely.

When the harvest was good they said
Some god has breathed on our fields.

It is well known that one
Of my forefathers was a god.

Who but a god could have moved   30
Those giant blocks of stone?

It burned like fire up there
High up on the battlements.

It was never hot inside the city.
There was always a cool breeze.

———

It seems now we have lost
The way of pleasing heaven.

Thesmophoriazusae
(*or* Euripides at Bay)
by Aristophanes
Translated by William Arrowsmith

CHORUS

The Choral Interlude at *last*! Time for us to step forward
and put in a good word or two in praise of women.
                                              God knows,
we could use a little kindness now and then, what with you
   men
constantly trotting out your libellous clichés and nasty little
labels, calling us Albatrosses, Millstones-around-the-Necks-of-
   Honest-Men, Harpies, Holy Terrors,
Royal Pains, and God knows what
sexist rubbish. Talk about poor Pandora! Why,
to hear you talk,
every human evil is entirely women's doing: *viz.*,
Squabbling,   10
Feuding, Revolution, Total War, Arthritis, Hemorrhoids,
and you name it.
              Now:
If we're such bloody Millstones around your aching male necks,
why do you idiots insist on marrying Millstones?
I mean:
why settle down with an Albatross when you don't have to?
And why put this nasty Albatross in a little gilded cage
and then go green with jealousy every time she flies the coop
or even peeps out the bars? Why all this furious fuss
to keep your Harpy in her place—"in the kitchen," of
   course,   20

"where she belongs"?

It's crazy.

Or suppose a girl steps out,
and you can't momentarily locate your personal Albatross:
you fly off the handle and start climbing the walls.
Whereas
if we're the Royal Pains you say we are, you ought to be
     whooping it up
and thanking God your Royal Pain has flown the little nest.
But that's too *rational* for men, isn't it?
Or suppose we get bored with our steady diet of conjugal bliss
and spend the night at a girlfriend's place: you poor twerps
literally tear the joint to pieces, looking for your   30
lost pet Albatross or your missing Millstone.
And what happens if one of us Holy Terrors so much as looks
     out
the window? *Presto,* there's a gaggle of men down below
drooling and gaping at the legs of this Holy Terror.
And if the Albatross is shy and tries to hide, you men promptly
go berserk with impatience waiting for this Albatross to
     brighten up
your life. Which only proves your obvious inferiority to women;
if you're not inferior, how come you're always underneath us,
staring up?

We can prove our case,
and we propose to do just that. You say we're worse   40
than men, but we're *demonstrably* superior. Take, for
     instance,
a typical sample of men and women—
a few representative cases chosen at random.
Charminos, you'll admit, is a notorious loser. It
isn't *every* admiral, after all,
who succeeds in losing an entire fleet in a single naval battle.
Well, compare the man with Nausimache.
She's certainly notorious; in fact, she's a whore.
Has she ever lost a navel encounter? Nary a one.
Or contrast the cases of Cleophon and Salabaccho.   50

He's a politician, she's a whore. But which is worse?
Clearly, Cleophon. Why? Because he screws the whole city
   en masse,
and his service charge makes poor Salabaccho look like a piker.
Or compare the sexes of past and present.
Modern men are effeminate and degenerate; they're losers to
   a man.
Show us one *man* who can compare with the *wives* of the men
   who fought
and won at Marathon. You can't. Because they're not heroes.
Hell, they're not even heroines.
                              Or take the case of Euboule.
You men treat her with contempt: she's a "woman of easy
   virtue."
Well, easy or not, there's more virtue in that little hustler's
   twat   60
than you'll find in any Senator whose term is presently
   expiring.
No comment, Senator?
                            In conclusion, we women claim our sex
is indisputably superior. You don't catch women embezzling
   public funds
and then driving up to the Akropolis the next day in a brand-
   new
wide-track super de luxe sports chariot. No, it takes a *man*
to embezzle in a big way. Whereas if a woman steals at all,
it's usually nothing but petty larceny—a little chickenfeed,
   say,
or something of the sort. And she steals it from her husband,
and she pays it back with interest too, that very same day.

What man among you so-called men can claim as much?   70
What are you men but conglomerate deadbeats, fatcats?
Overstuffedshirt, loudmouth, cheap-ass gluttons,
professional plumbers, grafters, contractors, swindlers
on the make, the take, traffickers in slaves
(black and white), exploiters of the other sex?

In fact, are you even *men*? Frankly, we wonder.
God knows, we're women (and damned proud of it too)!
Our traditions and our attributes—they're *ours*.
Distaff, spindle, loom, knit one purl two—
you name it, we can find it. It's *ours*, still.   80
But you! What have you sexless zeroes got?
Where's your *spear*? Your *shaft*? Your *thew*? Your *thrust*?
Your *sinew*? Your *spine*? Your *backbone*? Boys,
where are your BALLS?

57. Marathon: celebrated battle between Athenians and Persians, 490 B.C.
62. No comment, Senator?: *(To a putative Senator in the audience)*, translator's
     stage direction.

Thesmophoriazusae
(*or* Euripides at Bay)
by Aristophanes
Translated by William Arrowsmith

AGATHON

Trojan dancers   take this torch   (*as* KORYPHAIOS)
by Kore and Demeter blessed,
sing your freedom
                    dance such joy
you bring the gods who make us free
you bring the gods who make us glad.

Teach my feet   to follow yours   (*as* CHORUS)
what god   what goddess   shall I sing?
O leader master
teach my movements to adore
divinities who make me dance!   10

Muse of singing   dancing words   (*as* KORYPHAIOS)
by your beauty   weave him here:

bright Apollo   Golden Bow
dance him down
as once his weaving song compelled
tier by tier   the stones of Troy
by singing bound
is beauty made   this towered place.

Lovely words best call Apollo: (*as* CHORUS)
O god of sudden light in mortal darkness blazing,   · 20
power whose shining
crowns with god all loveliness of mortal song,
illuminate my singing!

Now sing the goddess of the greening oaks: (*as* KORYPHAIOS)
O Purity
            Presence of high and lonely places
You whose virgin eyes disclose
                                    miraculous
the virgin world!

Purity becomes her best: (*as* CHORUS)
Come, O golden Leto's goddess child:
With pure and virgin words I pray: 30
O Artemis
            unapproachable Virgin
be with us now.

Now sing the lady Leto   sing the lovely lyre (*as* KORYPHAIOS)
whose oriental strings
                    beat
                        ecstatic time
and circling feet   wildly weaving
                            trace
their graceful arabesques in glory of the Goddess.

——

I glorify the mother, Leto   (*as* CHORUS)
I praise her lovely lyre:
                    O mother of music
Your golden progeny is song!
                              And lo!
the deep male voice of the shining god   40
in answer rings:
Apollo!

Sings   (*as* KORYPHAIOS)
        and from immortal eyes
sudden glory breaks
                    a splendor falls
on blinded mortal vision.
Wherefore I sing:
                    praise the shining of Apollo!

Hail, Apollo, splendid son of holy Leto!   (*as* CHORUS)

2. Kore and Demeter: Kore is Persephone, whose mother, Demeter, was the
   goddess of the earth's fruits. The festival of the Thesmophoria commemorated
   the introduction of the laws and regulations of civilized life, which were as-
   cribed to Demeter since agriculture is the basis of civilization.
29. Leto: goddess worshiped as the mother of both Artemis, the virgin huntress,
   and Apollo, god of medicine, music, archery, and prophecy.

The Cyclops
by Euripides
Translated by Roger Lancelyn Green

POLYPHEMUS

Midget, the really wise man's god is gain:
All else is mere pretence, vaunting and vain.

What of each sea-girt pile and sanctuary?
My father's temples are no use to me.

I scorn the bolt of Zeus you call divine!
How do I know his power is more than mine?
That's all that counts.
                        And when the rain comes down
I've got my snug, dry cave, in which I drown
The thunder with loud belches, feasting there
On some roast game, or veal, and banish care   10
With gurgling vats of milk. And when the snow
Comes from the bitter north, why then I blow
The embers to a blaze, throw on a tree,
Don a warm fur—and what's the snow to me!

The earth bears grass, whether it will or not,
To feed my flocks and herds. So tell me what
I need with sacrifice—which none deserve?
My belly is the only god I serve!
It's simple sense that man's first care should be
To please himself: no other deity   20
Is half so pleasing as a well-fed man.

As for the fool who forms himself a plan,
A code of rules to make him sick and sad,
I wish him joy of it, and think he's mad.
I've got more sense than to deny myself!

So to the pot you go: nor prayers nor pelf
Shall save you. Here's true hospitality:
A warm place in my—belly—presently!

Come in! The cauldron waits, the water boils:
My welcome frees a man from all his toils!   30

26. pelf: wealth.

The Persians
by Aeschylus
Translated by Philip Vellacott

MESSENGER

Some Fury, some malignant Power,
Appeared, and set in train the whole disastrous rout.

A Hellene from the Athenian army came and told
Your son Xerxes this tale: that, once the shades of night
Set in, the Hellenes would not stay, but leap on board,
And, by whatever secret route offered escape,
Row for their lives. When Xerxes heard this, with no thought
Of the man's guile, or of the jealousy of the gods,
He sent this word to all his captains: "When the sun
No longer flames to warm the earth, and darkness holds   10
The court of heaven, range the main body of our fleet
Threefold, to guard the outlets and the choppy straits."
Then he sent other ships to row right round the isle,
Threatening that if the Hellene ships found a way through
To save themselves from death, he would cut off the head
Of every Persian captain. By these words he showed
How ignorance of the gods' intent had dazed his mind.

Our crews, then, in good order and obediently,
Were getting supper; then each oarsman looped his oar
To the smooth rowing-pin; and when the sun went down   20
And night came on, the rowers all embarked, and all
The heavy-armed soldiers; and from line to line they called,
Cheering each other on, rowing and keeping course
As they were ordered.
                    All night long the captains kept
Their whole force cruising to and fro across the strait.
Now night was fading; still the Hellenes showed no sign
Of trying to sail out unnoticed; till at last

Over the earth shone the white horses of the day,
Filling the air with beauty. Then from the Hellene ships
Rose like a song of joy the piercing battle-cry,   30
And from the island crags echoed an answering shout.

The Persians knew their error; fear gripped every man.
They were no fugitives who sang that terrifying
Paean, but Hellenes charging with courageous hearts
To battle. The loud trumpet flamed along their ranks.
At once their frothy oars moved with a single pulse,
Beating the salt waves to the bo'suns' chant; and soon
Their whole fleet hove clear into view; their right wing first,
In precise order, next their whole array came on,
And at that instant a great shout beat our ears: 40
"Forward, you sons of Hellas! Set your country free!
Set free your sons, your wives, tombs of your ancestors,
And temples of your gods. All is at stake: now fight!"
Then from our side in answer rose the manifold
Clamour of Persian voices; and the hour had come.

At once ship into ship battered its brazen beak.
A Hellene ship charged first, and chopped off the whole stern
Of a Phoenician galley. Then charge followed charge
On every side. At first by its huge impetus
Our fleet withstood them. But soon, in that narrow space,   50
Our ships were jammed in hundreds; none could help another.
They rammed each other with their prows of bronze; and some
Were stripped of every oar. Meanwhile the enemy
Came round us in a ring and charged. Our vessels heeled
Over; the sea was hidden, carpeted with wrecks
And dead men; all the shores and reefs were full of dead.

Then every ship we had broke rank and rowed for life.
The Hellenes seized fragments of wrecks and broken oars
And hacked and stabbed at our men swimming in the sea
As fishermen kill tunnies or some netted haul.   60
The whole sea was one din of shrieks and dying groans,

Till night and darkness hid the scene.

> > > If I should speak

For ten days and ten nights, I could not tell you all
That day's agony. But know this: never before
In one day died so vast a company of men.

But there is more, and worse.

> > > Opposite Salamis

There is an island—small, useless for anchorage—
Where Pan the Dancer treads along the briny shore.
There Xerxes sent them, so that, when the enemy,
Flung from their ships, were struggling to the island
　　beach,   70
The Persian force might without trouble cut them down,
And rescue Persian crews from drowning in the sea:
Fatal misjudgement!

> > > When in the sea-battle Heaven

Had given glory to the Hellenes, that same day
They came, armed with bronze shields and spears, leapt from
　　their ships,
And made a ring round the whole island, that our men
Could not tell where to turn. First came a shower of blows
From stones slung with the hand; then from the drawn
　　bowstring
Arrows leapt forth to slaughter; finally, with one
Fierce roar the Hellenes rushed at them, and cut and
　　carved   80
Their limbs like butchers, till the last poor wretch lay dead.

This depth of horror Xerxes saw; close to the sea
On a high hill he sat, where he could clearly watch
His whole force both by sea and land. He wailed aloud,
And tore his clothes, weeping; and instantly dismissed
His army, hastening them to a disordered flight.

He who died quickest, was luckiest. The handful who
　　survived,
Suffering untold hardship, struggled on through Thrace

To safety, and now at last have reached their native earth.

So, well may Persia's cities mourn their young men lost. 90
I have spoken truth; yet all I have told is but a part
Of all the evil God sent to strike Persia down.

The Bacchae
by Euripides
Translated by Kenneth Cavander

HERDSMAN

Our herds of cattle are topping the rise of the hills,
Grazing as they go, and the sun's rays are just
Beginning to warm the grass, when I see three
Circles of women—the dancers!

One of them is round Autonoë,
The second with Agave, your mother,
And the third is with Ino.
They are all asleep, lying every way,
Some propped against pine-tree trunks,
Others curled up modestly on a pile   10
Of oak leaves, pillowed on the earth—
None of the drunkenness you talked about,
None of the obscene abandon, or the wild
Music—no love among the bushes.

All at once, your mother stands up. She cries out
And wakes the rest of the women, says she can hear
The lowing of cattle. They shake the sleep petals
From their eyes, and all stand upright,
A marvel of calm and order . . . Young girls,
Old women, maidens who have never slept   20
With a man.
           First, they let their hair tumble

Down their shoulders. Then, the ones whose fawn-skins
Have come loose from the brooches pinning them, fasten them
Back on their shoulders, and belt the spotted hides
With snakes—
And those snakes were live—I saw their tongues
Flicker . . .
One of them might carry a fawn, cradled
In her arms, or a wild wolf cub, and gives it her own
Milk—   30
You see, some had left newborn babies at home
And so their breasts were full . . .

They all weave strands of ivy, oak leaves,
Tendrils of flowering briony in their hair.
Then one of them winds ivy on a branch,
Taps a rock, and out of the rock spouts
Water—running water! Fresh as dew!
Another drops her wand, a little twig,
On to the earth, and where she drops it some force
Sends up a spring—a wine-spring! Some   40
Feel they'd like to drink fresh milk.
They scrape the tips of their fingers on the earth
And they have milk—fountains of milk! From all
Their ivy-covered branches sweet honey
Drips, cascades down . . . Oh, if you
Had been there and seen all this, you would have been
On your knees, praying—not criticizing—but praying
For help and guidance.

All we herdsmen and shepherds hold
A meeting, we begin to talk, we compare   50
Stories—
Because these were fantastic things the women were doing,
We could hardly believe our eyes . . .
Someone who knows his way in the city, knows
How they make speeches there, he stands up
And makes one himself:

"You inhabitants of the majestic mountain acres, allow
me to propose to you that we hunt down Agave, mother
of Pentheus, from the midst of her Dionysiac festivities,
and thereby do our royal master in Thebes . . . a great   60
good turn . . . "

Applause!

We decide to lay in ambush for the women
In the undergrowth,
We hide in the leaves,
We wait.
The hour for their rites approaches . . .
The sticks with the ivy begin to beat out a rhythm.
It gets in your blood, that rhythm.
"Iacchos!" they howl in unison,   70
"Bromios!"
"Son of Zeus!"

The whole mountain sways to that one beat, beat, beat:
The wild beasts join in,
Everything moves,
Everything's running, running, Agave is racing towards
me, she's coming near, nearer, almost touches me, I leap
out—I wanted to catch her, you see—I jump from my
safe hiding place and—
She gives a screech: 80
"Look, my swift hounds, we are being hunted
By these men. Follow me!
Follow me!
Branches—get branches and arm yourselves!"

We turn and run—
If we hadn't we would have been torn to shreds
By the Bacchae . . .

As it is, they descend on our heifers grazing
In the long grass. They have nothing in their hands,
Those women—nothing metal. But imagine you see   90
One of them, just with her hands, tearing a young
Well-grown heifer in two, while it screams . . .
Others have found full-grown cows and are wrenching them
Limb from limb. Ribs, hooves, toss
Up in the air, drop to the ground. Parts
Of our animals hang from the branches of pine trees,
Dripping there, blood spattering the leaves.
Bulls with surging horns, invincible
Till now, are tripped, sprawl full length
On the ground, while a mob of hands, girls'   100
Hands, rip them apart. Faster than you can
Blink your royal eyes the flesh is peeled
Off their bones.

Then down, like flocks of birds, so fast
Their feet never touch the ground, they sweep to the Valley
Sleeping between the hills. Here, on the banks
Of the Asopos, the grain grows deep in the farmlands,
Little towns, Hysiai, Erythrai, snuggle
Beneath the slopes of Kithairon . . .
Like an invading army those women mill   110
Through the valley, they tear it apart, chaos! Children
Snatched from their beds . . . Anything they can pick up,
And carry on their backs, stays there—nothing
Holds it on, but it never slips to the ground,
Even the bronze, the iron—they put live coals
In their hair—and nothing burns them!
The people are furious, being plundered by these women,
And rush to defend themselves. Then what happens?

—It was a terrible sight to see, master . . .

No spear, no weapon, nothing so much as scratches   120
The Bacchae. But one of those wooden sticks they carry

Draws blood at once. They throw them—and men run
For their lives—that isn't human, there's some other power
At work . . .
                         At last, they go, back to the mountains
Where they came from, back to the springs of water
Which Dionysos sent them. They wash away
The blood . . . and the snakes lick off the dirt and gore
From the women's cheeks with their tongues . . .

This power, master, whoever he is, whatever
He is . . . let him into Thebes! He   130
Is great. And one thing above all they say
He has done, I've heard that he gave mankind
The grape . . . And the grape is the best grave—for grief.
If there were no wine
There would be no love,
There would be no joy in life.

34. briony: climbing plant or vine.
70. Iacchos: a name associated with Dionysos. Bacchus and Bromios are other
    names for the god, the latter meaning "noisy" or "boisterous."
109. Kithairon: a lofty mountain range northwest of Athens, sacred to Dionysos
    and the Muses. The river and towns mentioned are in the general vicinity.

THE AGE
OF
SHAKESPEARE

Sixteenth- and Seventeenth-Century

English Monologues

Introduction

Speak the speech, I pray you, as I pronounced it to you,
trippingly on the tongue . . . Suit the action to the word,
the word to the action, with this special observance,
that you o'erstep not the modesty of nature. For anything so o'erdone is from the purpose of playing, whose
end, both at the first and now, was and is, to hold, as
'twere, the mirror up to nature; to show virtue her own
feature, scorn her own image, and the very age and body
of the time his form and pressure.
                    —William Shakespeare (from *Hamlet*)

Whether working with an actor on a prepared monologue or
attending a fully mounted production, I am repeatedly im-
pressed by the importance of achieving a public dimension in
presenting Elizabethan and Jacobean material. It was an age
of expansion and intrigue, when the scope of even the smallest
action might be hard to measure, and when even the most
intimate moment was likely to be overheard or interrupted.
As anyone who has performed Shakespeare outdoors will con-
firm, there is a special energy, something akin to improvisa-
tion, that begins to take over. I urge the actor to seek those
external circumstances in each monologue that will keep him
engaged and active.

The Texts
In spelling and punctuation, I have generally kept each monologue modern, without resorting to rewrites that might sacrifice the ambiguities which make this material so rich in nuance
and texture.

I once had the misfortune of seeing a production of *Richard
III* performed by an American company with a reputation for
doing classical material well. Clearly no one had bothered to
inform the actors that final syllables are not always pronounced. The result was a highly affected form of speech that

sounded like a poor imitation of British acting, while violating the most basic cadences of Shakespeare's rhythms.

Shakespeare, and most other dramatists of his era, wrote smoothly constructed verse lines in iambic pentameter, a meter chosen because it was—and still is—most natural to the melodies of spoken English. Only where an exceptional stress was desired did the author break the meter, and such lapses are often the actor's clues to key moments in a scene. Whether or not the final syllable in "banished," for example, is pronounced usually depends on where the word appears in a line. Romeo's monologue contains both two- and three-syllable versions of the word. Rather than give a short course in scansion, I have employed an apostrophe for unsounded vowels ("banish'd," for example) wherever there might be doubt. When a final syllable is to be pronounced, however, please note that it need not be stressed. A pulse or brief pause in the rhythm of the line may often suffice and sound less forced. In prose passages, where verse scansion does not apply, all words should be pronounced as naturally as possible.

An apostrophe also appears in place of the omitted letter in a contraction. There is a wide variety of contractions in this material, most often for metrical consistency, but sometimes to indicate an offhand or casual manner on the part of a character. So, when Jaques says "I met a fool i' the forest" he is being glib, but when Caliban mentions "the rest o' th' island" he is careless in the manner of one whose understanding of language is colloquial and incomplete. The "i" and the "o" should be pronounced exactly as they would be in the original words "in" and "of."

The Friends

As varied as the worlds of Shakespeare's plays are, there are kinds of characters he never tackled, and an actor with classical interests who concentrates exclusively on Shakespeare might be compared, in a modern context, with someone studying Tennessee Williams while completely ignoring Albee, Shepard, or Mamet. There are qualities inherent in the work of other Elizabethan and Jacobean dramatists that simply do not exist in Shakespeare's, and there are roles and language that might more clearly demonstrate a particular actor's strengths.

These monologues are representative of some of Shakespeare's predecessors, competitors, and collaborators and range from Marlowe's robustly imaginative characterizations to the richly textured tapestries of Webster and Tourneur. At first, some of the pieces may sound just a bit alien to an ear attuned to Shakespeare's rhythms and sounds, but I believe that among them an actor is likely to find at least one voice that is particularly close to his own.

WILLIAM SHAKESPEARE

HEROIC

Among Shakespeare's most interesting characters are the villains, rebels, and outcasts in this section. As articulate as he is charming and urbane, the Bastard in *King John* values his intellect, and his illegitimacy affords him just the right distance from the rest of society to be able to indulge his politics, even justify them, without the faintest moral scruple. The monologue has a simple three-part structure, moving from contemplation of the world at large to specific and personal application. "Commodity" may be interpreted variously as convenience, profit, advantage, or just plain business.

Working to overthrow the system the Bastard uses to his advantage, Jack Cade of *Henry VI, Part 2* is the prototype of the crass revolutionary, high on his newfound power. He is semiliterate, an arrogant champion of benighted stupidity, and the speech is direct and unsubtle, but a couple of sudden transitions and a beat or two improvised on the spot can hint at potential violence and make the scene terribly exciting. The Gloucester monologue from *Henry VI, Part 3* anticipates the Richard of *Richard III*, and reveals a character at once more direct, more fun, and less forgivable than anything encountered in the later play. The fun in the scene comes from

Richard's humor and unabashed candor and is balanced by his bitterness and obsessive need. Any extreme physical deformity, particularly in an audition, is to be discouraged. A shorter version may begin with line 11, 23, or 25 and end on line 29, 48, or 58. Tyrrell, a hardened criminal enlisted by Richard III to murder the young princes in the tower, experiences the deed through the eyes of his hired assassins and seems amazed at the force of his own reaction, collecting a mouthful of suppressed venom for Richard's entrance on line 23.

More open in their vitriolic furor, and reminiscent of the commedia Pantalone, are Shakespeare's nastiest old men, Shylock and Timon. Playing Antonio like a large fish, Shylock casts about to discover how badly the man needs a loan. When Antonio reaches his limit and rails at him (after line 24), Shylock gently concedes, only to set his famous condition a few lines later. The "equal pound/ Of your fair flesh" should take the audience by surprise, and it can really shock if Shylock reveals his enjoyment of the game at the very end of the scene. Timon, in self-imposed exile, has not yet cut himself loose from his Athenian roots ("our youth"), and his wild joy in caustic invention is a means by which he tries to hide the pain of separation.

Aaron of *Titus Andronicus* is a character of pure evil, a simpler model for Iago, and his confession, this catalogue of crimes, Gothic by any standard, can be treated seriously and with anger, or as a tongue-in-cheek mockery of a credulous audience—a deliberate attempt to shock with each succeeding horror. A shorter version of the piece runs from line 11 through line 47. Othello's final monologue has a rhythmic intensity that is slow and rich in vowel sounds. Although perhaps unfashionable today because of its extreme stateliness, Paul Robeson's reading* of the piece makes excellent listening and inspiration. His rendition sings of power and the joy of words, and is a good lesson in pacing the material, as the actor com-

---

* *Paul Robeson at Carnegie Hall;* recorded May 9, 1958; Vanguard Recording Society, New York (VSD 2035).

fortably stretches a mere twenty-one lines to a full two minutes. Othello speaks from absolute contempt for his audience,
an attitude that can be useful to compensate for audition nerves.
The last two lines may be a bit too much to handle, but I
include them in honor of Mr. Robeson, who did so well by
them.

Even in an age dominated by a woman as absolute monarch
and characterized by a wealth of dramas about women, Shakespeare cannot be matched in writing powerful female characters. Portrayed as a fascinating fanatic, *Henry VI, Part 1*'s
Joan speaks with a kind of inevitability, and her perfect confidence in her spiritual credentials, martial prowess, and beauty
may well put one in mind of the modern political activism of
a Jane Fonda or a Bernadette Devlin. Margaret is one of the
great ranting women of all time and is all too often played
without any real intelligence or clarity. This speech from *Henry
VI, Part 3* is a fine example of persuasive rhetoric and perfectly
structured metaphor—the ship of state. The woman is an
effective leader, not by force alone but by careful manipulation
of emotional and political factors. She honors the dead (Warwick and Montague) but encourages the living (Oxford, Somerset, her French allies, and her son Ned—Edward, Prince of
Wales). The enemy (the brothers Edward, Clarence, and Richard) are dehumanized to the point where defection to their
ranks becomes unthinkable. Finally, rather than building to
the usual rallying cry, Margaret rests her case with deceptive
simplicity.

Just as subtle in her own way, Goneril treats her father,
King Lear, as if he were a backward child and responds to his
rage and the Fool's insolence with cold equanimity, insisting
that he give up a portion of his royal retinue. This speech is
a composite, and the indicated beats should be treated as
Lear's attempts to interrupt her. Hermione of *The Winter's
Tale* and Katharine of *Henry VIII* are each victims of a hus-
band's whim, faced with the humiliation of open accusation.
Their strength is in righteous pride. The public formality of
Hermione's monologue is tempered by the oddly scanned,

disjointed language, suggesting the pain just below the surface of her defense. Katharine's speech has more of the feeling of an actual courtroom scene and could be treated as a partially prepared plea, emphasizing her status as a foreigner not wholly at home with the English language.

Constance's (*King John*) son Arthur is a prime pawn in a political struggle that takes him to prison and Constance to the French king to enlist his sympathy. Her talk of madness is best played in a controlled manner, the scene building to an overt emotional climax only when Constance sees that she is making no headway with her audience. Furthermore, the French court (King Philip, Lewis the Dauphin, and Cardinal Pandulph) should be regarded as individuals to whom she appeals one at a time, so the structure of the scene becomes an exercise of intellect and power rather than a simple emotional outburst. Eleanor in *Henry VI, Part 2*, a victim of political plots against her husband, has been accused of conspiracy and witchcraft and is being led through the streets of London ("with Papers pinned upon her back, in a white sheet, her feet bare, and a taper burning in her hand") to be shamed prior to imprisonment. She is met by the Duke, her husband, who refuses to help her, pleading the law and his reputation. The special richness of this scene derives from conflicting emotional elements: public humiliation, genuine concern for her husband, and scorn for his naïveté and weakness. A more exemplary marriage is Lady Percy's to Hotspur, in *Henry IV, Part 2*. A widow, she uses her husband's memory to inspire her father-in-law, the Earl of Northumberland, to battle. She is quite simply a woman of practical maturity, capable of leadership and action.

King John

(Act II, Scene 1)

THE BASTARD

Mad world! mad kings! mad composition!

John, to stop Arthur's title in the whole,
Hath willingly departed with a part;
And France, whose armour conscience buckled on,
Whom zeal and charity brought to the field
As God's own soldier, rounded in the ear
With that same purpose-changer, that sly devil,
That broker, that still breaks the pate of faith,
That daily break-vow, he that wins of all,
Of kings, of beggars, old men, young men, maids,   10
Who having no external thing to lose
But the word "maid," cheats the poor maid of that,
That smooth-fac'd gentleman, tickling Commodity,

Commodity, the bias of the world;
The world, who of itself is peized well,
Made to run even upon even ground,
Till this advantage, this vile-drawing bias,
This sway of motion, this Commodity,
Makes it take head from all indifferency,
From all direction, purpose, course, intent: 20
And this same bias, this Commodity,
This bawd, this broker, this all-changing word,
Clapp'd on the outward eye of fickle France,
Hath drawn him from his own determin'd aid,
From a resolv'd and honourable war,
To a most base and vile-concluded peace.

And why rail I on this Commodity?
——

But for because he hath not woo'd me yet.
Not that I have the power to clutch my hand
When his fair angels would salute my palm;   30
But for my hand, as unattempted yet,
Like a poor beggar, raileth on the rich.
Well, whiles I am a beggar, I will rail,
And say there is no sin but to be rich;
And being rich, my virtue then shall be
To say there is no vice but beggary.
Since kings break faith upon Commodity,
Gain, be my lord, for I will worship thee!

4. France: King of France.
8. pate: head.
14. bias: tendency, generally away from the straight and narrow.
15. peized: poised or balanced.
22. bawd: pimp or procuress.
30. angels: coins.

Henry VI, Part 2

(Act IV, Scene 7)

JACK CADE

So, sirs:—Now go some and pull down the Savoy;
others to the inns of court: down with them all. Away!
burn all the records of the realm: my mouth shall be the
parliament of England.

Ah! thou say, thou serge, nay,
thou buckram lord; now art thou within point-blank of
our jurisdiction regal.

Be it known unto thee by these
presence, even the presence of Lord Mortimer, that I
am the besom that must sweep the court clean of such
filth as thou art. Thou hast most traitorously corrupted
the youth of the realm in erecting a grammar-school; and   10
whereas, before, our fore-fathers had no other books but
the score and the tally, thou hast caused printing to be

used; and, contrary to the king, his crown, and dignity, thou hast built a paper-mill. It will be proved to thy face that thou hast men about thee that usually talk of a noun and a verb, and such abominable words as no Christian ear can endure to hear. Thou hast appointed justices of peace, to call poor men before them about matters they were not able to answer. Moreover, thou hast put them in prison; and because they could not read, thou hast   20 hanged them; when indeed only for that cause they have been most worthy to live.

                         Away with him! and do as I command ye.

                           The proudest peer in the realm shall not wear a head on his shoulders, unless he pay me tribute; there shall not a maid be married, but she shall pay to me her maidenhead, ere they have it; men shall hold of me *in capite;* and we charge and command that their wives be as free as heart can wish or tongue can tell.

             Up Fish Street! down St. Magnus' corner! kill and   30 knock down! throw them into the Thames!

1. Savoy: palace in London.
2. inns of court: law colleges.
4. say: a kind of silk cloth; Cade's pun on Lord Say's name is especially insulting as the quality of cloth declines from silk to wool (serge) to the coarsest linen (buckram).
8. besom: broom.
12. the score and the tally: primitive method of accounting.
27. *in capite:* legal term for holdings received directly from the king.

Henry VI, Part 3
(Act III, Scene 2)

RICHARD, EARL OF GLOUCESTER
Ay, Edward will use women honourably.

Would he were wasted, marrow, bones, and all,

That from his loins no hopeful branch may spring
To cross me from the golden time I look for!

And yet, between my soul's desire and me—
The lustful Edward's title buried,—
Is Clarence, Henry, and his son young Edward,
And all the unlook'd for issue of their bodies,
To take their rooms, ere I can place myself:
A cold premeditation for my purpose!   10

Why then, I do but dream on sovereignty;
Like one that stands upon a promontory,
And spies a far-off shore where he would tread,
Wishing his foot were equal with his eye;
And chides the sea that sunders him from thence,
Saying, he'll lade it dry to have his way:
So do I wish the crown, being so far off,
And so I chide the means that keep me from it,
And so I say I'll cut the causes off,
Flattering me with impossibilities.   20
My eye's too quick, my heart o'erweens too much,
Unless my hand and strength could equal them.

Well, say there is no kingdom then for Richard;
What other pleasure can the world afford?

I'll make my heaven in a lady's lap,
And deck my body in gay ornaments,
And witch sweet ladies with my words and looks.
O miserable thought! and more unlikely
Than to accomplish twenty golden crowns.
Why, love foreswore me in my mother's womb: 30
And, for I should not deal in her soft laws,
She did corrupt frail nature with some bribe,
To shrink mine arm up like a wither'd shrub;
To make an envious mountain on my back,

Where sits deformity to mock my body;
To shape my legs of an unequal size;
To disproportion me in every part,
Like to a chaos, or an unlick'd bear-whelp
That carries no impression like the dam.
And am I then a man to be belov'd?   40

O monstrous fault! to harbour such a thought.

Then, since this earth affords no joy to me
But to command, to check, to o'erbear such
As are of better person than myself,
I'll make my heav'n to dream upon the crown;
And, whiles I live, to account this world but hell,
Until my mis-shap'd trunk that bears this head
Be round impaled with a glorious crown.

And yet I know not how to get the crown,
For many lives stand between me and home: 50
And I, like one lost in a thorny wood,
That rents the thorns and is rent with the thorns,
Seeking a way and straying from the way;
Not knowing how to find the open air,
But toiling desperately to find it out,
Torment myself to catch the English crown:
And from that torment I will free myself,
Or hew my way out with a bloody axe.

Why, I can smile, and murder while I smile,
And cry, "Content," to that which grieves my heart,   60
And wet my cheeks with artificial tears,
And frame my face to all occasions.
I'll drown more sailors than the mermaid shall;
I'll slay more gazers than the basilisk;
I'll play the orator as well as Nestor,

Deceive more slily than Ulysses could,
And, like a Sinon, take another Troy.
I can add colours to the chameleon,
Change shapes with Proteus for advantages,
And set the murderous Machiavel to school.   70

Can I do this, and cannot get a crown?
Tut! were it farther off, I'll pluck it down.

1. Edward, one of Richard's elder brothers known for his lascivious habits, has
   just left the scene.
64. basilisk: a mythical serpent (also cockatrice) with the ability to kill by eye
   contact anyone it catches looking at it, hence "gazers." This is a strong actor's
   image, and one frequently associated with the character.
67. Sinon: the Greek who thought up the wooden horse scheme.

Richard III

(Act IV, Scene 3)

TYRRELL

The tyrannous and bloody act is done;
The most arch deed of piteous massacre
That ever yet this land was guility of.

Dighton and Forrest, whom I did suborn
To do this piece of ruthless butchery,
Albeit they were flesh'd villains, bloody dogs,
Melting with tenderness and mild compassion,
Wept like to children in their death's sad story.
"O! thus," quoth Dighton, "lay the gentle babes:"
"Thus, thus," quoth Forrest, "girdling one another   10
Within their alabaster innocent arms:
Their lips were four red roses on a stalk
Which in their summer beauty kiss'd each other.
A book of prayers on their pillow lay;
Which one," quoth Forrest, "almost chang'd my mind;

But, O, the devil"
          —there the villain stopp'd;
When Dighton thus told on: "We smothered
The most replenished sweet work of nature,
That from the prime creation e'er she fram'd."

Hence both are gone with conscience and remorse;   20
They could not speak;
          and so I left them both,
To bear this tidings to the bloody king:
And here he comes.

If to have done the thing you gave in charge
Beget your happiness, be happy then,
For it is done.

6. flesh'd: made fierce and eager for the hunt, as with dogs fed exclusively with raw meat.

The Merchant of Venice
(Act I, Scene 3)

SHYLOCK

Signior Antonio, many a time and oft
In the Rialto you have rated me
About my moneys and my usances:

Still have I borne it with a patient shrug,
For sufferance is the badge of all our tribe.

You call me misbeliever, cut-throat dog,
And spet upon my Jewish gaberdine,
And all for use of that which is mine own.

Well then, it now appears you need my help:

Go to then; you come to me, and you say,   10
"Shylock, we would have moneys:" you say so;
You, that did void your rheum upon my beard,
And foot me as you spurn a stranger cur
Over your threshold:
                              moneys is your suit.
What should I say to you?
                              Should I not say,
"Hath a dog money? Is it possible
A cur can lend three thousand ducats?" or
Shall I bend low, and in a bondman's key,
With bated breath, and whispering humbleness,
Say this:—   20
"Fair sir, you spet on me on Wednesday last;
You spurn'd me such a day; another time
You call'd me dog; and for these courtesies
I'll lend you thus much moneys?"

Why, look you, how you storm!
I would be friends with you, and have your love,
Forget the shames that you have stain'd me with,
Supply your present wants, and take no doit
Of usance for my moneys, and you'll not hear me:

This kindness will I show—   30
Go with me to a notary, seal me there
Your single bond; and, in a merry sport,
If you repay me not on such a day,
In such a place, such sum or sums as are
Express'd in the condition, let the forfeit
Be nominated for an equal pound
Of your fair flesh, to be cut off and taken
In what part of your body it pleaseth me.

2. Rialto: in Venice, location of the exchange. rated: chided, upbraided.
3. usances: interest on money, usury.
12. rheum: saliva.

18. bondman's key: a slave's tone of voice.
25. Antonio has replied firmly that he is likely to behave so again and asks that if Shylock decides to lend the money he lend it not "as to thy friends" but "rather to thine enemy."
30. Antonio has finally begun to listen.
36. equal pound: an exact pound.

Timon of Athens
(Act IV, Scene 1)

TIMON

Let me look back upon thee.
                    O thou wall,
That girdles in those wolves, dive in the earth,
And fence not Athens!
                    Matrons, turn incontinent!
Obedience fail in children! slaves and fools,
Pluck the grave wrinkled senate from the bench,
And minister in their steads! To general filths
Convert, o' the instant, green virginity!
Do't in your parents' eyes! Bankrupts, hold fast;
Rather than render back, out with your knives,
And cut your trusters' throats! Bound servants, steal!—   10
Large-handed robbers your grave masters are,—
And pill by law. Maid, to thy master's bed;
Thy mistress is o' the brothel! Son of sixteen,
Pluck the lin'd crutch from thy old limping sire,
With it beat out his brains!
                    Piety, and fear,
Religion to the gods, peace, justice, truth,
Domestic awe, night-rest and neighborhood,
Instruction, manners, mysteries and trades,
Degrees, observances, customs and laws,
Decline to your confounding contraries,   20
And let confusion live!
                    Plagues incident to men,

Your potent and infectious fevers heap
On Athens, ripe for stroke! Thou cold sciatica,
Cripple our senators, that their limbs may halt
As lamely as their manners! Lust and liberty
Creep in the minds and marrows of our youth,
That 'gainst the stream of virtue they may strive,
And drown themselves in riot! Itches, blains,
Sow all the Athenian bosoms, and their crop
Be general leprosy! Breath infect breath,   30
That their society, as their friendship, may
Be merely poison!
              Nothing I'll bear from thee
But nakedness, thou detestable town!
Take thou that too, with multiplying bans!
Timon will to the woods; where he shall find
The unkindest beast more kinder than mankind.

The gods confound—hear me, you good gods all—
The Athenians both within and out that wall!
And grant, as Timon grows, his hate may grow
To the whole race of mankind, high and low!   40
Amen.

12. pill: pillage, rob, plunder.
17. neighborhood: friendship.
28. blains: blisters.
34. bans: curses.

Titus Andronicus

(Act V, Scene 1)

AARON
'Twas Tamora's two sons that murder'd Bassianus;

They cut thy sister's tongue and ravish'd her,
And cut her hands and trimm'd her as thou saw'st.

Why, she was wash'd, and cut, and trimm'd, and 'twas
Trim sport for them that had the doing of it.

Indeed, I was their tutor to instruct them.
That codding spirit had they from their mother,
As sure a card as ever won the set;
That bloody mind, I think, they learn'd of me
As true a dog as ever fought at head.   10

Well, let my deeds be witness of my worth.

I train'd thy brethren to that guileful hole
Where the dead corpse of Bassianus lay;
I wrote the letter that thy father found,
And hid the gold within the letter mention'd,
Confederate with the queen and her two sons:
And what not done, that thou hast cause to rue,
Wherein I had no stroke of mischief in it.
I play'd the cheater for thy father's hand,
And, when I had it, drew myself apart,   20
And almost broke my heart with extreme laughter.
I pry'd me through the crevice of a wall
When, for his hand, he had his two sons' heads;
Beheld his tears, and laugh'd so heartily,
That both mine eyes were rainy like to his:
And when I told the empress of this sport,
She swounded almost at my pleasing tale,
And for my tidings gave me twenty kisses.

Few come within the compass of my curse,
Wherein I did not some notorious ill: 30
As kill a man, or else devise his death;
Ravish a maid, or plot the way to do it;
Accuse some innocent, and forswear myself;
Set deadly enmity between two friends;
Make poor men's cattle break their necks;
Set fire on barns and hay-stacks in the night,

And bid the owners quench them with their tears,
Oft have I digg'd up dead men from their graves,
And set them upright at their dear friends' doors,
Even when their sorrows almost were forgot;   40
And on their skins, as on the bark of trees,
Have with my knife carved in Roman letters,
"Let not your sorrow die, though I am dead."

Tut! I have done a thousand dreadful things
As willingly as one would kill a fly,
And nothing grieves me heartily indeed
But that I cannot do ten thousand more.

If there be devils, would I were a devil,
To live and burn in everlasting fire,
So I might have your company in hell,   50
But to torment you with my bitter tongue!

2. The speech is addressed to Lucius, Titus's one surviving son.
4. The image is one of meat dressed for cooking.
7. codding: lecherous, lustful.
12. train'd: enticed.
19. hand: refers to an actual hand, cut off and exchanged for the severed heads
    of Titus's other two sons.
27. swounded: swooned, fainted.
29. compass: range.

Othello

(Act V, Scene 2)

OTHELLO

Soft you;
   a word or two before you go.

I have done the state some service, and they know't;
No more of that.
     I pray you, in your letters,

When you shall these unlucky deeds relate,
Speak of me as I am; nothing extenuate,
Nor set down aught in malice: then, must you speak
Of one that lov'd not wisely but too well;
Of one not easily jealous, but, being wrought,
Perplex'd in the extreme; of one whose hand,
Like the base Indian, threw a pearl away   10
Richer than all his tribe; of one whose subdu'd eyes,
Albeit unused to the melting mood,
Drop tears as fast as the Arabian trees
Their med'cinable gum.
                              Set you down this;
And say besides, that in Aleppo once,
Where a malignant and a turban'd Turk
Beat a Venetian and traduc'd the state,
I took by the throat the circumcised dog,
And smote him thus.

  (Stabs himself)

I kiss'd thee ere I kill'd thee; no way but this,   20
Killing myself to die upon a kiss.

17. traduc'd: shamed.
18. circumcised dog: barbarian; Robeson uses "damned heathen dog."
19. for the stabbing ("thus") I recommend a sudden, sharp, nonspecific gesture
    rather than a blow to the stomach.

Henry VI, Part 1

(Act I, Scene 2; Act III, Scene 3)

JOAN LA PUCELLE (or JOAN OF ARC)

Look on thy country,
          look on fertile France,
And see the cities and the towns defac'd
By wasting ruin of the cruel foe.
As looks the mother on her lowly babe
When death doth close his tender dying eyes,
See, see the pining malady of France;
Assign'd am I to be the English scourge.

This night the siege assuredly I'll raise:
Expect Saint Martin's summer, halcyon days,
Since I have entered into these wars.   10
Glory is like a circle in the water,
Which never ceaseth to enlarge itself,
Till by broad spreading it disperse to nought;
With Henry's death the English circle ends.

Dauphin, I am by birth a shepherd's daughter,
My wit untrain'd in any kind of art.
Heaven and our Lady gracious hath it pleas'd
To shine on my contemptible estate;
Lo!
    whilst I waited on my tender lambs,
And to sun's parching heat display'd my cheeks,   20
God's mother deigned to appear to me,
And in a vision full of majesty
Will'd me to leave my base vocation
And free my country from calamity:
Her aid she promis'd and assur'd success;
In complete glory she reveal'd herself;
And, whereas I was black and swart before,

With those clear rays which she infus'd on me,
That beauty am I bless'd with which you see.
Ask me what questions thou canst possible   30
And I will answer unpremeditated:
My courage try by combat, if thou dar'st,
And thou shalt find that I exceed my sex.
Resolve on this, thou shalt be fortunate
If thou receive me for thy warlike mate.

9. Saint Martin's summer, halcyon days: fair weather after winter has set in, i.e.,
    prosperity after misfortune. St. Martin's feast day is November 11.
16. art: artifice.
27. black and swart: her former complexion, tanned perhaps from outdoor work,
    and definitely unfashionable.

Henry VI, Part 3

(Act V, Scene 4)

QUEEN MARGARET

Great lords, wise men ne'er sit and wail their loss,
But cheerly seek how to redress their harms.

What though the mast be now blown overboard,
The cable broke, the holding anchor lost,
And half our sailors swallow'd in the flood?
Yet lives our pilot still: is't meet that he
Should leave the helm and like a fearful lad
With tearful eyes add water to the sea,
And give more strength to that which hath too much;
Whiles in his moan the ship splits on the rock,   10
Which industry and courage might have sav'd?
Ah! what a shame! ah, what a fault were this.

Say, Warwick was our anchor; what of that?
And Montague our top-mast; what of him?
Our slaughter'd friends the tackles; what of these?

Why, is not Oxford here another anchor?
And Somerset, another goodly mast?
The friends of France our shrouds and tacklings?
And, though unskilful, why not Ned and I
For once allow'd the skilful pilot's charge?   20
We will not from the helm, to sit and weep,
But keep our course, though the rough wind say no,
From shelves and rocks that threaten us with wrack.
As good to chide the waves as speak them fair.

And what is Edward but a ruthless sea?
What Clarence but a quicksand of deceit?
And Richard but a ragged fatal rock?
All those the enemies to our poor bark.
Say you can swim; alas! 'tis but a while:
Tread on the sand; why, there you quickly sink: 30
Bestride the rock; the tide will wash you off,
Or else you famish; that's a threefold death.

This speak I, lords, to let you understand,
In case some one of you would fly from us,
That there's no hop'd-for mercy with the brothers
More than with ruthless waves, with sands and rocks.
Why, courage, then! what cannot be avoided
'Twere childish weakness to lament or fear.

King Lear

(Act I, Scene 4)

GONERIL

Not only, sir, this your all-licens'd fool,
But other of your insolent retinue
Do hourly carp and quarrel, breaking forth
In rank and not-to-be-endured riots.
                                        Sir,

I had thought, by making this well known unto you,
To have found a safe redress; but now grow fearful,
By what yourself too late have spoke and done,
That you protect this course, and put it on
By your allowance; which if you should, the fault
Would not 'scape censure, nor the redresses sleep,   10
Which in the tender of a wholesome weal,
Might in their working do you that offence,
Which else were shame, that then necessity
Will call discreet proceeding.

I would you would make use of your good wisdom,
Whereof I know you are fraught; and put away
These dispositions which of late transport you
From what you rightly are.
                                        I do beseech you
To understand my purposes aright:
As you are old and reverend, should be wise.   20

Here do you keep a hundred knights and squires;
Men so disorder'd, so debauch'd, and bold,
That this our court, infected with their manners,
Shows like a riotous inn: epicurism and lust
Make it more like a tavern or a brothel
Than a grac'd palace. The shame itself doth speak
For instant remedy;
                                        be then desir'd
By her that else will take the thing she begs,
A little to disquantity your train;
And the remainder, that shall still depend,   30
To be such men as may besort your age,
Which know themselves and you.

7. too late: so recently.
11. Which . . . weal: which in my desire to bring matters to a happy state.
12–14. Might . . . proceeding: the necessity for my actions will cancel whatever
          shame you may feel at my seemingly unfilial offense to you.
16. fraught: loaded.

The Winter's Tale

(Act III, Scene 2)

HERMIONE

Since what I am to say must be but that
Which contradicts my accusation, and
The testimony on my part no other
But what comes from myself, it shall scarce boot me
To say "Not guilty:"
                 mine integrity
Being counted falsehood, shall, as I express it,
Be so receiv'd.
             But thus: if powers divine
Behold our human actions, as they do,
I doubt not then but innocence shall make
False accusation blush, and tyranny   10
Tremble at patience.
               You, my lord, best know,—
Who least will seem to do so,—my past life
Hath been as continent, as chaste, as true,
As I am now unhappy; which is more
Than history can pattern, though devis'd
And play'd to take spectators. For behold me,
A fellow of the royal bed, which owe
A moiety of the throne, a great king's daughter,
The mother to a hopeful prince, here standing
To prate and talk for life and honour 'fore   20
Who please to come and hear.

For Polixenes,—
With whom I am accus'd,—I do confess
I lov'd him as in honour he requir'd,
With such a kind of love as might become
A lady like me; with a love even such,
So and no other, as yourself commanded:

Which not to have done I think had been in me
Both disobedience and ingratitude
To you and toward your friend, whose love had spoke,   30
Even since it could speak, from an infant, freely
That it was yours.
                    Now, for conspiracy,
I know not how it tastes, though it be dish'd
For me to try how: all I know of it
Is that Camillo was an honest man;
And why he left your court, the gods themselves,
Wotting no more than I, are ignorant.

Sir, spare your threats:
The bug which you would fright me with I seek.

To me can life be no commodity: 40

The crown and comfort of my life, your favour,
I do give lost; for I do feel it gone,
But know not how it went.
                    My second joy,
And first-fruits of my body, from his presence
I am barr'd, like one infectious.
                    My third comfort,
Starr'd most unluckily, is from my breast,
The innocent milk in its most innocent mouth,
Hal'd out to murder: myself on every post
Proclaim'd a strumpet: with immodest hatred
The child-bed privilege denied, which 'longs   50
To women of all fashion:
                    lastly, hurried
Here to this place, i' the open air, before
I have got strength of limit.
                    Now, my liege,
Tell me what blessings I have here alive,
That I should fear to die?
                    Therefore proceed.

But yet hear this; mistake me not; no life,
I prize it not a straw:—but for mine honour,
Which I would free, if I shall be condemn'd
Upon surmises, all proofs sleeping else
But what your jealousies awake, I tell you   60
'Tis rigour and not law.
                              Your honours all,
I do refer me to the oracle:

Apollo be my judge!

4. boot: avail; such protestations are most likely to be of no avail.
14–16. which is more . . . to take spectators: history can offer no precedent for
        her unhappiness, no parallel, not even if it were performed as drama in
        such a manner as to move the audience to tears.
17. owe: own, possess.
18. moiety: half.
20. prate: tattle, talk idly.
37. Wotting: knowing.
38. Leontes has just threatened Hermione with death, the "bug" to which she
        refers in the next line.
43. My second joy: her son Mamillius.
45. My third comfort: her infant daughter Perdita.
46. Starr'd most unluckily: born under an unfavorable astrological aspect.
48. Hal'd: drawn, pulled.
49. strumpet: whore.
53. strength of limit: strength to go out.

Henry VIII
(Act II, Scene 4)

QUEEN KATHARINE
Sir, I desire you do me right and justice;
And to bestow your pity on me;
                              for
I am a most poor woman, and a stranger,
Born out of your dominions; having here
No judge indifferent, nor no more assurance

Of equal friendship and proceeding.
                                   Alas! sir,
In what have I offended you? what cause
Hath my behavior given to your displeasure,
That thus you should proceed to put me off
And take your good grace from me?
                                   Heaven witness,   10
I have been to you a true and humble wife,
At all times to your will conformable;
Ever in fear to kindle your dislike,
Yea, subject to your countenance, glad or sorry
As I saw it inclin'd.
                        When was the hour
I ever contradicted your desire,
Or made it not mine too?
                            Or which of your friends
Have I not strove to love, although I knew
He were mine enemy? what friend of mine
That had to him deriv'd your anger, did I   20
Continue in my liking? nay, gave notice
He was from thence discharg'd.
                                 Sir, call to mind
That I have been your wife, in this obedience
Upward of twenty years, and have been blest
With many children by you: if, in the course
And process of this time, you can report,
And prove it too, against mine honour aught,
My bond to wedlock, or my love and duty,
Against your sacred person, in God's name
Turn me away; and let the foul'st contempt   30
Shut door upon me, and so give me up
To the sharp'st kind of justice.
                                  Please you, sir,
The king, your father, was reputed for
A prince most prudent, of an excellent
And unmatch'd wit and judgment: Ferdinand,
My father, King of Spain, was reckon'd one

The wisest prince that there had reign'd by many
A year before:
                    it is not to be question'd
That they had gather'd a wise council to them
Of every realm, that did debate this business,   40
Who deem'd our marriage lawful.
                              Wherefore I humbly
Beseech you, sir, to spare me, till I may
Be by my friends in Spain advis'd, whose counsel
I will implore: if not, i' the name of God,
Your pleasure be fulfill'd!

5. indifferent: impartial.

King John
(Act III, Scene 4)

CONSTANCE

No,
    I defy all counsel, all redress,
But that which ends all counsel, true redress,
Death,
            death: O amiable lovely death!
Thou odoriferous stench! sound rottenness!
Arise forth from the couch of lasting night,
Thou hate and terror to prosperity,
And I will kiss thy detestable bones,
And put my eyeballs in thy vaulty brows,
And ring these fingers with thy household worms,
And stop this gap of breath with fulsome dust,   10
And be a carrion monster like thyself:

Come, grin on me; and I will think thou smil'st
And buss thee as thy wife!
                          Misery's love,
O! come to me.

I am not mad:
        this hair I tear is mine;
My name is Constance; I was Geoffrey's wife;
Young Arthur is my son, and he is lost!
I am not mad:
        I would to heaven I were!
For then 'tis like I should forget myself:
O! if I could, what grief should I forget.   20
Preach some philosophy to make me mad,
And thou shalt be canoniz'd, cardinal;
For being not mad but sensible of grief,
My reasonable part produces reason
How I may be deliver'd of these woes,
And teaches me to kill or hang myself:

If I were mad, I should forget my son,
Or madly think a babe of clouts were he.
I am not mad:
          too well, too well I feel
The different plague of each calamity.   30

Grief fills the room up of my absent child,
Lies in his bed, walks up and down with me,
Puts on his pretty looks, repeats his words,
Remembers me of all his gracious parts,
Stuffs out his vacant garments with his form:
Then have I reason to be fond of grief.

Fare you well: had you such a loss as I,
I could give better comfort than you do.
I will not keep this form upon my head
When there is such disorder in my wit.   40

O Lord!
        my boy, my Arthur, my fair son!
My life, my joy, my food, my all the world!
My widow-comfort, and my sorrows' cure!

10. fulsome: disgusting, nauseous.
13. buss: kiss.
15. Although actual tearing of the hair is discouraged, some other activity, sep-
    arating strand from strand, for instance, might serve as a sign of distraction.
31–36. This section is in direct response to King Philip's accusation that Con-
    stance is "as fond of grief as of your child."

Henry VI, Part 2

(Act II, Scene 4)

ELEANOR, DUCHESS OF GLOUCESTER

Come you, my lord, to see my open shame?

Now thou dost penance too. Look! how they gaze.
See! how the giddy multitude do point,
And nod their heads, and throw their eyes on thee.
Ah, Gloucester, hide thee from their hateful looks,
And, in thy closet pent up, rue my shame,
And ban thine enemies, both mine and thine!
Ay, Gloucester, teach me to forget myself;
For whilst I think I am thy wedded wife,
And thou a prince, protector of this land,   10
Methinks I should not thus be led along,
Mail'd up in shame, with papers on my back,
And follow'd with a rabble that rejoice
To see my tears and hear my deep-fet groans.

The ruthless flint doth cut my tender feet,
And when I start, the envious people laugh,
And bid me be advised how I tread.

Ah, Humphrey! can I bear this shameful yoke?
Trow'st thou that e'er I'll look upon the world,
Or count them happy that enjoy the sun?   20
No; dark shall be my light, and night my day;
To think upon my pomp shall be my hell.

Sometime I'll say, I am Duke Humphrey's wife;
And he a prince and ruler of the land:
Yet so he rul'd and such a prince he was
As he stood by whilst I, his forlorn duchess,
Was made a wonder and a pointing-stock
To every idle rascal follower.

But be thou mild and blush not at my shame;
Nor stir at nothing till the axe of death   30
Hang over thee, as, sure, it shortly will;
For Suffolk, he that can do all in all
With her that hateth thee, and hates us all,
And York, and impious Beaufort, that false priest,
Have all lim'd bushes to betray thy wings;
And, fly thou how thou canst, they'll tangle thee:
But fear not thou, until thy foot be snar'd,
Nor never seek prevention of thy foes.

5. Gloucester: pronounced GLAW-ster.
6. closet: private room.
14. deep-fet: deep-fetched, profound.
19. Trow'st thou: do you believe?
35. lim'd bushes: set traps, as when birdlime, a sticky substance, would be
    smeared on branches to catch birds.

Henry IV, Part 2

(Act II, Scene 3)

LADY PERCY
O! yet for heaven's sake, go not to these wars.

The time was, father, that you broke your word
When you were more endear'd to it than now;
When your own Percy, when my heart's dear Harry,
Threw many a northward look to see his father
Bring up his powers; but he did long in vain.

Who then persuaded you to stay at home?

There were two honours lost, yours and your son's:
For yours, may heavenly glory brighten it!

For his, it stuck upon him as the sun   10
In the grey vault of heav'n; and by his light
Did all the chivalry of England move
To do brave acts: he was indeed the glass
Wherein the noble youth did dress themselves:
He had no legs that practic'd not his gait;
And speaking thick, which nature made his blemish,
Became the accents of the valiant;
For those that could speak low and tardily,
Would turn their own perfections to abuse,
To seem like him: so that, in speech, in gait,   20
In diet, in affections of delight,
In military rules, humours of blood,
He was the mark and glass, copy and book,
That fashion'd others.
                    And him, O wondrous him!
O miracle of men! him did you leave,—
Second to none, unseconded by you,—
To look upon the hideous god of war
In disadvantage; to abide a field
Where nothing but the sound of Hotspur's name
Did seem defensible: so you left him.   30

Never, O! never, do his ghost the wrong
To hold your honour more precise and nice
With others than with him: let them alone.
The marshal and the archbishop are strong:
Had my sweet Harry had but half their numbers,
Today might I, hanging on Hotspur's neck,
Have talk'd of Monmouth's grave.

13. glass: mirror.
15. He . . . gait: there were none (with legs) who did not emulate his walk.

16. thick: rapidly, too quickly.
21. affections of delight: inclinations to enjoyment, and therefore pleasures.
24. The beat here indicated is not necessary, but it may help if the momentum is too difficult to sustain.
26. unseconded: unsupported.
32. precise and nice: exact, punctilious, and scrupulous.

ROMANCE AND COMEDY

Most of these men's monologues share an intensity that makes each character seem possessed—by an idea, a spirit, love itself, or perhaps by the very language of the world he inhabits. Romeo's outrage at being banished, for instance, has all the youthful energy and brashness that any young actor could wish for. The images literally fly. They must be allowed to flow and transform without interruption or intellectual interference, so only a couple of actor's beats are indicated. Special attention should be paid here to sounds, the harsh sibilants of "cutt'st," "smil'st," "kisses sin," "poison mix'd," "ghostly confessor," "profess'd," and the like. They reinforce a quick, jagged breathing pattern that sets the rhythm for the speech.

Although well phrased, Berowne's praise of the fair sex in *Love's Labour's Lost* is less rhetorical than it appears and should be full of all the fire and fanaticism of which only a convert is capable. Here too, passion, not logic, predominates. In *Twelfth Night,* Sebastian tries to be reasonable but soon discovers that his attraction to the lovely Olivia (thanks to mistaken identity, he seems to be engaged to her) cannot be explained away. His is a perfect juvenile monologue, at once ingenuous and intelligent.

Richard III's is one of the most blatantly romantic speeches ever written, as it precipitates Lady Anne's reversal from vengeful hatred to a yielding tolerance that leads to marriage later in the play. Although the scene is usually played as a closely intimate one, the presence of Henry's funeral party provides a public dimension. I have left in the stage directions for clarity. At first reading, Parolles's speech in *All's Well That Ends Well* also sounds like a seduction, but its actual purpose is much more ambiguous. He is speaking to Helena, his best friend's betrothed, and so there is a friendship, a common history, an intimacy that finally makes the monologue seem an argument *for* virginity. From *As You Like It* come both

Jaques's entertainment, epitomizing the perfect philosopher-wit—cool, calculating, dry as a martini—and Duke Senior's mature pastoral, characterized by a deliberate, almost plodding lyricism.

Although language obviously remains important, the monologues that follow demand a stronger physical emphasis. Bottom's awakening in *A Midsummer Night's Dream*, for instance, is filled with the reorientation, discovery, and confusion that often accompany such occasions. Trinculo's bid for shelter in *The Tempest* is also very much involved with not only a physical artifact but the deteriorating weather as well. Caliban, Trinculo's "bedfellow," is something of a monster, and, as such, is not particularly funny. But his scene can actually be quite moving if there is a sense of great violence, forcibly contained and expressed through a grounded physical stance that allows the power to come at once from within and from below.

Even Don Adriano de Armado, of *Love's Labour's Lost*, although taking himself most seriously, needs to be fiercely animated. He is a bit like Ford in *The Merry Wives of Windsor* actually, who takes himself *too* seriously. We laugh because he cannot. Tightly wound nerves and rapid, manic shifts in focus can help make this an intensely funny monologue, and the beats in the speech should be dictated by a relentless inner logic derived from a strong personal image—the more bizarre the better—of what "cuckold" means to the actor. Launce's monologue from *Two Gentlemen of Verona* is my favorite audition piece actually, maybe because it doesn't matter what kind of character work the actor does since the star is, of course, Crab the dog, and the success of the scene depends on how visible he becomes to an audience. A friend once developed a version of the piece punctuated entirely by Crab's (imaginary) pulls on a leash (also imaginary). The dog in that version seemed very large.

Shakespeare's romantic women express their passions and obsessions more subtly. Highly formal in structure, Juliet's monologue, for example, offers a chance to convey intense

personal longing with great energy and drive; the formality functions as a lid, barely keeping under control the maelstrom within. The momentum of the piece leaves little opportunity for good breathing pauses. The simplest structural beats occur before each "Come . . . ," but I have indicated alternative beats that halt the rhythm and so build tension instead of reinforcing the formality. In *The Merchant of Venice*, Portia, too, covers her simple vow of love with a binding care, a legalistic shrewdness to which attention must be paid. It is *Twelfth Night*'s Viola, however, who is the complete mistress of subtext. First, disguised as a man, she obliquely expresses her love for her patron, Duke Orsino. Then, still in disguise, she woos Olivia on his behalf. In courtly fashion, and inspired by her own love for the Duke, Viola speaks directly for him, unwittingly capturing Olivia's affections for herself. Later Olivia must try to reconcile her romantic inclinations and the social forms that are clearly important to her. She is a proud and complex woman, and a serious treatment of the role will reveal depths in her worthy of an Ibsen heroine. In this speech, her vulnerability is especially important.

Tamora, Aaron's consort in *Titus Andronicus*, was probably written to show how wanton and lascivious the Queen of the Goths could be. Out of context, however, there is a rare lyrical simplicity in her speech, and the piece should be played slowly and gently, as a kind of love-lullaby. Cressida, an exception to most of Shakespeare's heroines, turns out to be the perfect ingenue, sweet and charming without being cloying. Emotion makes her babble in a manner embarrassingly familiar to most people, until she finally gathers enough control to manage the very formal avowal at the end. It is possible, of course, that she is only pretending to lose control, but I think the scene is more fun if played honestly. There is little doubt about Helena's sincerity in *All's Well* as she first comes to realize the depth of her love for Bertram and then confesses her feelings to her friend (and Bertram's mother) the Countess. Her images are complex, resonating at times with religious fervor, but her own understanding of them is complete and

requires that the logic be worked out as thoroughly by the actor.

The mechanics are deceptively important when attempting *Cymbeline*'s Imogen. For her, both the letter—no mere prop—and its bearer, Pisanio, become her means to reach Milford-Haven and her husband, Posthumus. As in Hermione's speech in *The Winter's Tale*, Shakespeare employs inconsistent, often interrupted rhythms to suggest the depth of feeling underneath. Rosalind of *As You Like It* is perhaps Shakespeare's wittiest woman, but she seldom speaks in monologue form. Her quips and quick rejoinders are, in fact, among her most distinctive traits. In man's attire and under the name Ganymede, she baits Orlando and offers to cure him of his love for Rosalind. Naturally, she loves Orlando and is only testing his perseverance, and the effectiveness of this composite depends on the vividness with which Orlando's presence can be conjured up. Phebe, on the other hand, is a real diz, a wacky shepherdess who has no idea how odd she is. Her scene must be played rapidly and with absolute seriousness. I used to think it best for her to ignore Silvius, her devoted dog's-body, and concentrate on the fading form of Rosalind/Ganymede, but recent experience has suggested that she might really be quite pleased by Silvius's attentions, using her (feigned?) infatuation with another to keep him on the string.

An anomaly in several ways, Julia's scene in *Two Gentlemen* depends on a real letter (use a prop) and, once the maid Lucetta is sent away in line 4, is best played in a private and self-indulgent manner. I include the composite from Joan's trial scene in *Henry VI, Part 1* in this section because I believe that Shakespeare meant it to be funny; there are tremendous comic possibilities in her rapid decline from holiness to pregnancy to ranting witchery. Each section should embody a separate characterization, full and distinct, so that the sudden shifts will take the audience by surprise, while allowing the actor a character range that is rare in classical monologues.

Romeo and Juliet

(Act III, Scene 3)

ROMEO

There is no world without Verona walls,
But purgatory, torture, hell itself.

Hence banished is banish'd from the world,
And world's exile is death; then "banished,"
Is death mis-term'd. Calling death "banished,"
Thou cutt'st my head off with a golden axe,
And smil'st upon the stroke that murders me.
'Tis torture, and not mercy: heav'n is here,
Where Juliet lives; and every cat and dog
And little mouse, every unworthy thing,   10
Live here in heaven and may look on her;
But Romeo may not: more validity,
More honourable state, more courtship lives
In carrion flies than Romeo: they may seize
On the white wonder of dear Juliet's hand,
And steal immortal blessing from her lips,
Who, even in pure and vestal modesty,
Still blush, as thinking their own kisses sin;
Flies may do this, but I from this must fly:
They are free men, but I am banished.   20
And sayst thou yet that exile is not death?
Hadst thou no poison mix'd, no sharp-ground knife,
No sudden mean of death, though ne'er so mean,
But "banished" to kill me? "Banished!"

O friar! the damned use that word in hell;
Howlings attend it: how hast thou the heart,
Being a divine, a ghostly confessor,
A sin-absolver, and my friend profess'd,
To mangle me with that word "banished"?

25. This the only real shift in focus, as Romeo begins to deal directly with the Friar who has brought him the news.

Love's Labour's Lost

(Act IV, Scene 3)

BEROWNE
Have at you, then, affection's men-at-arms:

Consider what you first did swear unto,
To fast, to study, and to see no woman;
Flat treason 'gainst the kingly state of youth.

Say, can you fast? your stomachs are too young,
And abstinence engenders maladies.
And where that you have vow'd to study, lords,
In that each of you hath forsworn his book,
Can you still dream and pore and thereon look?
For when would you, my lord, or you, or you,   10
Have found the ground of study's excellence
Without the beauty of a woman's face?

From women's eyes this doctrine I derive:

They are the ground, the books, the academes,
From whence doth spring the true Promethean fire.
Why, universal plodding poisons up
The nimble spirits in the arteries,
As motion and long-during action tires
The sinewy vigour of the traveller.
Now, for not looking on a woman's face,   20
You have in that forsworn the use of eyes,
And study too, the causer of your vow;
For where is any author in the world
Teaches such beauty as a woman's eye?
Learning is but an adjunct to ourself,
And where we are our learning likewise is:

Then when ourselves we see in ladies' eyes,
Do we not likewise see our learning there?
O!
  we have made a vow to study, lords,
And in that vow we have forsworn our books: 30
For when would you, my liege, or you, or you,
In leaden contemplation have found out
Such fiery numbers as the prompting eyes
Of beauty's tutors have enrich'd you with?
Other slow arts entirely keep the brain,
And therefore, finding barren practisers,
Scarce show a harvest of their heavy toil;
But love, first learned in a lady's eyes,
Lives not alone immured in the brain,
But, with the motion of all elements,   40
Courses as swift as thought in every power,
And gives to every power a double power,
Above their functions and their offices.

It adds a precious seeing to the eye;
A lover's eyes will gaze an eagle blind;
A lover's ear will hear the lowest sound,
When the suspicious head of theft is stopp'd:
Love's feeling is more soft and sensible
Than are the tender horns of cockled snails:
Love's tongue proves dainty Bacchus gross in taste. 50
For valour, is not Love a Hercules,
Still climbing trees in the Hesperides?
Subtle as Sphinx; as sweet and musical
As bright Apollo's lute, strung with his hair;
And when Love speaks, the voice of all the gods
Makes heaven drowsy with the harmony.

Never durst poet touch a pen to write
Until his ink were temper'd with Love's sighs;
O! then his lines would ravish savage ears,
And plant in tyrants mild humility.   60

From women's eyes this doctrine I derive:
They sparkle still the right Promethean fire;
They are the books, the arts, the academes,
That show, contain, and nourish all the world;
Else none at all in aught proves excellent.

Then fools you were these women to forswear,
Or, keeping what is sworn, you will prove fools.
For wisdom's sake, a word that all men love,
Or for love's sake, a word that loves all men,
Or for men's sake, the authors of these women;   70
Or women's sake, by whom we men are men,
Let us once lose our oaths to find ourselves,
Or else we lose ourselves to keep our oaths.
It is religion to be thus forsworn;
For charity itself fulfills the law;
And who can sever love from charity?

Advance your standards, and upon them, lords!

25. adjunct: attendant.
33. numbers: rhythmical cadence; poetry.
41. power: physical or intellectual function.
47. When . . . stopp'd: when even a thief wouldn't hear.
48. Here and for the next twelve lines, Love is personified, which might suggest
    some physicalization for the actor.
52. Hesperides: garden where Hercules performed one of his labors, picking
    golden apples.

Twelfth Night
(Act IV, Scene 3)

SEBASTIAN

This is the air;
                that is the glorious sun;
This pearl she gave me, I do feel't and see't;

And though 'tis wonder that enwraps me thus,
Yet 'tis not madness.

                  Where's Antonio then?
I could not find him at the Elephant;
Yet there he was, and there I found this credit,
That he did range the town to seek me out.
His counsel now might do me golden service;
For though my soul disputes well with my sense
That this may be some error, but no madness,   10
Yet doth this accident and flood of fortune
So far exceed all instance, all discourse,
That I am ready to distrust mine eyes,
And wrangle with my reason that persuades me
To any other trust but that I am mad
Or else the lady's mad: yet, if 'twere so,
She could not sway her house, command her followers,
Take and give back affairs and their dispatch
With such a smooth, discreet, and stable bearing
As I perceive she does.
                      There's something in't   20
That is deceivable.
                  But here the lady comes.

4. There is a major shift in focus and perception here.
5. Elephant: local inn or tavern.
21. deceivable: delusive, not what it seems. Olivia's entrance probably serves
best as an interruption to speculation that might otherwise go on longer.

Richard III

(Act I, Scene 2)

RICHARD, DUKE OF GLOUCESTER

Those eyes of thine from mine have drawn salt tears,
Sham'd their aspects with store of childish drops;

———

These eyes, which never shed remorseful tear;
No, when my father York and Edward wept
To hear the piteous moan that Rutland made
When black-fac'd Clifford shook his sword at him;
Nor when thy warlike father like a child,
Told the sad story of my father's death,
And twenty times made pause to sob and weep,
That all the standers-by had wet their cheeks,   10
Like trees bedash'd with rain: in that sad time,
My manly eyes did scorn an humble tear;
And what these sorrows could not thence exhale,
Thy beauty hath, and made them blind with weeping.

I never su'd to friend, nor enemy;
My tongue could never learn sweet smoothing words;
But, now thy beauty is propos'd my fee,
My proud heart sues, and prompts my tongue to speak.

Teach not thy lip such scorn, for it was made
For kissing, lady, not for such contempt.   20
If thy revengeful heart cannot forgive,
Lo! here I lend thee this sharp-pointed sword;
Which if thou please to hide in this true breast,
And let the soul forth that adoreth thee,
I lay it open to the deadly stroke,
And humbly beg the death upon my knee.
   (He lays his breast open: she offers at it with his sword)
Nay, do not pause; for I did kill King Henry;
But 'twas thy beauty that provoked me.
Nay, now dispatch; 'twas I that stabb'd young Edward;
   (She again offers at his breast)
But 'twas thy heavenly face that set me on.   30
   (She lets fall the sword)
Take up the sword again, or take up me.

All's Well That Ends Well

(Act I, Scene 1)

PAROLLES

Are you meditating on virginity?

Man is enemy to virginity, and you may not barricado it
against him. Man, sitting down before you, will under-
mine you and blow you up. Virginity being blown down,
man will quicklier be blown up: marry in blowing him
down again, with the breach yourselves made, you lose
your city.

It is not politic in the commonwealth of nature
to preserve virginity. Loss of virginity is rational increase, and there was never virgin got till virginity was
first lost. That you were made of is metal to make virgins.   10
Virginity, by being once lost, may be ten times found:
by being ever kept, it is ever lost. 'Tis too cold a companion: away with't!

There's little can be said in't; 'tis
against the rule of nature. To speak on the part of virginity is to accuse your mothers, which is most infallible
disobedience. He that hangs himself is a virgin: virginity
murders itself, and should be buried in highways, out of
all sanctified limit, as a desperate offendress against nature. Virginity breeds mites, much like a cheese, con-
sumes itself to the very paring, and so dies with feeding   20
his own stomach. Besides, virginity is peevish, proud,
idle, made of self-love, which is the most inhibited sin
in the canon. Keep it not; you cannot choose but lose
by't! Out with't! within the year it will make itself two,
which is a goodly increase, and the principal itself not
much the worse. Away with't!

'Tis a commodity that will
lose the gloss with lying; the longer kept, the less worth:

off with't, while 'tis vendible; answer the time of request.

Virginity, like an old courtier, wears her cap out
of fashion; richly suited, but unsuitable. Your virginity,   30
your old virginity, is like one of our French withered
pears; it looks ill, it eats drily; marry, 'tis a withered pear;
it was formerly better; marry, yet 'tis a withered pear.

Will

you anything with it?

2–3. Man . . . against him: Helena's line has been interpolated for clarity of
   argument.
17–18. should . . . limit: like other suicides, virginity cannot demand rest in
   holy ground.
28. vendible: saleable.
28–29. answer . . . request: meet the demand.

As You Like It
(Act II, Scene 7)

JAQUES
A fool, a fool! I met a fool i' the forest,
A motley fool;
        a miserable world!
As I do live by food, I met a fool
Who laid him down and bask'd him in the sun,
And rail'd on Lady Fortune in good terms,
In good set terms, and yet a motley fool.

"Good morrow, fool," quoth I. "No, sir," quoth he,
"Call me not fool till heav'n hath sent me fortune."
And then he drew a dial from his poke,
And, looking on it with lack-lustre eye,   10
Says very wisely, "It is ten o'clock;
Thus may we see," quoth he, "how the world wags:
'Tis but an hour ago since it was nine,
And after one hour more 'twill be eleven;

And so, from hour to hour we ripe and ripe,
And then from hour to hour we rot and rot,
And thereby hangs a tale."
                          When I did hear
The motley fool thus moral on the time,
My lungs began to crow like chanticleer,
That fools should be so deep-contemplative,   20
And I did laugh sans intermission
An hour by his dial.
                    O noble fool!
A worthy fool! Motley's the only wear;
It is my only suit. I must have liberty
Withal, as large a charter as the wind,
To blow on whom I please; for so fools have:
And they that are most galled with my folly,

They most must laugh.
Invest me in my motley; give me leave   30
To speak my mind, and I will through and through
Cleanse the foul body of th'infected world,
If they will patiently receive my medicine.

2. motley: multicolored suit traditionally worn by professional jester or clown.
6. set: proper.
9. poke: pocket.
19. chanticleer: rooster.
25. charter: recorded right, privilege.
27. galled: harassed.

As You Like It
(Act II, Scene 1)

DUKE SENIOR
Now, my co-mates and brothers in exile,
Hath not old custom made this life more sweet
Than that of painted pomp? Are not these woods
More free from peril than the envious court?

Here feel we but the penalty of Adam,
The seasons' difference; as, the icy fang
And churlish chiding of the winter's wind,
Which, when it bites and blows upon my body,
Even till I shrink with cold, I smile and say
"This is no flattery: these are counsellors,   10
That feelingly persuade me what I am."
Sweet are the uses of adversity,
Which like the toad, ugly and venomous,
Wears yet a precious jewel in his head;
And this our life exempt from public haunt,
Finds tongues in trees, books in the running brooks,
Sermons in stones, and good in every thing.

Come, shall we go and kill us venison?
And yet it irks me, the poor dappled fools,
Being native burghers of this desert city,   20
Should in their own confines with forked heads
Have their round haunches gor'd.

A Midsummer Night's Dream
(Act IV, Scene 1)

BOTTOM

When my cue comes, call me, and I will answer: my next is,
"Most fair Pyramus."

Heigh-ho! Peter Quince!

Flute, the bellows-
mender!
Snout, the tinker! Starveling!

God's my life! stolen hence, and
left me asleep!

I have had a most rare vision. I have had a
dream, past the wit of man to say what dream it was: man

is but an ass, if he go about to expound this dream.
Methought I was—
　　　　　　　　　there is no man call tell what.
Methought I was,—
　　　　　　　　　and methought I had,—
　　　　　　　　　　　　　　but man
is but a patched fool, if he will offer to say what methought I had. The eye of man hath not heard, the ear　　10
of man hath not seen, man's hand is not able to taste,
his tongue to conceive, nor his heart to report, what
my dream was.
　　　　　　I will get Peter Quince to write a ballad
of this dream: it shall be called Bottom's Dream, because it hath no bottom; and I will sing it in the latter
end of a play, before the duke: peradventure, to make
it the more gracious, I shall sing it at her death.

1. When my cue comes: Bottom and his friends were rehearsing a play, *Pyramus
and Thisbe*, in the forest when the mischievous Puck placed the head of an
ass on him. Bottom's subsequent romance with Titania, Queen of the Fairies,
is the dream he recalls with his "methought"s, and the physical possibilities
include mimes of ass's ears, echoes of hee-haws, etc., and much time should
be taken to explore them.
17. her death: Thisbe's death in the play.

The Tempest
(Act II, Scene 2)

TRINCULO
Here's neither bush nor shrub to bear off any weather
at all, and another storm brewing;
　　　　　　　　　I hear it sing i' the
wind: yond same black cloud, yond huge one, looks
like a foul bombard that would shed his liquor. If it
should thunder as it did before, I know not where to
hide my head: yond same cloud cannot choose but fall

by pailfuls.
—What have we here?
a man or a fish?
Dead
or alive?
A fish: he smells like a fish; a very ancient and fish-like smell; a kind of not of the newest Poor-John.
A
strange fish! Were I in England now,—as once I was,— 10
and had but this fish painted, not a holiday fool there but would give a piece of silver: there would this monster make a man; any strange beast there makes a man. When they will not give a doit to relieve a lame beggar, they will lay out ten to see a dead Indian.
Legged like
a man! and his fins like arms!
Warm, o' my troth!
I do
now let loose my opinion, hold it no longer; this is no fish, but an islander, that hath lately suffered by a thunderbolt. (*Thunder*)
Alas! the storm is come again: my best way is to creep under his gaberdine; there is 20 no other shelter hereabout:
misery acquaints a man with strange bedfellows. I will here shroud till the dregs of the storm be past.

4. bombard: large leather jug.
9. Poor-John: coarse dried salted fish, usually hake; a type of poor fare.
11. painted: as to advertise a fair booth.
14. doit: smallest coin.
20. gaberdine: loose upper garment.
22. shroud: take shelter.

The Tempest
(Act I, Scene 2)

CALIBAN

As wicked dew as e'er my mother brush'd
With raven's feather from unwholesome fen
Drop on you both! A south-west blow on ye,
And blister you all o'er!
                    I must eat my dinner.
This island's mine, by Sycorax my mother,
Which thou tak'st from me. When thou camest first,
Thou strok'dst me, and mad'st much of me; wouldst give me
Water with berries in't; and teach me how
To name the bigger light, and how the less,
That burn by day and night: and then I lov'd thee   10
And show'd thee all the qualities o' th' isle,
The fresh springs, brine-pits, barren place and fertile.
Curs'd be I that did so!—All the charms
Of Sycorax: toads, beetles, bats, light on you!
For I am all the subjects that you have,
Which first was mine own king; and here you sty me
In this hard rock, whiles you do keep from me
The rest o' th' island. Oh ho! Oh ho!

You taught me language; and my profit on't
Is, I know how to curse: the red plague rid you,   20
For learning me your language!

2. fen: bog.
3. both: Prospero's daughter, Miranda, is also present.

Love's Labour's Lost

(Act I, Scene 2)

DON ADRIANO DE ARMADO

I do affect the very ground, which is base, where her shoe, which is baser, guided by her foot, which is basest, doth tread.

I shall be forsworn,—which is a great argument of falsehood,—if I love. And how can that be true love which is falsely attempted?

Love is a familiar; Love is a devil: there is no evil angel but Love.

Yet was Samson so tempted, and he had an excellent strength; yet was Solomon so seduced, and he had a very good wit. Cupid's butt-shaft is too hard for Hercules' club, and therefore too much odds for a Spaniard's rapier.

The first and second clause will not serve my turn; the passado he respects not, the duello he regards not: his disgrace is to be called boy, but his glory is, to subdue men.   10

Adieu, valour! rust, rapier! be still, drum! for your manager is in love; yea, he loveth.

Assist me some extemporal god of rhyme, for I am sure I shall turn sonneteer.

Devise, wit; write, pen; for I am for whole volumes in folio.

1. affect: love.
5. familiar: demon or attendant spirit.
10. first . . . clause: referring to the proper protocol of a duel. passado: forward thrust with the sword, one foot being advanced at the same time. duello: established code of duelists.
17. in folio: reference is probably to the size of the pages, a folio having the largest.

The Merry Wives of Windsor
(Act II, Scene 2)

FORD

What a damned Epicurean rascal is this!
My heart is
ready to crack with impatience. Who says this is im-
provident jealousy? My wife hath sent to him, the hour
is fixed, the match is made. Would any man have thought
this? See the hell of having a false woman! My bed shall
be abused, my coffers ransacked, my reputation gnawn
at; and I shall not only receive this villainous wrong, but
stand under the adoption of abominable terms, and by
him that does me this wrong. Terms! names! Amaimon
sounds well; Lucifer, well; Barbason, well; yet they are   10
devils' additions, the names of fiends: but Cuckold! Wittol!—Cuckold! the devil himself hath not such a name.
Page is an ass, a secure ass: he will trust his wife; he will
not be jealous. I will rather trust a Fleming with my butter,
Parson Hugh the Welshman with my cheese, an Irish-
man with my aqua-vitae bottle, or a thief to walk my am-
bling gelding, than my wife with herself: then she plots,
then she ruminates, then she devises; and what they think
in their hearts they may effect, they will break their
hearts but they will effect. God be praised for my jealousy!   20

Eleven o'clock the hour: I will prevent this, detect my
wife, be revenged on Falstaff, and laugh at Page. I will
about it; better three hours too soon than a minute too
late. Fie, fie, fie! cuckold! cuckold! cuckold!

1. Epicurean: given to luxury, sensual.
11. wittol: another word for cuckold, a betrayed husband.
14–16. Ford lists three nationalities and their traditional predilections: the Flem-
     ish were reputed to like butter, the Welsh to thrive on cheese, and the
     Irish to consume great quantities of hard liquor.

Two Gentlemen of Verona
(Act IV, Scene 4)

LAUNCE

When a man's servant shall play the cur with him,
look you, it goes hard; one that I brought up of a puppy;
one that I saved from drowning, when three or four of
his blind brothers and sisters went to it. I have taught
him, even as one would say precisely, "Thus would I
teach a dog." I was sent to deliver him as a present to
Mistress Silvia from my master, and I came no sooner
into the dining-chamber but he steps me to her trencher
and steals her capon's leg. O! 'tis a foul thing when a cur
cannot keep himself in all companies. I would have, as   10
one should say, one that takes upon him to be a dog
indeed, to be, as it were, a dog in all things. If I had not
had more wit than he, to take a fault upon me that he
did, I think verily he had been hanged for't: sure as I
live, he had suffered for't: you shall judge. He thrusts
me himself into the company of three or four gentleman-
like dogs under the duke's table: he had not been there—
bless the mark—a pissing-while, but all the chamber
smelt him. "Out with the dog!" says one; "What cur is
that?" says another; "Whip him out," says the third; "Hang   20
him up," says the duke. I, having been acquainted with
the smell before, knew it was Crab, and goes me to the
fellow that whips the dogs: "Friend," quoth I, "you mean
to whip the dog?" "Ay, marry, do I," quoth he. "You do
him the more wrong," quoth I; " 'Twas I did the thing
you wot of." He makes me no more ado, but whips me
out of the chamber. How many masters would do this
for his servant? Nay, I'll be sworn, I have sat in the stocks
for puddings he hath stolen, otherwise he had been ex-
ecuted; I have stood on the pillory for geese he hath   30
killed, otherwise he had suffered for't; thou thinkest not

of this now. Nay, I remember the trick you served me
when I took my leave of Madam Silvia: did not I bid thee
still mark me and do as I do? When didst thou see me
heave up my leg and make water against a gentlewoman's
farthingale? Didst thou ever see me do such a trick?

8. me: the reflexive is colloquial, and not grammatically literal.
8. trencher: plate.
26. wot: know.
31. There is a mid-sentence change of focus here.
36. farthingale: hoop petticoat.

Romeo and Juliet

(Act III, Scene 2)

JULIET

Gallop apace, you fiery-footed steeds,
Towards Phoebus' lodging;
              such a waggoner
As Phaëthon would whip you to the west,
And bring in cloudy night immediately.
Spread thy close curtain, love-performing night!
That runaway's eyes may wink, and Romeo
Leap to these arms, untalk'd of and unseen!
Lovers can see to do their amorous rites
By their own beauties;
            or, if love be blind,
It best agrees with night. Come, civil night,   10
Thou sober-suited matron, all in black,
And learn me how to lose a winning match,
Play'd for a pair of stainless maidenhoods:
Hood my unmann'd blood, bating in my cheeks,
With thy black mantle; till strange love, grown bold,
Think true love acted simple modesty.
Come, night! come, Romeo! come, thou day in night!
For thou wilt lie upon the wings of night,
Whiter than new snow on a raven's back.
Come, gentle night; come,
            loving, black-brow'd night,   20
Give me my Romeo:
         and, when he shall die,
Take him and cut him out in little stars,
And he will make the face of heaven so fine
That all the world will be in love with night,
And pay no worship to the garish sun.
O!
   I have bought the mansion of a love,

But not possess'd it, and, though I am sold,
Not yet enjoy'd. So tedious is this day
As is the night before some festival
To an impatient child that hath new robes   30
And may not wear them.
                                    O! here comes my nurse.

2. Phoebus: Apollo, the sun-god; the "fiery-footed steeds" pull the sun's chariot
    across the sky, a chariot once recklessly stolen by Phaëthon.
14. bating: beating, fluttering, flapping; the term is used in falconry, as is "hood,"
    a covering for the falcon's eyes and head.

The Merchant of Venice
(Act III, Scene 2)

PORTIA

You see, my Lord Bassanio, where I stand,
Such as I am:
                   though for myself alone
I would not be ambitious in my wish,
To wish myself much better, yet, for you
I would be trebled twenty times myself;
A thousand times more fair, ten thousand times
More rich;
That only to stand high in your account,
I might in virtues, beauties, livings, friends,
Exceed account:
                   but the full sum of me   10
Is sum of nothing; which, to term in gross,
Is an unlesson'd girl, unschool'd, unpractis'd;
Happy in this, she is not yet so old
But she may learn; happier than this,
She is not bred so dull but she can learn;
Happiest of all is that her gentle spirit
Commits itself to yours to be directed,
As from her lord, her governor, her king.

Myself and what is mine to you and yours
Is now converted:
                    but now I was the lord   20
Of this fair mansion, master of my servants,
Queen o'er myself; and even now, but now,
This house, these servants, and this same myself
Are yours, my lord.
                    I give them with this ring;
Which when you part from, lose, or give away,
Let it presage the ruin of your love,
And be my vantage to exclaim on you.

 9. livings: property, possessions, fortune.
11. term in gross: state in broad terms.
20. but now: just now.
27. And . . . you: and I will have the right to cry out against you.

Twelfth Night

(Act II, Scene 4)

Viola

Say that some lady, as perhaps there is,
Hath for your love as great a pang of heart
As you have for Olivia: you cannot love her;
You tell her so; must she not then be answer'd?

I know too well what love women to men may owe:
In faith, they are as true of heart as we.
My father had a daughter lov'd a man,
As it might be, perhaps, were I a woman,
I should your lordship. And what's her history?
A blank, my lord. She never told her love,   10
But let concealment, like a worm i' the bud,
Feed on her damask cheek: she pin'd in thought,
And with a green and yellow melancholy,

She sat like Patience on a monument,
Smiling at grief. Was this not love indeed?
We men may say more, swear more; but indeed
Our shows are more than will, for still we prove
Much in our vows, but little in our love.

Sir, shall I to this lady?

19. Viola has been asked to serve as Orsino's emissary to Olivia.

Twelfth Night
(Act I, Scene 5)

VIOLA

Good madam, let me see your face;
'Tis beauty truly blent, whose red and white
Nature's own sweet and cunning hand laid on:
Lady, you are the cruell'st she alive,
If you will lead these graces to the grave
And leave the world no copy.

I see you what you are: you are too proud;
But, if you were the devil, you are fair.
My lord and master loves you
With adorations, with fertile tears,   10
With groans that thunder love, with sighs of fire.
O! such love could be but recompens'd,
Though you were crown'd the nonpareil of beauty.

If I did love you in my master's flame,
With such a suff'ring, such a deadly life,
In your denial I would find no sense;
I would not understand. Sweet lady, I would
Make me a willow cabin at your gate,
And call upon my soul within the house;
Write loyal cantons of contemned love,   20

And sing them loud even in the dead of night;
Holla your name to the reverb'rate hills,
And make the babbling gossip of the air
Cry out, "Olivia!" O! you should not rest
Between the elements of air and earth,
But you should pity me!

2. blent: blended.
20. cantons: songs. contemned: despised.

Twelfth Night
(Act III, Scene 1)

OLIVIA
O world! how apt the poor are to be proud.

If one should be a prey, how much the better
To fall befjore the lion than the wolf!
   (*Clock strikes*)
The clock upbraids me with the waste of time.
Be not afraid, good youth, I will not have you:
And yet, when wit and youth is come to harvest,
Your wife is like to reap a proper man:
There lies your way, due west.
                        But stay:
I prithee, tell me what thou think'st of me.

O! what a deal of scorn looks beautiful   10
In the contempt and anger of his lip.
A murderous guilt shows not itself more soon
Than love that would seem hid; love's night is noon.

Cesario, by the roses of the spring,
By maidhood, honour, truth, and every thing,
I love thee so, that, maugre all thy pride,

Nor wit nor reason can my passion hide.
Do not extort thy reasons from this clause,
For that I woo, thou therefore hast no cause;
But rather reason thus with reason fetter,   20
Love sought is good, but giv'n unsought is better.

4. The imagined striking of a clock can be used to develop Olivia's skittishness,
    another manifestation of her vulnerability.
10–13. These lines may be played as an aside or directly to Viola.
14. Cesario: the man's name Viola has chosen.
16. maugre: despite.
18. clause: interference.

Titus Andronicus
(Act II, Scene 3)

TAMORA
My lovely Aaron, wherefore look'st thou sad,
When every thing doth make a gleeful boast?

The birds chant melody on every bush,
The snake lies rolled in the cheerful sun,
The green leaves quiver with the cooling wind,
And make a chequer'd shadow on the ground.

Under their sweet shade, Aaron, let us sit,
And, whilst the babbling echo mocks the hounds,
Replying shrilly to the well-tun'd horns,
As if a double hunt were heard at once,   10
Let us sit down and mark their yelping noise;
And after conflict, such as was suppos'd
The wandering prince and Dido once enjoy'd,
When with a happy storm they were surpris'd,
And curtain'd with a counsel-keeping cave,
We may, each wreathed in the other's arms,
Our pastimes done, possess a golden slumber;

While hounds and horns and sweet melodious birds
Be unto us as is a nurse's song
Of lullaby to bring her babe asleep.   20

Troilus and Cressida
(Act III, Scene 2)

CRESSIDA
Boldness comes to me now, and brings me heart:

Prince Troilus, I have lov'd you night and day
For many weary months, for I was won, my lord,
With the first glance that ever—
                                 —pardon me—
If I confess much you will play the tyrant.
I love you now; but, till now, not so much
But I might master it: in faith, I lie;
My thoughts were like unbridled children, grown
Too headstrong for their mother. See, we fools!
Why have I blabb'd? who shall be true to us   10
When we are so unsecret to ourselves?
But, though I lov'd you well, I woo'd you not;
And yet, good faith, I wish'd myself a man,
Or that we women had men's privilege
Of speaking first. Sweet, bid me hold my tongue;
For in this rapture I shall surely speak
The thing I shall repent. See, see! your silence,
Cunning in dumbness, from my weakness draws
My soul of counsel from me. Stop my mouth.

My lord, I do beseech you, pardon me;   20
'Twas not my purpose thus to beg a kiss:

I am asham'd: O heavens! what have I done?
For this time I will take my leave, my lord.

I have a kind of self resides with you;
But an unkind self, that itself will leave,
To be another's fool. I would be gone.
If I be false, or swerve a hair from truth,
When time is old and hath forgot itself,
When waterdrops have worn the stones of Troy,
And blind oblivion swallow'd cities up,   30
And mighty states characterless are grated
To dusty nothing, yet let memory,
From false to false, among false maids in love
Upbraid my falsehood! when they have said "as false
As air, as water, wind, or sandy earth,
As fox to lamb, as wolf to heifer's calf,
Pard to the hind, or stepdame to her son;"
Yea, let them say, to stick the heart of falsehood,
"As false as Cressid."

20. Cressida has shied away from an attempted kiss.
37. Pard: leopard.

All's Well That Ends Well
(Act I, Scenes 1 and 3)

HELENA
I think not on my father;

And these great tears grace his remembrance more
Than those I shed for him.
                              What was he like?

I have forgot him: my imagination
Carries no favour in't but Bertram's.
I am undone: there is no living, none,
If Bertram be away.
                              It were all one

That I should love a bright particular star
And think to wed it, he is so above me:
In his bright radiance and collateral light   10
Must I be comforted, not in his sphere.
The ambition in my love thus plagues itself:
The hind that would be mated by the lion
Must die for love.
                        'Twas pretty, though a plague,
To see him every hour; to sit and draw
His arched brows, his hawking eye, his curls,
In our heart's table; heart too capable
Of every line and trick of his sweet favour:
But now he's gone, and my idolatrous fancy
Must sanctify his reliques.   20
    (*To the Countess*) Then, I confess,
Here on my knee, before high heaven and you
That before you, and next unto high heaven,
I love your son.

My friends were poor, but honest; so's my love:
Be not offended, for it hurts not him
That he is lov'd of me: I follow him not
By any token of presumptuous suit;
Nor would I have him till I do deserve him;
Yet never know how that desert should be.   30
I know I love in vain, strive against hope;
Yet, in this captious and intenible sieve
I still pour in the waters of my love,
And lack not to lose still. Thus, Indian-like,
Religious in mine error, I adore
The sun, that looks upon his worshipper,
But knows of him no more.
                        My dearest madam,
Let not your hate encounter with my love
For loving where you do: but, if yourself,
Whose aged honour cites a virtuous youth,   40
Did ever in so true a flame of liking

Wish chastely and love dearly, that your Dian
Was both herself and Love; O! then, give pity
To her, whose state is such that cannot choose
But lend and give where she is sure to lose;
That seeks not to find that her search implies,
But, riddle-like, lives sweetly where she dies.

5. favour: present or love token; also appearance, form, and therefore face. Appears again in line 18.
10. collateral: indirect.
13. hind: female red deer.
17. table: tablet. capable: susceptible.
32. captious: capacious. intenible: incapable of retaining.
33. waters: tears.
34. And . . . still: despite all this watering, Helena still has tears to spare. Indianlike: in this complex reference, she compares herself to a sun-worshiping pagan who persists in the error of his ways.

Cymbeline
(Act III, Scene 2)

IMOGEN

O! learn'd indeed were that astronomer
That knew the stars as I his characters;
He'd lay the future open.
                              You good gods,
Let what is here contain'd relish of love,
Of my lord's health, of his content, yet not
That we two are asunder; let that grieve him,—
Some griefs are med'cinable; that is one of them,
For it doth physic love,—of his content,
All but in that!
                    Good wax, thy leave. Bless'd be
You bees that make these locks of counsel! Lovers   10
And men in dangerous bonds pray not alike;
Though forfeiters you cast in prison, yet
You clasp young Cupid's tables.
                              Good news, gods!

Justice, and your father's wrath, should he take me in his dominion, could not be so cruel to me, as you, O the dearest of creatures, would not even renew me with your eyes. Take notice that I am in Cambria, at Milford-Haven; what your own love will out of this advise you, follow. So, he wishes you all happiness, that remains loyal to his vow, and your, increasing in love,   20

                     Leonatus Posthumus.

O! for a horse with wings! Hear'st thou, Pisanio?
He is at Milford-Haven; read, and tell me
How far 'tis thither. If one of mean affairs
May plod it in a week, why may not I
Glide thither in a day? Then, true Pisanio,—
Who long'st, like me, to see thy lord; who long'st,—
But in a fainter kind:—O! not like me,
For mine's beyond beyond; say, and speak thick;—
Love's counsellor should fill the bores of hearing,   30
To the smothering of the sense,—how far it is
To this same blessed Milford; and, by the way,
Tell me how Wales was made so happy as
T'inherit such a haven; but, first of all,
How we may steal from hence, and, for the gap
That we shall make in time, from our hencegoing
And our return, to excuse; but first, how get hence.
Why should excuse be borne or ere begot?
We'll talk of that hereafter.
                   Prithee, speak,
How many score of miles may we well ride   40
'Twixt hour and hour? I have heard of riding wagers,
Where horses have been nimbler than the sands
That run i' the clock's behalf.
                  But this is foolery;
Go bid my woman feign a sickness; say
She'll home to her father; and provide me presently
A riding-suit, no costlier than would fit

A franklin's housewife.

I see before me, man; nor here, nor here,
Nor what ensues, but have a fog in them
That I cannot look through.
Away, I prithee;   50
Accessible is none but Milford way.

2. characters: handwriting.
4. relish: taste.
9. wax: sealing wax; this section of the speech covers the business of undoing the letter's seal.
10–13. Lovers . . . tables: Imogen is saying that letters bearing penalties come open easily enough, so why can't she open a love letter?
17. Cambria: ancient name for the western part of England.
35–38. How . . . begot: she is asking for help in inventing an excuse for her absence, then considers that she may be gone and returned before any excuse is necessary.
39. Prithee, speak: Pisanio has, of course, had no chance to get a word in; nor does he get one now.
47. franklin: yeoman or small landowner.
49. them: her eyes.

As You Like It
(Act III, Scene 2)

ROSALIND

There is a man haunts the forest, that abuses our young plants with carving "Rosalind" on their barks; hangs odes upon hawthorns, and elegies on brambles; all, forsooth, deifying the name of Rosalind: if I could meet that fancy-monger, I would give him some good counsel, for he seems to have the quotidian of love upon him.

My uncle taught me how to know a man in love: a lean cheek, which you have not; an unquestionable spirit, which you have not; a beard neglected, which you have not: but I pardon you for that, for simply, your having   10
in beard is a younger brother's revenue. Then, your hose should be ungartered, your bonnet unbanded, your sleeve

unbuttoned, your shoe untied, and everything about you demonstrating a careless desolation.

But, in good sooth, are you he that hangs the verses on the trees, wherein Rosalind is so admired?

Love is merely a madness, and, I tell you, deserves as well a dark house and a whip as madmen do; and the reason why they are not so punished and cured is, that the lunacy is so ordinary that the whippers are in love   20
too.
        Yet I profess curing it by counsel. I cured one so; and in this manner.
                    He was to imagine me his love, his mistress; and I set him every day to woo me. At which time would I, being but a moonish youth, grieve, be effeminate, changeable, longing and liking; proud, fan-tastical, apish, shallow, inconstant, full of tears, full of smiles, for every passion something, and for no passion truly anything, as boys and women are, for the most part, cattle of this colour; would now like him, now loathe him; then entertain him, then forswear him; now weep   30
for him, then spit at him; that I drove my suitor from his mad humour of love to a living humour of madness, which was, to forswear the full stream of the world, and to live in a nook merely monastic.
                    And thus I cured him; and this way will I take upon me to wash your liver as clean as a sound sheep's heart, that there shall not be one spot of love in't. I would cure you, if you would but call me Rosalind, and come every day to my cote and woo me.

Nay, you must call me Rosalind.   40

4. fancy-monger: dream-peddler, poet.
6. quotidian: a fever which recurs daily.
24. moonish: capricious.

As You Like It

(Act III, Scene 5)

PHEBE
Know'st thou the youth that spoke to me erewhile?

Think not I love him, though I ask for him.
'Tis but a peevish boy; yet he talks well;
But what care I for words? Yet words do well,
When he that speaks them pleases those that hear.
It is a pretty youth: not very pretty:
But sure, he's proud; and yet his pride becomes him.
He'll make a proper man. The best thing in him
Is his complexion; and faster than his tongue
Did make offense his eye did heal it up.   10
He is not very tall; yet for his years he's tall.
His leg is but so so; and yet 'tis well.
There was a pretty redness in his lip,
A little riper and more lusty red
Than that mix'd in his cheek; 'twas just the difference
Betwixt the constant red and mingled damask.

There be some women, Silvius, had they mark'd him
In parcels as I did, would have gone near
To fall in love with him; but, for my part,
I love him not nor hate him not; and yet   20
Have more cause to hate him than to love him:
For what had he to do to chide at me?
He said mine eyes were black and my hair black;
And, now I am remember'd, scorn'd at me.

I marvel why I answer'd not again.

But that's all one; omittance is no quittance.
I'll write to him a very taunting letter,

And thou shalt bear it. Wilt thou, Silvius?
I'll write it straight;
The matter's in my head and in my heart: 30
I will be bitter with him and passing short.
Go with me, Silvius.

26. omittance is no quittance: passing up the chance before doesn't strike out
the debt.

Two Gentlemen of Verona
(Act I, Scene 2)

JULIA
This babble shall not henceforth trouble me.
Here is a coil with protestation!—(*Tears the letter*)

Go, get you gone, and let the papers lie:
You would be fing'ring them, to anger me.

O hateful hands, to tear such loving words!

Injurious wasps, to feed on such sweet honey
And kill the bees that yield it with your stings!
I'll kiss each several paper for amends.

Look, here is writ "kind Julia:" unkind Julia!
As in revenge of thy ingratitude,   10
I throw thy name against the bruising stones,
Trampling contemptuously on thy disdain.

And here is writ "love-wounded Proteus:"
Poor wounded name! my bosom, as a bed
Shall lodge thee till thy wound be throughly heal'd;
And thus I search it with a sovereign kiss.
But twice or thrice was "Proteus" written down:

Be calm, good wind, blow not a word away
Till I have found each letter in the letter,
Except mine own name; that some whirlwind bear   20
Unto a ragged, fearful-hanging rock,
And throw it thence into the raging sea!

Lo! here in one line is his name twice writ,
"Poor forlorn Proteus, passionate Proteus,
To the sweet Julia:"—that I'll tear away;

And yet I will not, sith so prettily
He couples it to his complaining names:
Thus will I fold them one upon another:
Now kiss, embrace, contend, do what you will.

2. coil: turmoil, bustle, confusion. Julia is saying that there's too much ado about
a lover's declaration.
16. search: probe, sound for depth.

Henry VI, Part 1
(Act V, Scene 4)

JOAN LA PUCELLE (or JOAN OF ARC)
First, let me tell you whom you have condemn'd:

Not me begotten of a shepherd swain,
But issu'd from the progeny of kings;
Virtuous and holy; chosen from above,
By inspiration of celestial grace,
To work exceeding miracles on earth.
I never had to do with wicked spirits:
But you,—that are polluted with your lusts,
Stain'd with the guiltless blood of innocents,
Corrupt and tainted with a thousand vices,—   10
Because you want the grace that others have,

You judge it straight a thing impossible
To compass wonders but by help of devils.
No misconceived! Joan of Arc hath been
A virgin from her tender infancy,
Chaste and immaculate in very thought;
Whose maiden blood, thus rigorously effus'd,
Will cry for vengeance at the gates of heaven.

Will nothing turn your unrelenting hearts?
Then, Joan, discover thine infirmity;   20
That warranteth by law to be thy privilege.
I am with child, ye bloody homicides:
Murder not then the fruit within my womb,
Although ye hale me to a violent death.

No pity yet?
Then lead me hence; with whom I leave my curse:
May never glorious sun reflex his beams
Upon the country where you make abode;
But darkness and the gloomy shade of death
Environ you, till mischief and despair   30
Drive you to break your necks or hang yourselves!

17. effus'd: lost, spilled.

King Lear

It has been my experience that material from *King Lear* must be treated in a manner altogether different from any more standard approach appropriate to the other plays. *King Lear* is perhaps the most theatrical play ever written, rich in nuance and diversity of style. Its multiple themes, plots, and characterizations resonate with the complexity of a Bach fugue, and some critics have doubted whether the play can be effectively produced at all.

Its dramatic structure is that of a morality play, as Lear and the others in the story journey across a bleak, forbidding landscape toward revelation and death. In his travels, each pilgrim must divest himself of all the trappings of civilized life until, ordeal by ordeal, he is stripped down to his basic humanity so that he may take on a new, archetypal personality. As the naked person ("the thing itself," as Lear puts it), he may then play out his role in the larger context of history, the elements, the stars, and all of the most primal human and natural forces.

Lear and his fellow travelers share the awareness of their place in moral and physical matrices in a manner reminiscent of the Greek tragic heroes. This is a consciousness I find best represented today in the work of our finest science fiction and fantasy writers. Arthur C. Clarke, Ursula K. Le Guin, Orson Scott Card, Theodore Sturgeon, John Crowley, J. R. R. Tolkien, and others have created worlds in which each single being, however diminutive, may perform an action of cosmic import. This is very much in keeping with Elizabethan cosmology in general and with Lear's universe in particular. Imagined worlds like Earthsea, Appalachee, Aegypt, and Middle Earth are compact but never self-contained, as their creators attempt to make manifest and to support a presumed continuum of world mythology. The scale of vision of these contemporary writers shifts rapidly from galaxies to grains of sand, and they can relate minute personal moral decisions to monumental issues. I do not believe any portion of *King Lear* (even Goneril's admittedly limited spectacle included earlier) can be understood or performed fully without such broadness of vision, and I heartily recommend these writers as part of the actor's homework.

Lear's storm is generated by the words he speaks and their component sounds. Every vowel and consonant must be explored fully, extended and exaggerated, before the speech can have much meaning. Lear not only speaks about—and to— the storm, he creates the very elements with his words and *becomes* the storm himself. His creation, like most creative acts, cannot be rushed, and the momentum of the scene, although powerful, is slow.

Edmund is the prime villain of the play, and his position is confirmed by his repudiation of cosmic or astrological influence. By insisting that he is a self-made man, he closes himself off from all possible revelation; he is doomed to remain what he is. As most such persons, he thoroughly enjoys himself, and that enjoyment is the keynote of the scene. Later, his brother Edgar, a victim of Edmund's plot of disinheritance, hides from his pursuers and decides to disguise himself as a "Bedlam beggar," a kind of itinerant lunatic, the poorest creature imaginable. It is an excellent disguise under the circumstances, for such people were believed to travel under God's protection and so were seldom disturbed. Some physical transformation should be accomplished during this scene.

I have prepared a composite of several of the Fool's speeches to serve as raw material for the actor, and it is meant to be adaptable to whatever sense of sequence he may choose. Some of it may be sung, some spoken; parts may be intimate moments with Lear, other parts may be public; the environment may change several times as the storm arrives and passes. It is necessary, however, that the actor make a specific and careful decision about the meaning and subtext of literally every word. A clearly defined physical structure, which might evolve either from a deliberately architectural use of space or from a well-developed physical characterization, will provide unity for the scene. An imaginative gymnast or mime might discover tremendous opportunities here. A shorter version of the piece runs from line 19 through line 45.

King Lear

(Act III, Scene 2)

LEAR

Blow, winds, and crack your cheeks! rage! blow!

You cataracts and hurricanoes, spout
Till you have drench'd our steeples, drown'd the cocks!
You sulph'rous and thought-executing fires,
Vaunt-couriers to oak-cleaving thunderbolts,
Singe my white head! And thou, all-shaking thunder,
Strike flat the thick rotundity o' th' world,
Crack Nature's moulds, all germens spill at once
That make ingrateful man!
Rumble thy bellyful! Spit, fire! spout, rain!   10
Nor rain, wind, thunder, fire, are my daughters:
I tax not you, you elements, with unkindness;
I never gave you kingdom, call'd you children,
You owe me no subscription: then, let fall
Your horrible pleasure; here I stand, your slave,
A poor, infirm, weak, and despis'd old man.
But yet I call you servile ministers,
That will with two pernicious daughters join
Your high-engender'd battles 'gainst a head
So old and white as this. O! Ho! 'tis foul!   20

Come on, my boy. How dost, my boy? Art cold?
I am cold myself. Where is this straw, my fellow?
The art of our necessities is strange,
And can make vile things precious. Come, your hovel.

Poor fool and knave, I have one part in my heart
That's sorry yet for thee.

8. germens: germs, seeds.

(Act I, Scene 2)

EDMUND

This is the excellent foppery of the world that when
we are sick in fortune—often the surfeit of our own behavior—we make guilty of our disasters the sun, the
moon, and stars; as if we were villains by necessity; fools
by heavenly compulsion; knaves, thieves, and treachers
by spherical predominance; drunkards, liars, and adul-
terers by an enforced obedience of planetary influence;
and all that we are evil in by a divine thrusting on.
An
admirable evasion of whoremaster man, to lay his goatish
disposition to the charge of a star! My father compounded   10
with my mother under the Dragon's tail, and my nativity
was under Ursa Major, so that it follows I am rough and
lecherous. 'Sfoot! I should have been that I am, had the
maidenliest star in the firmament twinkled on my bastardizing. Edgar—
 (*Enter* EDGAR)
Pat! he comes, like the catastrophe of the old comedy.
My cue is villainous melancholy, with a sigh like Tom o'
Bedlam—O these eclipses do portend these divisions!
(*Humming sadly*) Fa, sol, la, me.

1. foppery: folly
5. treachers: traitors, treacherous ones: rhymes with "lechers."
11–12. Dragon's tail . . . Ursa Major: the constellation Draco, or the Dragon,
 as charted in Shakespeare's time included the configuration known as
 Ursa Major, or the Great Bear; it was considered an unfavorable natal
 aspect.
14. bastardizing: Edgar is Gloucester's legitimate son; Edmund, his illegitimate.
16. catastrophe: in classical drama, the plot device that brings about the de-
 nouement of the play; Edgar's entrance interrupts Edmund's musing.

(Act II, Scene 3)

EDGAR

I heard myself proclaim'd,
And by the happy hollow of a tree
Escap'd the hunt.
                    No port is free, no place
That guard and most unusual vigilance
Does not attend my taking.
                    While I may 'scape
I will preserve myself; and am bethought
To take the basest and most poorest shape
That ever penury, in contempt of man,
Brought near to beast. My face I'll grime with filth,
Blanket my loins, elf all my hairs in knots,   10
And with presented nakedness outface
The winds and persecutions of the sky.

The country gives me proof and precedent
Of Bedlam beggars who, with roaring voices,
Strike in their numb'd and mortified bare arms
Pins, wooden pricks, nails, sprigs of rosemary;
And with this horrible object, from low farms,
Poor pelting villages, sheep-cotes, and mills,
Sometimes with lunatic bans, sometime with prayers,
Enforce their charity.
                    "Poor Turlygood, poor Tom!"   20
That's something yet! Edgar I nothing am.

5. taking: capture.
14. Bedlam: the Hospital of St. Mary of Bethlehem in London, used as an asylum
    for the mentally deranged.
18. pelting: paltry.
19. bans: curses.

(Act II, Scene 4; Act III, Scene 2)

FOOL

We'll set thee to school to an ant, to teach thee there's
no labouring i' the winter.
                        All that follow their noses are
led by their eyes but blind men, and there's not a nose
among twenty but can smell him that's stinking. Let go
thy hold when a great wheel runs down a hill, lest it
break thy neck with following it; but the great one that
goes up the hill, let him draw thee after. When a wise
man gives thee better counsel, give me mine again: I
would have none but knaves follow it, since a fool gives
it.   10

That sir which serves and seeks for gain,
    And follows but for form,
Will pack when it begins to rain,
    And leave thee in the storm.
But I will tarry; the Fool will stay
    And let the wise man fly.
The knave turns fool that turns away;
    The Fool no knave, perdy.

O nuncle, court holy-water in a dry house is better than
this rain-water out o' door. Good nuncle, in; ask they   20
daughters' blessing! Here's a night pities neither wise
man nor Fool. He that has a house to put his head in
has a good head-piece.

The codpiece that will house
    Before the head has any,
The head and he shall louse:
    So beggars marry many.
The man that makes his toe
    What he his heart should make
Shall of a corn cry woe,   30

And turn his sleep to wake.
For there was never yet fair woman but she made mouths
  in a glass.

He that has and a little tiny wit—
  With heigh-ho, the wind and the rain—
Must make content with his fortunes fit,
  Though the rain it raineth every day.
This is a brave night to cool a courtesan! I'll speak a
prophecy ere I go:

When priests are more in word than matter;   40
When brewers mar their malt with water;
When nobles are their tailors' tutors;
No heretics burn'd, but wenches' suitors;
Then shall the realm of Albion
Come to great confusion.

When every case in law is right;
No squire in debt, nor no poor knight;
When slanders do not live in tongues,
Nor cutpurses come not to throngs;
When usurers tell their gold i' th' field,   50
And bawds and whores do churches build;
Then comes the time, who lives to see't
That going shall be us'd with feet.

This prophecy Merlin shall make, for I live before his
time.

54. The last line may have been the inspiration for T. H. White's Merlin in *The
   Once and Future King*. White is, in any case, an excellent source for an
   imaginative context for this piece.

SHAKESPEARE'S FRIENDS

SERMONS, PRAYERS, TALES, AND DREAMS

Most of the monologues in this section are characterized by a moral passion and almost evangelical fervor. Even the pursuit of evil has a fanatically religious tone to it. The first is the classic revenge monologue, and Vendice is the perfect instrument of vengeance—watching from a distance, judging, cold as steel, while the villains of *The Revenger's Tragedy* parade before him in a dumb show as he speaks. He carries with him the skull of his dead mistress, a macabre reminder of his motive for revenge and an image for the grave proximity of life to death. If properly used, a fist may substitute for the skull, but there must not be the slightest touch of comedy about it. A shorter version of the speech may begin with line 14 and end in the middle of line 38.

Hieronimo's spur to vengeance in *The Spanish Tragedy* is his son Horatio, murdered by Lorenzo and Balthazar. A couple of porters are looking for Lorenzo, and in a series of strikingly visual images reminiscent of the Doré illustrations for Dante's *Inferno*, Hieronimo tells them where they can find him. Then, inspired by this imaginative outburst, he rejects suicide and commits himself to a path of righteous killing. When confronted with Annabella's confessed passion for her brother in *'Tis Pity She's a Whore*, the Friar responds to her plea for solace with a sermon worthy of the hellfire preachings of Jonathan Edwards or Cotton Mather. His objective is clearly to frighten her out of her sin, but an interesting range of interpretive possibilities opens up when we consider the degree to which he may enjoy, perhaps even relish, his task, more ecclesiastical ghoul than counselor. And it is with equal zest that Romelio's "meditation" in *The Devil's Law-Case* cites the horrors of the physical grave.

Although taken from a less sophisticated pre-Shakespearean morality play, Juventus's monologue in *Lusty Juventus* is actually quite complex theatrically. Juventus is not only the Everyman hero but also the actor playing him and the preacher/moralist who warns the audience about the dangers of sin. These three functions overlap and interact consistently in a manner that is more common today to nightclub and comedy routines. The stiffness and relative formality of the speech should be consciously used, and the image of a pulpit may be useful. It should help also to treat Satan, God, Knowledge, Good Counsel, etc., as real characters, grifters perhaps, trying to work the same audience, and not as abstractions.

Barabas is the *Jew of Malta,* an outrageously likeable villain at perpetual war with the Christian government of the island. He is recruiting an evil servant, Ithamore, to aid him in his revenge on his enemies. As a job description, this speech is unequaled; as a catalogue of crimes, it compares only to Aaron's confession in *Titus Andronicus.* There is an explosively imaginative energy operating here, a riot of invention that Marlowe could perhaps justify only in so exotic a character and setting. By contrast, Faustus's scene emphasizes an intense emotional state that takes him through a hallucinatory experience, a richly kaleidoscopic "trip" that seems almost drug-induced with its amorphous sense of time and sudden shifts of vision. In the story, Faustus has reaped the benefits of his pact with Mephistopheles and must pay the price, but I suggest this modern association for the actor who doesn't believe in classical devils. Faustus is a man possessed by something horrible, and so the actor must evoke a personal terror of his own to be convincing. Lines 32 through 50 may be omitted for a shorter version.

The actor who wishes to take his hallucination further has but to attempt the First Madman in *The Honest Whore, Part 1,* a delicious opportunity to create a totally subjective, constantly transforming world. From a very different kind of entertainment, a short masque called *Cupid and Death,* comes the dispassionate Chamberlain's speech. As master of ceremonies for the monumental contest between the title figures, the Chamberlain sustains an attitude of haughty superiority perhaps akin to Sir John Gielgud's butler in the film *Arthur*.

The women represented here exhibit considerable emotional range, and even when committed to some melodramatic mad scene seem capable of fine nuance. Lady More's dream in *Sir Thomas More* vividly portends her husband's falling-out with King Henry VIII, his imprisonment in the Tower, and his death. Its relative simplicity and the easy sympathy it commands make this one of the best women's audition pieces I know. Similarly low-key, Emilia's recollection of her lost friend in *The Two Noble Kinsmen* is charged with a rare and intense sensuality. Her plea for understanding, although for the benefit of others, is all the more poignant for the undertone of her own personal grief. For *The Changeling*'s Beatrice, a sense of place is all-important. If a real book is used to read from, the other impedimenta—closet, key, vials—can be indicated simply, without the scene becoming an exercise in mime. Intense curiosity is the most important motivating factor in the scene. In *The Maid's Tragedy*, Evadne, also sneaking about in the middle of the night, has a more deadly purpose, killing the king who has dishonored her. The scene's vocal variety helps make it especially exciting: whispers at the start, calling to wake the king, and the hissing violence of the last section.

Isabella is Hieronimo's wife and counterpart, mourning the same Horatio's murder. Kyd has her tearing apart the arbor where her son was killed, driving herself to a suicidal frenzy, and finally stabbing herself. It is a scene about extremes, demanding extremes in the performance, and I suggest a choice of two completely opposing approaches. If the words are allowed to carry the emotional burden, the physical expression can be limited to a couple of sudden moves: a quick turn toward the ghost, perhaps a contraction for the stabbing. Otherwise, the scene must become entirely physical, a dance, words released by movement, Isabella literally becoming the arbor, the wind, the pine, and the knife. Under no circumstances should props be used. The Jailor's Daughter's developing madness in *The Two Noble Kinsmen* is another challenge.

In this case melodrama can be best avoided by playing her need for Palamon and her isolation. The images she creates, if they are real enough for the actor, become the projected landscape of the Daughter's mind, giving the scene great pathos and strong dramatic impact. More accustomed to the restraint of court, Webster's Duchess of Malfi is about to be imprisoned, but her fish story is a model of sardonic humor summoned to cover despair.

The Revenger's Tragedy
by Cyril Tourneur

(Act I, Scene 1)

VENDICE

Duke! royal lecher!
             go, grey-hair'd adultery!
And thou his son, as impious steep'd as he:
And thou his bastard, true begot in evil:
And thou his duchess, that will do with devil:
Four excellent characters!
               O, that marrowless age
Should stuff the hollow bones with damn'd desires;
And, 'stead of heat, kindle infernal fires
Within the spendthrift veins of a dry duke,
A parch'd and juiceless luxur.
              O God! one,
That has scarce blood enough to live upon;   10
And he to riot it, like a son and heir!
O, the thought of that
Turns my abused heart-strings into fret.

Thou sallow picture of my poison'd love,
   (Views the skull in his hand)
My study's ornament, thou shell of death,
Once the bright face of my betrothed lady,
When life and beauty naturally fill'd out
These ragged imperfections;
When two heav'n-pointed diamonds were set
In those unsightly rings—then 'twas a face   20
So far beyond the artificial shine
Of any woman's bought complexion,
That the uprightest man (if such there be,
That sin but seven times a day) broke custom,
And made up eight with looking after her.

But, O accursed palace!
Thee, when thou wert apparell'd in thy flesh,
The old duke poisoned,
Because thy purer part would not consent
Unto his palsied lust; for old men lustful   30
Do show like young men angry, eager, violent,
Outbidden like their limited performances.
O, 'ware an old man hot and vicious!
"Age, as in gold, in lust is covetous."

Vengeance, thou murder's quit-rent, and whereby
Thou show'st thyself tenant to tragedy;
O keep thy day, hour, minute, I beseech,
For those thou hast determined.
                                    Hum! who e'er knew
Murder unpaid? faith, give revenge her due,
She has kept touch hitherto:
                            be merry, merry,   40
Advance thee.
                O thou terror to fat folks,
To have their costly three-pil'd flesh worn off
As bare as this; for banquets, ease, and laughter
Can make great men, as greatness goes by clay;
But wise men little are more great than they.

  9. luxur: one regularly employed in lust and lasciviousness.
 13. fret: worry, vexation; also the ridge or stop on a stringed instrument. This
     is a pun referring to "heart-strings."
 41. terror: addressing the skull once again.

The Spanish Tragedy
by Thomas Kyd
(Act III, Scenes 11 and 12)

HIERONIMO

There is a path upon your left-hand side
That leadeth from a guilty conscience
Unto a forest of distrust and fear—

A darksome place, and dangerous to pass:
There shall you meet with melancholy thoughts,
Whose baleful humours if you but uphold,
It will conduct you to despair and death—

Whose rocky cliffs when you have once beheld,
Within a hugy dale of lasting night,
That, kindled with the world's iniquities,   10
Doth cast up filthy and detested fumes:

Not far from thence, where murderers have built
A habitation for their cursed souls,
There, in a brazen cauldron, fix'd by Jove,
In his fell wrath, upon a sulphur flame,
Yourselves shall find Lorenzo bathing him
In boiling lead and blood of innocents.
    (*Exeunt* PORTERS)
Hieronimo, 'tis time for thee to trudge.

Down by the dale that flows with purple gore
Standeth a fiery tower; there sits a judge   20
Upon a seat of steel and molten brass,
And 'twixt his teeth he holds a fire-brand,
That leads unto the lake where hell doth stand.

Away, Hieronimo! to him be gone;
He'll do thee justice for Horatio's death.

Turn down this path: thou shalt be with him straight;

Or this, and then thou need'st not take thy breath:
This way or that way?
                    —Soft and fair, not so:

For if I hang or kill myself, let's know
Who will revenge Horatio's murder then?   30

No, no! fie, no! pardon me, I'll none of that.
   (He flings away the dagger and rope)
This way I'll take,
                    and this way comes the king:
   (He takes them up again)
And here I'll have a fling at him, that's flat;
And, Balthazar, I'll be with thee to bring,
And thee, Lorenzo!
                    Here's the king—
                              —nay, stay;
And here, ay here—there goes the hare away.

27. breath: the rope is his first alternative, the dagger his second.
34. bring: teach a lesson; bring to heel, perhaps.
36. there . . . away: there begins the chase.

'Tis Pity She's a Whore
by John Ford
(Act III, Scene 6)

FRIAR
I am glad to see this penance;
                    for, believe me,
You have unripp'd a soul so foul and guilty
As I must tell you true, I marvel how

The earth hath borne you up: but weep, weep on,
These tears may do you good;
                              weep faster yet,
Whiles I do read a lecture.
                              Wretched creature,
Almost condemn'd alive. There is a place—
List, daughter—in a black and hollow vault,
Where day is never seen; there shines no sun,
But flaming horror of consuming fires,   10
A lightless sulphur, chok'd with smoky fogs
Of an infected darkness; in this place
Dwell many thousand thousand sundry sorts
Of never-dying deaths; there damned souls
Roar without pity; there are gluttons fed
With toads and adders; there is burning oil
Pour'd down the drunkard's throat; the usurer
Is forc'd to sup whole draughts of molten gold;
There is the murderer forever stabb'd,
Yet can he never die; there lies the wanton   20
On racks of burning steel, whiles in his soul
He feels the torment of his raging lust.
There stands these wretched things
Who have dream'd out whole years in lawless sheets
And secret incests, cursing one another:
Then you will wish each kiss your brother gave
Had been a dagger's point; then shall you hear
How he will cry, "O would my wicked sister
Had first been damn'd, when she did yield to lust!"

But soft, methinks I see repentance work   30
New motions in your heart;
                              say, how is't with you?

2. unripp'd: exposed.

The Devil's Law-Case
by John Webster
(Act II, Scene 3)

ROMELIO

Denied Christian burial—
                              I pray what does that,

Or the dead lazy march in the funeral
Or the flattery in the epitaphs, which shows
More sluttish far than all the spiders' webs
Shall ever grow upon it:
                              what do these
Add to our well-being after death?

Not a scruple.
                    Very well then:

I have a certain meditation,
If I can think of 't, somewhat to this purpose;
I'll say it to you, while my mother there   10
Numbers her beads.

    You that dwell near these graves and vaults,
    Which oft do hide physicians' faults,
    Note what a small room does suffice
    To express men's good;
                              their vanities
    Would fill more volume in small hand,
    Than all the evidence of church-land.
    Funerals hide men in civil wearing,
    And are to the drapers a good hearing,
    Make the heralds laugh in their black raiment,   20
    And all die worthies die worth payment.

To the altar offerings, though their fame,
And all the charity of their name,
'Tween heaven and this yield no more light
Than rotten trees, which shine i' th' night.

O look the last act be the best i' th' play,
And then rest, gentle bones;
                          yet pray,
That when by the precise you are viewed,
A supersedeas be not sued,
To remove you to a place more airy,   30
That in your stead they may keep chary
Stockfish, or seacoal, for the abuses
Of sacrilege have turned graves to viler uses.

How then can any monument say,
"Here rest these bones till the last day,"
When time swift both of foot and feather
May bear them the sexton knows not whither?

What care I then, though my last sleep
Be in the desert, or in the deep,
No lamp, nor taper, day and night,   40
To give my charnel chargeable light?
I have there like quantity of ground,
And at the last day I shall be found.

Now I pray leave me.

1. what does that: what good is it.
2. or: either.
4. sluttish: unclean, nasty.
16. hand: handwriting.
17. evidence: title deeds.
19. a good hearing: good news.
21. And all . . . payment: all die honored who leave enough money to pay for their funerals.
25. rotten trees: refers to the phenomenon of a glow frequently given off by decaying vegetation in marshes and other nasty places.

28. the precise: refers specifically to the Puritans, who would seek to take over
   any building, even a charnel-house, for business purposes, and thus for the
   storage of fish or seacoal (coal).
29. supersedeas: a writ used to interfere with legal proceedings.
41. chargeable: expensive.

Lusty Juventus
by Richard Wever

JUVENTUS
O sinful flesh, thy pleasures are but vain.

Now I find it true, as the scripture doth say,
Broad and pleasant is the path which leadeth unto pain,
But unto eternal life full narrow is the way.

He that is not led by God's spirit surely goeth astray;
And all that ever he doth shall be clean abhorr'd;
Although he brag and boast never so much of God's
   word.

O subtle Satan, full deceitful is thy snare;
Who is able thy falsehood to disclose?
What is the man, that thou dost favour or spare,   10
And dost not tempt him eternal joys to lose?

Not one in the world, surely I suppose.

Therefore happy is the man, which doth truly wait,
Always to refuse thy deceitful and crafty bait.

When I had thought to live most christianly,
And followed the steps of Knowledge and Good Counsel,
Ere I was aware, thou hadst deceived me,
And brought me into the path which leadeth unto hell:
And of an earnest professor of Christ's gospel

Thou madest me an hypocrite, blind and pervert,   20
And from virtue unto vice thou hadst clean turn'd my
  heart.

All Christian people which be here present
May learn by me Hypocrisy to know,
With which the devil, as with a poison most pestilent,
Daily seeketh all men to overthrow:
Credit not all things unto the outward show,
But try them with God's word, that squire and rule most
  just,
Which never deceiveth them, that in him put their trust.

Let no flattering friendship, not yet wicked company,
Persuade you in no wise God's word to abuse;   30
But see that you stand steadfastly unto the verity,
And according to the rule thereof your doings frame and
  use,
Neither kindred nor fellowship shall you excuse,
When you shall appear before the judgment seat,
But your own secret conscience shall then give an audit.

All you that be young, whom I do now represent,
Set your delight both day and night on Christ's Testa-
  ment:
If pleasure you tickle, be not fickle, and suddenly slide,
But in God's fear everywhere see that you abide:
In your tender age seek for knowledge, and after wisdom
  run,   40
And in your old age teach your family to do as you have
  done:

Your bodies subdue into virtue, delight not in vanity;
Say not, "I am young, I shall live long," lest your days
  shorten'd be:
Do not incline to spend your time in toys, wanton and
  nice,

For idleness doth increase much wickedness and vice:
Do not delay the time, and say, "My end is not near;"
For with short warning the Lord coming shall suddenly
  appear.

19. professor: one who speaks or professes his beliefs.
26. Credit . . . show: don't believe everything you see.
32. use: accustom.
33. you excuse: inversion of excuse you.
36. Juventus is literally a representation of all young people.
44. nice: petty, insignificant, trifling.

The Jew of Malta
by Christopher Marlowe
(Act II, Scene 1)

BARABAS

Hast thou no trade?
                        then listen to my words,
And I will teach thee that shall stick by thee:
First, be thou void of these affections:
Compassion, love, vain hope, and heartless fear.
Be mov'd at nothing, see thou pity none,
But to thyself smile when the Christians moan.

As for myself, I walk abroad o' nights
And kill sick people groaning under walls.
Sometimes I go about and poison wells;
And now and then, to cherish Christian thieves,   10
I am content to lose some of my crowns,
That I may, walking in my gallery,
See 'em go pinion'd along by my door.
Being young, I studied physic, and began
To practice first upon the Italian;
There I enrich'd the priests with burials,
And always kept the sextons' arms in ure

With digging graves and ringing dead men's knells.
And after that was I an engineer,
And in the wars 'twixt France and Germany,   20
Under pretence of helping Charles the Fifth,
Slew friend and enemy with my stratagems.
Then after that was I an usurer,
And with extorting, cozening, forfeiting,
And tricks belonging unto brokery,
I fill'd the jails with bankrupts in a year,
And with young orphans planted hospitals,
And every moon made some or other mad,
And now and then one hang himself for grief,
Pinning upon his breast a long great scroll   30
How I with interest tormented him.
But mark how I am blest for plaguing them;
I have as much coin as will buy the town.

But tell me now, how hast thou spent thy time?

11. crowns: coins, money.
14. physic: medicine.
17. in ure: in use, busy.
24. cozening: cheating.
34. Although the last line may be omitted, it does provide a closing transition
    that shifts focus back to the audience—particularly useful in an audition, I
    should think.

Doctor Faustus
by Christopher Marlowe
(Act V, Scene 2)

FAUSTUS

Ah, Faustus,
Now hast thou but one bare hour to live,
And then thou must be damn'd perpetually!

Stand still, you ever moving spheres of heaven,
That time may cease, and midnight never come;
Fair Nature's eye, rise, rise again, and make
Perpetual day; or let this hour be but
A year, a month, a week, a natural day,
That Faustus may repent and save his soul!

O lente, lente currite, noctis equi!   10

The stars move still, time runs, the clock will strike,
The devil will come, and Faustus must be damn'd.

O, I'll leap up to my God!—Who pulls me down?—

See, see, where Christ's blood streams in the firmament!
One drop would save my soul, half a drop: ah, my Christ!—
Ah, rend not my heart for naming of my Christ!
Yet will I call on him: O, spare me, Lucifer—

Where is it now? 'tis gone: and see, where God
Stretcheth out his arm, and bends his ireful brows!
Mountains and hills, come, come, and fall on me,   20
And hide me from the heavy wrath of God!

No, no!
Then will I headlong run into the earth:
Earth, gape!
          O, no, it will not harbour me!
You stars that reign'd at my nativity,
Whose influence hath allotted death and hell,
Now draw up Faustus, like a foggy mist,
Into the entrails of yon lab'ring cloud
That, when you vomit forth into the air,
My limbs may issue from your smoky mouths,   30
So that my soul may but ascend to heaven!
   (The clock strikes)
Ah, half the hour is past! 'twill all be past anon.

O God,
If thou wilt not have mercy on my soul,
Yet for Christ's sake, whose blood hath ransom'd me,
Impose some end to my incessant pain;
Let Faustus live in hell a thousand years,
A hundred thousand, and at last be sav'd!

O, no end is limited to damned souls!
Why wert thou not a creature wanting soul?   40
Or why is this immortal that thou hast?
Ah, Pythagoras' *metempsychosis*, were that true,
This soul should fly from me, and I be chang'd
Unto some brutish beast! all beasts are happy,
For, when they die,
Their souls are soon dissolv'd in elements;
But mine must live still to be plagu'd in hell.
Curs'd be the parents that engender'd me!

No, Faustus, curse thyself, curse Lucifer
That hath depriv'd thee of the joys of heaven.   50
    (The clock strikes twelve)
O, it strikes, it strikes! Now, body, turn to air,
Or Lucifer will bear thee quick to hell!
O soul, be changed into little water-drops,
And fall into the ocean, ne'er be found!
    (Thunder. Enter the DEVILS*)*
My God, my God, look not so fierce on me!
Adders and serpents, let me breathe a while!
Ugly hell, gape not! come not, Lucifer!
I'll burn my books!—Ah, Mephistopheles!

10. *O lente . . . equi:* oh slowly, slowly run, horses of the night. This line and
    the last four lines are optional.
42. Pythagoras' *metempsychosis:* theory of transmigration of souls.
52. quick: alive.

The Honest Whore, Part 1
by Thomas Dekker
(Act V, Scene 2)

FIRST MADMAN

God speed the plough, thou shalt not speed me. No, I
am neither fish nor flesh.

Dost not see, fool?

There's a
fresh salmon in't; if you step one foot further, you'll
be over shoes, for you see I'm over head and ears in
the salt-water: and if you fall into this whirlpool where
I am, y'are drowned: y'are a drowned rat.

I am fishing
here for five ships, but I cannot have a good draught,
for my net breaks still, and breaks;

but I'll break some
of your necks an I catch you in my clutches. Stay, stay,
stay, stay, stay, where's the wind?

where's the wind?   10
where's the wind? where's the wind? Out, you gulls,
you goose-caps, you gudgeon-eaters! Do you look for
the wind in the heavens? Ha, ha, ha, ha! no, no! Look
there, look there, look there! the wind is always at
that door: hark how it blows, puff, puff, puff!

Do you
laugh at God's creatures?

Do you mock old age, you
rogues? Is this gray beard and head counterfeit that
you cry, ha, ha, ha?

Sirrah, art not thou my eldest
son?

Then th'art a fool, for my eldest son had a polt-
foot, crooked legs, a verjuice face, and a pear-coloured   20
beard. I made him a scholar, and he made himself a

fool.

      Sirrah, thou there: hold out thy hand.

                                Look, look, look, look! Has he not long nails, and short hair? Tenpenny nails, are they not? Such nails had my second boy.

      Kneel down, thou varlet, and ask thy father's blessing. Such nails had my middlemost son, and I made him a promoter: and he scrapt, and scrapt, and scrapt, till he got the devil and all: but he scrapt thus, and thus, and thus, and it went under his legs, till at length a company of kites, taking him for carrion, swept up all, all, all, all, all, all, all.   30

                  If you love your lives, look to yourselves: see, see, see, see, the Turk's galleys are fighting with my ships! Bounce goes the guns! Oooh! cry the men! Rumble, rumble, go the waters! Alas, there;

                                  'tis sunk, 'tis sunk: I am undone, I am undone!

                  You are the damned pirates have undone me: you are, by the Lord, you are, you are!—

      Stop 'em—you are!

                      Tame me? No, I'll be madder than a roasted cat.

7. draught: draw of the net.
11. gulls, goose-caps, gudgeon-eaters: fools, simpletons, dupes.
19. polt-foot: clubfoot. verjuice: sour, crabbed.
27. promoter: informer. scrapt: scraped; the most likely meaning relates to collection or the amassing of wealth by great effort, but other senses of the word meaning bowing and scratching are certainly to be considered in the actor's preparation.
30. kites: hawks.

Cupid and Death
by James Shirley

CHAMBERLAIN

Death and his train are gone,
I thank heaven he's departed.
                      I slept not
One wink tonight, nor durst I pray aloud
For fear of waking Death:
                      but he, at midnight,
Calls for a cup to quench his thirst; a bowl
Of blood I gave him for a morning's draught,
And had an ague all the while he drunk it.

At parting, in my own defence, and hope
To please him, I desir'd to kiss his hand,
Which was so cold, o' the sudden, sir, my mouth   10
Was frozen up, which, as the case stood
Then with my teeth, did me a benefit,
And kept the dancing bones from leaping out.

At length, fearing for ever to be speechless,
I us'd the strength of both my hands to open
My lips, and now felt every word I spake
Drop from it like an icicle.

What said Cupid? He was fast asleep.
The boy went drunk to bed.
                    But now he's up and ready,
And looks as fresh as if he had known no surfeit   20
Of virgin's tears, for whose fair satisfaction
He broke his leaden shafts, and vows hereafter
To shoot all flames of love into their servants.

But I have made my own revenge upon him,

For the hard-hearted baggage that he sent me;
And Death I have serv'd a trick for all his huffing.

They think not what artillery they carry
Along with them; I have chang'd their arrows.

How Death will fret to see his fury cozen'd!
But how will Love look pale when he shall find   30
What a mortality his arrows make
Among the lovers!
                    Let the god look to't,
I have put it past my care, and not expect
To see them again; or should I meet with Death,
I shall not fear him now; for Cupid, if
Lovers must only by his arrows fall,
I am safe, for, ladies, I defy you all.

  7. ague: malarial fever characterized by shivering; pronounced AY-gyoo.
29. cozen'd: fooled.

Sir Thomas More
by William Shakespeare and others unknown
(Act IV, Scene 3)

LADY MORE

Troth, son, I know not what; I am not sick,
And yet I am not well. I would be merry;
But something lies so heavy on my heart,
I cannot choose but sigh.
                              You are a scholar;
I pray you tell me, may one credit dreams?
Because tonight I had the strangest dream
That e'er my sleep was troubled with.
                              Methought 'twas night,
And the king and queen went on the Thames
In barges to hear music: my lord and I
Were in a little boat methought,—Lord, Lord,   10
What strange things live in slumbers!—and, being near,
We grappled to the barge that bore the king.

But after many pleasing voices spent
In that still moving music-house, methought
The violence of the stream did sever us
Quite from the golden fleet, and hurried us
Unto the bridge, which with unused horror
We enter'd at full tide: thence some slight shoot
Being carried by the waves, our boat stood still
Just opposite the Tower, and there it turn'd   20
And turn'd about, as when a whirlpool sucks
The circled waters: methought that we both cried,
Till that we sunk; where arm in arm we died.

5. credit: believe.

The Two Noble Kinsmen
by William Shakespeare and John Fletcher
(Act I, Scene 3)

EMILIA

I was acquainted
Once with a time, when I enjoy'd a playfellow:

You were at wars, when she the grave enrich'd
Who made too proud the bed, took leave o' th' moon
(Which then look'd pale at parting) when our count
Was each eleven.

You talk of Pirithous' and Theseus' love;
Theirs has more ground, is more maturely season'd,
More buckled with strong judgment, and their needs
The one of th'other may be said to water   10
Their intertangled roots of love;
                              but I
And she I sigh and spoke of were things innocent,
Lov'd for we did, and like the elements
That know not what, nor why, yet do effect
Rare issues by their operance, our souls
Did so to one another;
                       what she lik'd
Was then of me approv'd; what not, condemn'd—
No more arraignment; the flow'r that I would pluck
And put between my breasts (then but beginning
To swell about the blossom) O, she would long   20
Till she had such another, and commit it
To the like innocent cradle, where Pheonix-like
They died in perfume:
                      on my head no toy
But was her pattern; her affections (pretty,
Though happily hers careless were) I follow'd

For my most serious decking; had mine ear
Stol'n some new air, or at adventure hummed on
From musical coinage, why it was a note
Whereon her spirits would sojourn (rather dwell on)
And sing it in her slumbers.
                        This rehearsal   30
(Which, every innocent wots well, comes in
Like old importment's bastard) has this end,
That the true love 'tween maid and maid may be
More than in sex individual.

  5. count: age.
 18. arraignment: critical examination, consideration.
 22. Phoenix-like: refers to the ancient Oriental myth of the Phoenix, a wonderful
     bird of great beauty which, after living five hundred or six hundred years in
     the Arabian wilderness, the only one of its kind, built for itself a funeral pile
     of spices and aromatic gums, lighted the pile with the fanning of its wings,
     and was burned upon it. However, since from its ashes the Phoenix was
     revived in the freshness of youth, it often serves as an emblem of immortality.
 24. affections: affectations; airs, mannerisms, feignings.
 25. careless: artless, unstudied.
27–28. at adventure . . . coinage: improvised.
 31. wots: knows.
 32. old importment's bastard: a foreshadowing of adult experience.
 34. sex individual: couples of differing sexes.

The Changeling
by Thomas Middleton
(Act IV, Scene 1)

BEATRICE
This fellow has undone me endlessly;

Never was bride so fearfully distress'd.
The more I think upon th' ensuing night,
And whom I am to cope with in embraces,
One who's ennobled both in blood and mind,
So clear in understanding, that's my plague now,

Before whose judgment will my fault appear
Like malefactors' crimes before tribunals;

There is no hiding on't—the more I dive
Into my own distress.
                  How a wise man   10
Stands for a great calamity! There's no venturing
Into his bed, what course soe'er I light upon,
Without my shame, which may grow up to danger;
He cannot but in justice strangle me
As I lie by him, as a cheater use me.
'Tis a precious craft to play with a false die
Before a cunning gamester.
                      Here's his closet,
The key left in't, and he abroad i' th' park!

Sure 'twas forgot;
              I'll be so bold as look in't.
(She opens the closet)
Bless me!
          A right physician's closet 'tis,   20
Set round with vials; every one her mark too.
Sure he does practice physic for his own use,
Which may be safely call'd your great man's wisdom.

What manuscript lies here? "The Book of Experiment,
Call'd Secrets in Nature."
              So 'tis, 'tis so;

"How to know whether a woman be with child or no."
I hope I am not yet.
             If he should try though!
Let me see, "folio forty-five." Here 'tis;
The leaf tuck'd down upon't, the place suspicious.
"If you would know whether a woman be with child or
    not,   30
Give her two spoonfuls of white water in glass C."

—Where's that glass C? O, yonder, I see't now.

—"And if she be with child she sleeps full twelve
hours after; if not, not."

None of that water comes into my belly;
I'll know you from a hundred. I could break you now,
Or turn you into milk, and so beguile
The master of the mystery, but I'll look to you.

Ha! That which is next is ten times worse:
"How to know whether a woman be a maid or not."   40

If that should be applied, what would become of me?
Belike he has a strong faith of my purity,
That never yet made proof;
                              but this he calls
"A merry sleight, but true experiment, the author An-
tonius Mizaldus. Give the party you suspect the quantity of a spoonful of the water in the glass M, which,
upon her that is maid, makes three several effects:
'twill make her incontinently gape, then fall into a
sudden sneezing, last into a violent laughing; else dull,
heavy, and lumpish."   50

Where had I been?

I fear it, yet 'tis seven hours to bedtime.

1. undone me endlessly: damned me for eternity.
17. closet: private room; for the sake of the monologue, the bigger the better,
so that the space may be effectively used.
21. her: its.
33–34: these lines and lines 44–50 are prose.
51. Where had I been: what would have become of me?

The Maid's Tragedy
by Francis Beaumont and John Fletcher
(Act V, Scene 1)

EVADNE

The night grows horrible; and all about me
Like my black purpose.

                  O, the conscience
Of a lost virgin, whither wilt thou pull me?
To what things dismal as the depth of hell
Wilt thou provoke me?

                Let no woman dare
From this hour be disloyal, if her heart be flesh,
If she have blood, and can fear. 'Tis a daring
Above that desperate fool's that left his peace,
And went to sea to fight: 'tis so many sins,
An age cannot repent 'em; and so great,   10
The gods want mercy for. Yet I must through 'em:

I have begun a slaughter on my honour,
And I must end it there.

             —He sleeps.

                  Good Heavens!
Why give you peace to this untemperate beast,
That hath so long transgress'd you?

                  I must kill him,
And I will do it bravely: the mere joy
Tells me, I merit in it. Yet I must not
Thus tamely do it as he sleeps—that were
To rock him to another world:

                my vengeance
Shall take him waking, and then lay before him   20
The number of his wrongs and punishments.
I'll shape his sins like Furies, till I waken
His evil angel, his sick conscience,

And then I'll strike him dead.
　　　　　　　　　—My lord the King!

My lord!
　　　　—He sleeps, as if he meant to wake
No more. —My lord!
　　　　　　　—Is he not dead already?

—Sir! My lord!
　　　　　　Lie still; and, if the devil,
Your lust, will give you leave, repent.
　　　　　　　　　　　This steel
Comes to redeem the honour that you stole,
King, my fair name; which nothing but thy death　　　30
Can answer to the world.
　　　　　　　Stir not!
　　　　　　　　　If thou dost,
I'll take thee unprepar'd, thy fears upon thee,
That make thy sins look double, and so send thee
(By my revenge I will!) to look those torments
Prepar'd for such black souls.

The Spanish Tragedy
by Thomas Kyd
(Act IV, Scene 2)

ISABELLA

Tell me no more!
　　　　　O monstrous homicides!
Since neither piety nor pity moves
The king to justice or compassion,
I will revenge myself upon this place,
Where thus they murder'd my beloved son.
　(She cuts down the arbour)

Down with these branches and these loathsome boughs
Of this unfortunate and fatal pine!
Down with them, Isabella; rent them up,
And burn the roots from whence the rest is sprung!
I will not leave a root, a stalk, a tree,   10
A bough, a branch, a blossom, nor a leaf,
No, not an herb within this garden-plot,—

Accursed complot of my misery!
Fruitless forever may this garden be,
Barren the earth, and blissless whosoever
Imagines not to keep it unmanur'd!

An eastern wind, commix'd with noisome airs,
Shall blast the plants and the young saplings;
The earth with serpents shall be pestered,
And passengers, for fear to be infect,   20
Shall stand aloof, and, looking at it, tell:
"There, murder'd, died the son of Isabel."

Ay, here he died, and here I him embrace:

See, where his ghost solicits with his wounds
Revenge on her that should revenge his death.

Hieronimo, make haste to see thy son;
For sorrow and despair hath cited me
To hear Horatio plead with Rhadamanth.
Make haste, Hieronimo, to hold excus'd
Thy negligence in pursuit of their deaths   30
Whose hateful wrath bereav'd him of his breath.

Ah, nay, thou dost delay their deaths,
Forgives the murd'rers of thy noble son,
And none but I bestir me—to no end!

And as I curse this tree from further fruit,
So shall my womb be cursed for his sake;

And with this weapon will I wound the breast,
The hapless breast, that gave Horatio suck.
   (She stabs herself)

13. complot: accomplice, conspirator.
16. unmanur'd: uncultivated, untilled.
17. noisome: noxious, offensive, disgusting.
20. passengers: passersby.
28. Rhadamanth: in Greek mythology, one of the lords of the underworld.
29. hold excus'd: make excuses.

The Two Noble Kinsmen
by William Shakespeare and John Fletcher
(Act III, Scenes 2 and 4)

JAILOR'S DAUGHTER

He has mistook the brake I meant, is gone
After his fancy.
         'Tis now well nigh morning;
No matter, would it were perpetual night,
And darkness lord o' th' world.
           Hark, 'tis a wolf!
In me hath grief slain fear, and but for one thing
I care for nothing, and that's Palamon.

What if I halloo'd for him?
I cannot halloo: if I whoop'd, what then?
If he not answer'd, I should call a wolf,
And do him but that service.
         I have heard   10
Strange howls this livelong night, why may't not be
They have made prey of him? he has no weapons,
He cannot run, the jingling of his gyves
Might call fell things to listen, who have in them
A sense to know a man unarm'd, and can
Smell where resistance is.
         I'll set it down

He's torn to pieces; they howl'd many together
And then they fed on him: so much for that.

No, no, I lie. I have not clos'd mine eyes
Save when my lids scour'd off their brine; alas,   20
Dissolve my life, let not my sense unsettle
Lest I should drown, or stab, or hang myself.
O state of nature, fail together in me,
Since thy best props are warp'd!
                                        So, which way now?
The best way is the next way to the grave:
Each errant step besides is torment.

I am very cold, and all the stars are out too,
The little stars, and all, that look like aglets:
The sun has seen my folly. Palamon!

Alas no; he's in heaven.
                                        Where am I now?   30
Yonder's the sea, and there's a ship; how't tumbles!
And there's a rock lies watching under water;
Now, now, it beats upon it: now, now, now,
There's a leak sprung, a sound one; how they cry!
Spoon her before the wind, you'll lose all else:
Up with a course or two, and tack about, boys!
Good night, good night, y'are gone.
                                        I am very hungry.

Would I could find a fine frog; he would tell me
News from all parts o' th' world, then would I make
A carack of a cockleshell, and sail   40
By east and north-east to the King of Pigmies,
For he tells fortunes rarely.
                                        Now my father,
Twenty to one, is truss'd up in a trice
Tomorrow morning; I'll never say a word.
  (Sings)

For I'll cut my green coat a foot above my knee,
And I'll clip my yellow locks an inch below mine eye.
Hey nonny, nonny, nonny!
He'll buy me a white cut, forth for to ride,
And I'll go seek him, through the world that is so wide.
Hay nonny, nonny, nonny!   50

O for a prick now like a nightingale
To put my breast against. I shall sleep like a top else.

  1. brake: thicket.
13. gyves: chains; Palamon is an escaped prisoner.
19. A shorter version of the scene may begin here or with line 27, and any version
    may exclude the Ophelia-like song, lines 45–50.
28. aglets: ornaments at the ends of points or ribbons used for tying or lacing
    garments.
35. else: otherwise.
36. course: point of the compass or, occasionally, sails.
40. carack: large ship of burden, such as those formerly used by the Portuguese
    in trading with the East Indies. cockleshell: any bivalve shell, especially that
    of the scallop.
42. rarely: finely, splendidly, exceptionally well.
43. truss'd up: packed up, gone off, departed.
48. cut: common or work horse.
51. prick: of a thorn; as a nightingale might, according to tradition, prick its
    breast against a thorn in order to keep awake.

The Duchess of Malfi
by John Webster
(Act III, Scene 5)

THE DUCHESS

I prithee, who is greatest? can you tell?

Sad tales befit my woe: I'll tell you one.

A salmon, as she swam unto the sea,
Met with a dog-fish, who encounters her
With this rough language: "Why art thou so bold

To mix thyself with our high state of floods,
Being no eminent courtier, but one
That for the calmest and fresh time o' the year
Dost live in shallow rivers, rank'st thyself
With silly smelts and shrimps? and darest thou   10
Pass by our dog-ship without reverence?"
"O!" quoth the salmon, "sister, be at peace:
Thank Jupiter we both have pass'd the net!
Our value never can be truly known,
Till in the fisher's basket we be shown:
I' the market then my price may be the higher,
Even when I am nearest to the cook and fire."

So to great men the moral may be stretched;
Men oft are valued high, when they're most wretched.—

But come, whither you please. I am armed 'gainst
   misery;   20
Bent to all sways of the oppressor's will:
There's no deep valley but near some great hill.

18. stretched: the word is written to rhyme with "wretched," and so to have two
    syllables; I recommend that the rhyme be sacrificed and "stretched" kept to
    the more common single syllable.

ARGUMENTS AND ENTERTAINMENTS

Paris, conceived by Massinger as the chief Roman actor of his time, argues that virtue (or its absence) is mainly in the eye of the beholder, and his apologia for the actor's craft, like many of the other monologues to follow, provides an excellent opportunity for explicitly theatrical, controlled audience contact. More flamboyant, Carcurgus's act in *Misogonus* has all the fire of a good old medicine show. The choppy stiffness of the text can provide an effective base for a foreign accent, preferably one invented for the occasion. The giant of them all, though, is Sir Epicure Mammon from *The Alchemist*, whose excesses are cosmic in proportion.

James Shirley's anonymous Lord ————, with gracious urbanity and pastoral ardor, reduces the scale of things to a more human level in *The Lady of Pleasure* by enclosing whole worlds within a carefully constructed scene of courtship. Each image must fall deliciously from honeyed tongue to eager ear, encouraging the lady's quick capitulation. Vendice of *The Revenger's Tragedy*, in disguise, has been hired to seduce his own sister for the evil Duke's lust. Aghast to find their mother aiding him in the task, and in a hot, fierce parody of wooing, he goes at the job with a relentless vengeance in order to test his sister's chastity and perseverance.

In *The Honest Whore, Part 1*, Hippolito, too, employs all the intense intimacy, care, and timing of a love scene to literally seduce the harlot Bellafront away from her profession toward virtue. Pug, a minor devil sent to earth to prove himself in *The Devil Is an Ass*, is appalled by women's vanity and devious behavior and finally asks to be called home again. It is most fun when the monologue is kept conspiratorial until line 20, when Pug shifts tone and focus and becomes desperate.

In *Gallathea*, Diana, Roman goddess of the moon, the hunt, and chastity, admonishes the Nymphs, her followers, with gentle but firm authority to avoid the traps of her rival, Venus, and shun the society of men. Her righteous attitude is especially justified as they have just been caught flirting. Both Celestina in *The Lady of Pleasure* and Crispinella in *The Dutch Courtesan* argue against marriage. A widow, Celestina challenges the assumption that her first course of action must be to find a new husband, insisting rather that she may enjoy her position and take advantage of the wealth left to her by her first. Taken as a whole, her speech can be a compelling demand for personal and social freedom, and beside it Crispinella's piece has more the air of an entertainment, trivial, frivolous, espousing fun until the right man comes along. Neither is a soapbox lecture, and a parlor atmosphere (a couple of lady friends over for tea) should prevail.

Championing the opposing view, the Mother of *A Mad World, My Masters* is a bawd who bemoans the increasing difficulty in conning the customers and advises her daughter, the whore, to look for someone fool enough to marry her. The homespun, commonsense sound of the advice is in ironic contrast to the content. In *The Roman Actor*, Domitia, wife to Caesar and so Empress of Rome, is actor Paris's number-one fan. Self-possessed and confident, she tries to win him by force of logic and will, an uncommon enough tactic for a seduction. To make matters even more interesting, the placement of the scene is at least semipublic, and so Domitia may be interrupted at any moment (they are, in fact, overheard by Caesar), a factor adding spice and urgency. In defense of her virtue, the Countess has reminded King Edward III that he and she are already married and not to each other. Edward rashly responds that he will kill her husband, Lord Salisbury, and his own queen in order to have her. Her reply is strong and direct. The daggers can be a problem, but I believe the scene can be managed quite convincingly using simple mime.

The Roman Actor
by Philip Massinger
(Act I, Scene 3)

PARIS

Let a good actor in a lofty scene
Show great Alcides honour'd in the sweat
Of his twelve labours;
     or a bold Camillus
Forbidding Rome to be redeem'd with gold
From the insulting Gauls; or Scipio
After his victories imposing tribute
On conquer'd Carthage. If done to the life,
As if they saw their dangers, and their glories,
And did partake with them in their rewards,
All that have any spark of Roman in them,   10
The slothful arts laid by, contend to be
Like those they see presented.
       But 'tis urg'd
That we corrupt youth, and traduce superiors.

When do we bring a vice upon the stage
That does go off unpunish'd?
      Do we teach,
By the success of wicked undertakings,
Others to tread in their forbidden steps?

We show no arts of Lydian pandarism,
Corinthian poisons, Persian flatteries,
But mulcted so in the conclusion that   20
Even those spectators that were so inclin'd
Go home chang'd men.
      And, for traducing such
That are above us, publishing to the world
Their secret crimes, we are as innocent

As such as are born dumb.
                              When we present
An heir, that does conspire against the life
Of his dear parent, numb'ring every hour
He lives as tedious to him; if there be
Among the auditors one whose conscience tells him
He is of the same mould, we cannot help it.   30

Or bringing on the stage a loose adult'ress,
That does maintain the riotous expense
Of him that feeds her greedy lust, yet suffers
The lawful pledges of a former bed
To starve the while for hunger; if a matron,
However great in fortune, birth or titles,
Guilty of such a foul, unnatural sin,
Cry out, " 'Tis writ by me," we cannot help it.

Or when we show a judge that is corrupt,
And will give up his sentence as he favours   40
The person, not the cause; saving the guilty
If of his faction, and as oft condemning
The innocent out of particular spleen;
If any of this reverend assembly,
Nay, e'en yourself, my lord, that are the image
Of absent Caesar, feel something in your bosom
That puts you in remembrance of things past,
Or things intended, 'tis not in us to help it.

I have said, my lord; and now, as you find cause,
Or censure us, or free us with applause.   50

2. Alcides: Hercules.
3. Camillus: Roman commander who saved Rome from having to buy off the
    besieging Gauls.
5. Scipio: Scipio Africanus, victorious against Hannibal.
13. traduce: defame.
20. mulcted: punished; the alternate word may certainly be substituted unless
    the actor wants to value the original word for its sound.
28. he: the parent. him: the heir.

Misogonus
Author unknown
(Act III, Scene 3)

CACURGUS

Good Lord! what great diversity and alteration
Is there in the manner of diverse people and countries!

I am here derided of the men of this nation,
Because my garment is pied not like to their guise.
If they were in my country, all men would them scorn,
Because they are all in one hue like a company of crows.
For of the best gentlemen there diverse coloured garments
    be worn;
We most delight in pied gowns and little care for hose.

I am, by my country and birth, a true Egyptian;

I have seen the black Moors and the men of Cyne.   10
My father was also a natural Ethiopian.
I must needs be very cunning, I have it by kind.

I have been one and twenty mile beyond the moon.
Four year together I touched the sun when it rose.
Where I was born, when't is midnight, it is here noon.
I was five years with them that with their heels upward goes.
By profession I am a very good physician.

Before I could speak I had learn'd all arts liberal.
I am also a very skilful soothsayer and magician.
To speak at one word: I can do all things in general.   20
There is no sickness, disease or malady,
But I can tell only by viewing of the hand.
For every grief I can prescribe a present remedy.
I have all things that grows in the Indian land.

I can cure the ague, the measles and the French pock,
The tetter, the morphew, the bile, blain, and weal,
The megrim, the maidens, and the hitchcock,
The toothache or anything at one word I can heal.

My head is so full of the supermundal science
That I am faint to bind it, lest my brains should crow.   30
This nightcap was given me when doctor I did commence;
Good Lord, good Lord, what things do I know!

Neither do I care for any great gains winning;
I do all for Godsake and not for any gain;
And before I do deal, if any man doubt of my cunning,
That they may know't, I will tell their thought, certain!

Therefore, if there be any man or woman in this country
That would have their pains and aches now cur'd,
Let them come: I will judge of it only by palmistry,
Which if I can, that I can help them they may be assur'd. 40

4. pied: multicolored, usually in patches.
10. Cyne: probably China.
25. French pock: pox, venereal disease.
26. tetter, skin disease or scab. morphew: a leprous eruption. weal: pustule, or
     mark raised on the skin by a lashing.
27. megrim: migraine. hitchcock: might conceivably be an earlier form of "hitchy-
     koo," referring to a verminous or itchy body state.
31. This line may easily be omitted or used figuratively.

The Alchemist
by Ben Jonson
(Act II, Scene 2)

SIR EPICURE MAMMON

No. I'll have no bawds
But fathers and mothers: they will do it best,
Best of all others.
        And my flatterers

Shall be the pure and gravest of divines,
That I can get for money. My mere fools,
Eloquent burgesses, and then my poets
The same that writ so subtly of the fart,
Whom I will entertain still for that subject.
The few that would give out themselves to be
Court and town-stallions, and, each-where, bely　　　10
Ladies who are known most innocent, for them,—
These will I beg, to make me eunuchs of:
And they shall fan me with ten estrich tails
Apiece, made in a plume to gather wind.
We will be brave, Puffe, now we have the med'cine.
My meat shall all come in, in Indian shells,
Dishes of agate set in gold, and studded
With emeralds, sapphires, hyacinths, and rubies.
The tongues of carps, dormice, and camels' heels,
Boil'd in the spirit of sol, and dissolv'd pearl,　　　20
Apicius' diet, 'gainst the epilepsy:
And I will eat these broths with spoons of amber,
Headed with diamond and carbuncle.
My foot-boy shall eat pheasants, calvered salmons,
Knots, godwits, lampreys. I myself will have
The beards of barbel serv'd, instead of salads;
Oil'd mushrooms; and the swelling unctuous paps
Of a fat pregnant sow, newly cut off,
Drest with an exquisite and poignant sauce;
For which, I'll say unto my cook, *There's gold;*　　　30
Go forth, and be a knight.

1. bawds: procurers.
3. A beat here is probably necessary so that the momentum of the rest of the speech may be maintained without further pause.
6. burgesses: solid citizens.
10. bely: misrepresent; to lie about, slander.
21. Apicius (Marcus Gabius Apicius): a famous Roman epicure who lived during the reigns of Augustus and Tiberius. It is said that having spent one hundred million sesterces (about $3,600,000) in procuring and inventing rare dishes, he balanced his accounts and found that he had only ten million sesterces ($360,000) left. Unwilling to starve on such a pittance, he destroyed himself. His is the principal surviving book of Roman cookery.

25. knots, godwits: edible birds.
26. barbel: literally, bearded fish; a fish of the carp family, so called because of
    hairlike filaments hanging from its mouth.

The Lady of Pleasure
by James Shirley
(Act V, Scene 2)

LORD ———

Madam, you have heard
I can be constant,
    and if you consent
To grace it so, there is a spacious dwelling
Prepar'd within my heart for such a mistress.

Why, my good lady,
Your sex doth hold it no dishonour
To become mistress to a noble servant
In the now court Platonic way.
        Consider
Who 'tis that pleads to you; my birth and present
Value can be no stain to your embrace;   10

But these are shadows when my love appears,
Which shall, in his first miracle, return
Me in my bloom of youth, and thee a virgin;
When I, within some new Elysium,
Of purpose made and meant for us, shall be
In every thing Adonis, but in his
Contempt of love; and court thee from a Daphne
Hid in the cold rind of a bashful tree,
With such warm language and delight, till thou
Leap from that bay into the Queen of Love,   20
And pay my conquest with composing garlands
Of thy own myrtle for me.

———

Consent to be my mistress, Celestina,
And we will have it spring-time all the year;
Upon whose invitations, when we walk,
The winds shall play soft descant to our feet,
And breathe rich odours to re-pure the air:
Green bowers on every side shall tempt our stay,
And violets stoop to have us tread upon 'em.
The red rose shall grow pale, being near thy cheek,   30
And the white blush, o'ercome with such a forehead.

Here laid, and measuring with ourselves some bank,
A thousand birds shall from the woods repair,
And place themselves so cunningly behind
The leaves of every tree, that while they pay
Us tribute of their songs, thou shalt imagine
The very trees bear music, and sweet voices
Do grow in every arbour.
                           Here can we
Embrace and kiss, tell tales, and kiss again,
And none but Heaven our rival.   40

5. Celestina has responded to his use of the word "mistress."
16. Adonis: a youth beloved of Aphrodite and changed into an anemone at his
    death.
17. Daphne: beloved of Apollo. Her fate was to be transformed into a laurel tree.

The Revenger's Tragedy
by Cyril Tourneur
(Act II, Scene 1)

VENDICE
O, think upon the pleasure of the palace!

Secured ease and state! the stirring meats,
Ready to move out of the dishes, that e'en now

Quicken when they are eaten!
Banquets abroad by torchlight! music! sports!
Nine coaches waiting—hurry, hurry, hurry—

Who'd sit at home in a neglected room,
Dealing her short-liv'd beauty to the pictures,
That are as useless as old men, when those
Poorer in face and fortune than herself   10
Walk with a hundred acres on their backs,
Fair meadows cut into green foreparts? O,
It was the greatest blessing ever happened to woman
When farmers' sons agreed and met again
To wash their hands, and come up gentlemen!
The commonwealth has flourish'd ever since:
Lands that were mete by the rod, that labour's spar'd:
Tailors ride down, and measure 'em by the yard.
Fair trees, those com'ly foretops of the field,
Are cut to maintain head-tires—much untold.   20
All thrives but chastity; she lies a-cold.
Nay,
          shall I come nearer to you? mark but this:

Why are there so few honest women, but because 'tis
the poorer profession? that's accounted best that's best
followed; least in trade, least in fashion; and that's not
honesty, believe it; and do but note the love and dejected
price of it—

Lose but a pearl, we search, and cannot brook it:
But that once gone, who is so mad to look it?

4. Quicken: come to life.
5. sports: games.
11. hundred acres on their backs: allusion is to the richness of a court wardrobe,
     often comparable in worth to an entire farm.
17. mete: measured.
23. This is a curious shift into prose, suggesting a more intimate, parenthetical
     moment.
29. that: chastity.

The Honest Whore, Part 1
by Thomas Dekker
(Act II, Scene 1)

HIPPOLITO
Lend me your silence, and attention.

Methinks a toad is happier than a whore;
That with one poison swells, with thousands more
The other stocks her veins.
                                    Harlot?
                                            fie, fie!
You are the miserablest creatures breathing,
The very slaves of nature;
                                    mark me else:
You put on rich attires, others' eyes wear them,
You eat, but to supply your blood with sin:
And this strange curse e'en haunts you to your graves.
From fools you get, and spend it upon slaves.   10

Like bears and apes, you're baited and show tricks
For money; but your bawd the sweetness licks.
Indeed, you are their journey-women, and do
All base and damn'd works they list set you to;
So that you ne'er are rich;
                                    for do but show me,
In present memory, or in ages past,
The fairest and most famous courtesan,
Whose flesh was dear'st; that rais'd the price of sin,
And held it up; to whose intemp'rate bosom,
Princes, earls, lords, the worst has been a knight,   20
The mean'st a gentleman, have offer'd up
Whole hecatombs of sighs, and rain'd in showers
Handfuls of gold; yet, for all this, at last

Diseases suck'd her marrow, then grew so poor,
That she has begg'd e'en at a beggar's door.

And (wherein Heaven has a finger) when this idol,
From coast to coast, has leapt on foreign shores,
And had more worship than th'outlandish whores;
When several nations have gone over her,
When for each several city she has seen,   30
Her maidenhead has been new, and been sold dear;
Did live well there, and might have died unknown,
And undefam'd; back comes she to her own,
And there both miserably lives and dies,
Scorn'd e'en of those that once ador'd her eyes,
As if her fatal circled life thus ran,
Her pride should end there where it first began.

What, do you weep to hear your story read?
Nay, if you spoil your cheeks, I'll read no more.

12. bawd: pimp or procuress.
18. dear'st: most expensive.
22. hecatombs: public sacrifices; in Greece, at least a hundred oxen.
28. outlandish: foreign.

The Devil Is an Ass
by Ben Jonson
(Act II, Scene 5, and Act V, Scene 2)

PUG
It was a shrewd disheart'ning this at first!

Who would ha' thought a woman so well harness'd,
Or rather well-caparison'd, indeed,
That wears such petticoats, and lace to her smocks,
Broad seaming laces (as I see 'hem hang there)
And garters which are lost, if she can show 'hem,

Could ha' done this?
                    Hell!
                                why is she so brave?
It cannot be to please Duke Dottrel, sure,
Nor the dull pictures in her gallery,
Nor her own dear reflection, in her glass;   10

Yet that may be:
                    I have known many of 'hem,
Begin their pleasure, but none end it, there:
(That I consider, as I go along with it)
They may, for want of better company,
Or that they think the better, spend an hour,
Two, three, or four, discoursing with their shadow.

But sure they have a farther speculation.

No woman dress'd with so much care and study
Doth dress herself in vain.

O, call me home again, dear Chief, and put me   20
To yoking foxes, milking of he-goats,
Pounding of water in a mortar, laving
The sea dry with a nut-shell, gathering all
The leaves are fall'n this autumn, drawing farts
Out of dead bodies, making ropes of sand,
Catching the winds together in a net,
Must'ring of ants, and numb'ring atoms; all
That hell, and you thought exquisite torments, rather
Than stay me here a thought more:
                                I would sooner
Keep fleas within a circle, and be accountant   30
A thousand year which of 'hem and how far
Out-leap'd the other, than endure a minute
Such as I have within.
                    There is no hell

To a Lady of Fashion.
                                   All your tortures there
Are pastimes to it. 'Twould be a refreshing
For me, to be i' the fire again, from hence.

  3. caparison'd: covered or outfitted, referring usually to a horse.
  7. brave: fine, splendid, beautiful.
 22. laving: washing.

Gallathea
by John Lyly
(Act III, Scene 4)

DIANA

Now, ladies, doth not that make your cheeks blush that
makes mine ears glow,
or can you remember that without
sobs which Diana cannot think on without sighs?
What
greater dishonor could happen to Diana, or to her
nymphs,—shame—than that there can be any time so
idle that should make their heads so addle?
Your chaste
hearts, my nymphs, should resemble the onyx, which is
hottest when it is whitest; and your thoughts, the more
they are assaulted with desires, the less they should be
affected. You should think love like Homer's moly, a   10
white leaf and a black root, a fair show and a bitter
taste.
Of all trees the cedar is greatest and hath the smallest seeds; of all affections love hath the greatest name
and the least virtue.
Shall it be said, and shall Venus say
it; nay, shall it be seen, and shall wantons see it: that
Diana, the goddess of chastity, whose thoughts are always answerable to her vows, whose eyes never glanced
on desire, and whose heart abateth the point of Cupid's
arrows, shall have her virgins to become unchaste in
desires, immoderate in affection, untemperate in love,   20
in foolish love, in base love:
Eagles cast their evil feathers
in the sun, but you cast your best desires upon a shadow.

___

The birds
Ibes lose their sweetness when they lose their sights,
and virgins all their virtues with their unchaste thoughts.
"Unchaste" Diana calleth that that hath either any show
or suspicion of lightness.

O my dear nymphs, if you knew
how loving thoughts stain lovely faces, you would be as
careful to have the one as unspotted as the other beautiful.

Cast before your eyes the loves of Venus' trulls, their   30
fortunes, their fancies, their ends.

What are they else but
Silenus' pictures: without, lambs and doves; within, apes
and owls, who, like Ixion, embrace clouds for Juno, the
shadows of virtue instead of the substance? The eagle's
feathers consume the feathers of all others, and love's
desire corrupteth all other virtues.

I blush, ladies, that
you, having been heretofore patient of labors, should
now become 'prentices to idleness, and use the pen for
sonnets, not the needle for samplers.

And how is your
love placed?

Upon pelting boys, perhaps base of birth,   40
without doubt weak of discretion.

Ay, but they are fair.
O ladies, do your eyes begin to love colors, whose hearts
were wont to loathe them? Is Diana's chase become Venus'
court, and are your holy vows turned to hollow thoughts?

 2. ears glow: the belief implicit here is that when people are talking about you
    your ears will burn; thus gossip is that which makes Diana's ears glow.
 6. idle: idleness was a state considered especially conducive (medically) to love.
10. Homer's moly: herb mentioned in the *Odyssey*.
18. abateth: destroys, strikes off.
26. lightness: levity, wantonness.
32. Silenus' pictures: images of the gross satyr Silenus.
33. Ixion: making a pass at Juno, he was fooled by her husband Jupiter into
    embracing a cloud instead.
40. pelting: paltry.

42. colors: ruddy complexions.
43. chase: hunt.

The Lady of Pleasure
by James Shirley
(Act II, Scene 2)

CELESTINA

Shall we be so much
Cowards, to be frighted from our pleasure
Because men have malicious tongues, and show
What miserable souls they have?

                 No, cousin,
We hold our life and fortunes upon no
Man's charity; if they dare show so little
Discretion to traduce our fames, we will
Be guilty of so much wit to laugh at 'em.

My stars
Are yet kind to me; for, in a happy minute   10
Be it spoke, I'm not in love, and men shall never
Make my heart lean with sighing, nor with tears
Draw on my eyes the infamy of spectacles.

'Tis the chief principle to keep your heart
Under your own obedience; jest, but love not.
I say my prayers, yet can wear good clothes,
And only satisfy my tailor for 'em.
I will not lose my privilege.

One thing I'll tell you more, and this I give you
Worthy your imitation, from my practice: 20
You see me merry, full of song and dancing,
Pleasant in language, apt to all delights
That crown a public meeting; but you cannot

Accuse me of being prodigal of my favours
To any of my guests.
                    I do not summon,
By any wink, a gentleman to follow me
To my withdrawing chamber;
                            I hear all
Their pleas in court, nor can they boast abroad,
And do me justice, after a salute,
They have much conversation with my lip.   30
I hold the kissing of my hand a courtesy,
And he that loves me, must, upon the strength
Of that, expect till I renew his favour.

Some ladies are so expensive in their graces
To those that honour 'em, and so prodigal,
That in a little time they have nothing but
The naked sin left to reward their servants;
Whereas, a thrift in our rewards will keep
Men long in our devotion, and preserve
Ourselves in stock, to encourage those that honour us.   40

It takes not from the freedom of our mirth,
But seems to advance it, when we can possess
Our pleasures with security of our honour;

And, that preserv'd, I welcome all the joys
My fancy can let in.

29. salute: ordinary kiss of greeting.
33. expect: wait.
34. expensive: given to great expense, lavish.

The Dutch Courtesan
by John Marston
(Act III, Scene 1)

CRISPINELLA

Marry? No, faith;
          husbands are like lots in the lottery:
you may draw forty blanks before you find one that has
any prize in him.
          A husband generally is a careless, dom-
ineering thing that grows like coral, which as long as it
is under water is soft and tender, but as soon as it has
got his branch above the waves is presently hard, stiff,
not to be bowed but burst; so when your husband is a
suitor and under your choice, Lord, how supple he is,
how obsequious, how at your service, sweet lady! Once
married, got up his head above, a stiff, crooked, knobby,   10
inflexible, tyrannous creature he grows; then they turn
like water, more you would embrace, the less you hold.
                              I'll
live my own woman, and if the worst come to the worst,
I had rather prove a wag than a fool.

O, but a virtuous marriage, you say? There is no more
affinity betwixt virtue and marriage than betwixt a man
and his horse. Indeed, virtue gets up upon marriage
sometimes and manageth it in the right way, but marriage is of another piece; for as a horse may be without
a man, and a man without a horse, so marriage, you   20
know, is often without virtue, and virtue, I am sure,
more oft without marriage.
                    But thy match, sister—by my
troth, I think 'twill do well. He's a well-shaped, clean-
lipped gentleman, of a handsome but not affected fine-

ness, a good faithful eye, and a well-humored cheek.
Would he did not stoop in the shoulders, for thy sake!

See,
here he is.

14. wag: witty person.

A Mad World, My Masters
by Thomas Middleton
(Act I, Scene 1)

MOTHER

Every part of the world shoots up daily into more sub-
tlety.
   The very spider weaves her cauls with more art and
cunning to entrap the fly.
The shallow ploughman can distinguish now
'Twixt simple truth and a dissembling brow;
Your base mechanic fellow can spy out
A weakness in a lord, and learns to flout.

How dost behoove us then that live by sleight
To have our wits wound up to their stretch'd height!

Fifteen times thou know'st I have sold thy maidenhead 10
To make up a dowry for thy marriage, and yet
There's maidenhead enough for old Sir Bounteous still.
He'll be all his lifetime about it yet,
And be as far to seek when he has done.

The sums that I have told upon thy pillow!

I shall once see those golden days again;
Though fifteen, all thy maidenheads are not gone.
The Italian is not serv'd yet, nor the French;

The British men come for a dozen at once,
They engross all the market.
Tut, my girl,
'Tis nothing but a politic conveyance,
A sincere carriage, a religious eyebrow
That throws their charms over the worldlings' senses;
And when thou spiest a fool that truly pities
The false springs of thine eyes,
And honourably dotes upon thy love,
If he be rich, set him by for a husband.

Be wisely temper'd and learn this, my wench:
Who gets th'opinion for a virtuous name
May sin at pleasure, and ne'er think of shame.

2. cauls: webs.
6. mechanic fellow: mechanical, laborer.
21. politic conveyance: sharp management.
29. opinion: reputation.

The Roman Actor
by Philip Massinger
(Act IV, Scene 2)

DOMITIA

We could wish
That we could credit thee,
and cannot find
In reason but that thou, whom oft I have seen
To personate a gentleman, noble, wise,
Faithful, and gamesome, and what virtues else
The poet pleases to adorn you with,
But that (as vessels still partake the odour
Of the sweet, precious liquors they contain'd)
Thou must be really, in some degree,

The thing thou dost present.
                          Nay, do not tremble.   10
We seriously believe it, and presume
Our Paris is the volume in which all
Those excellent gifts the stage hath seen him grac'd with
Are curiously bound up.
                    Come, you would put on
A wilful ignorance, and not understand
What 'tis we point at.
               Must we, in plain language,
Against the decent modesty of our sex,
Say that we love thee, love thee to enjoy thee,
Or that in our desires thou art preferr'd,
And Caesar but thy second?
                   Thou in justice   20
(If from the height of majesty we can
Look down upon thy lowness and embrace it)
Art bound with fervour to look up to me.

You are coy,
Expecting I should court you.
                 Let mean ladies
Use prayers and entreaties to their creatures
To rise up instruments to serve their pleasures;
But for Augusta so to lose herself
That holds command o'er Caesar, and the world,
Were poverty of spirit.
              Thou must!
                  Thou shalt!   30
The violence of my passions knows no mean,
And in my punishments, and my rewards,
I'll use no moderation.
             Take this only
As caution from me: threadbare chastity
Is poor in the advancement of her servants,
But wantonness magnificent; and 'tis frequent
To have the salary of vice weigh down

The pay of virtue.
                        So,
                        without more trifling,
Thy sudden answer.
    (*Enter* CAESAR, *above*)
                                Why lose we time
And opportunity? These are but salads   40
To sharpen appetite.
                        Let us to the feast,
Where I shall wish that thou wert Jupiter,
And I Alcmena, and that I had power
To lengthen out one short night into three,
And so beget a Hercules.

    1. we: a royal "we" that she abandons almost immediately.
    2. credit: believe.
    28. Augusta: Domitia's formal title as Empress.
    39. sudden: immediate; the scene may end with Domitia's demand without entering upon the more urgent importunities of the last six and a half lines.
    43. Alcmena: wife to Amphytrion, visited by Zeus during her husband's absence. Hercules was one of the children of their union.

Edward III
Disputed authorship
(Act II, Scene 2)

COUNTESS OF SALISBURY
Keep but thy word, great king, and I am thine.

Stand where thou dost, I'll part a little from thee,
And see how I will yield me to thy hands.
    (*Turning suddenly upon him, and showing two daggers*)
Here by my side doth hang my wedding knives:
Take thou the one, and with it kill thy Queen,
And learn by me to find her where she lies;
And with this other I'll dispatch my love,
Which now lies fast asleep within my heart:

When they are gone, then I'll consent to love.

Stir not, lascivious king, to hinder me;   10
My resolution is more nimbler far,
Than thy prevention can be in my rescue,
And if thou stir, I strike; therefore, stand still,
And hear the choice that I will put thee to:

Either swear to leave thy most unholy suit
And never henceforth to solicit me;
Or else, by heaven, this sharp pointed knife
Shall stain thy earth with that which thou wouldst stain,
My poor chaste blood.
                              Swear, Edward, swear,
Or I will strike and die before thee here.   20

THE AGE OF STYLE

OF

STYLE

Restoration and

Eighteenth-Century

English Monologues

Introduction

In our Old Plays, the humour Love and Passion
Like Doublet, Hose, and Cloak, are out of fashion:
That which the World call'd Wit in Shakespears Age,
Is laught at, as improper for our Stage . . .
      —James Shirley
          (from the Prologue to the 1667 revival of
          Love Tricks or *The School of Compliments*)

When the English monarchy was restored in 1661, the London theatres began to reopen after sixteen years of Puritan rule and dark stages. It was a different world to which the players returned, socially self-conscious and artistically insecure, and to many it seemed a pale reflection of the vital theatricality of Shakespeare's age. This was an age of critics; the newly invented proscenium arch confined the action and distanced the audience from the play; women were allowed onstage; and "wit" became the buzzword of the time. In the passionate pursuit of this elusive quality, society developed into armed camps of "True Wits" and those considered "Witwoulds" or "False Wits."

In his 1690 *Essay Concerning Human Understanding*, philosopher John Locke defined wit as "lying most in the assemblage of ideas, and putting those together with quickness and variety . . . thereby to make up pleasant pictures and agreeable visions in the fancy." The critic Joseph Addison, citing Locke as his authority in a 1711 issue of *The Spectator*, proceeds further to point out that "every resemblance of ideas is not that which we call wit, unless it be such an one that gives delight and surprise." Until well into the eighteenth century, when an increasingly affluent middle class began frequenting the theatres demanding stories of moral value, the principal preoccupation for most writers and actors was with style rather then with content.

Acting Style

With the exception of a few tragedies, doomed to be replaced by newly developing operatic genres, Restoration and eighteenth-century drama took place in a room; the scale was domestic and the theatricality intimate. Therefore, to speak of style is not to speak of extravagance; rather, an economy of gesture is wanted. One look at the fashions of the age, emphasizing wigs, ruffs, gloves, and other accessories designed to cover rather than expose, suggests that restraint was the norm, and that behavior might be well rehearsed to avoid that unpremeditated move which might be misinterpreted or simply considered vulgar. A useful exercise for the actor is to invent an imaginary mirror—sometimes an invisible companion, friend, or lover, can serve even better—that can function as a kind of private reflector. By this means the actor can frequently check his image—his pose, his hair, his character mask—to make sure he is revealing only as much of his inner life as is required.

It's a simple technique, and the actor will find it equally useful when tackling any dramatic material that pits artifice against substance, especially with writers like Oscar Wilde, G. B. Shaw, and Tom Stoppard, who are among the natural descendants of Restoration comedy.

COMEDY OF WIT

It is most fitting to begin this section with a speech about wit itself, in this case the prologue to the 1671 premiere of George Villiers's *The Rehearsal* at the Theatre Royal, Drury Lane. It was spoken that night by John Lacy, the production's leading actor, who played Bayes, a dramatic poet intended to satirize John Dryden, William D'Avenant, and perhaps other "heroic" playwrights of the age. Lacy's (or Villiers's) attitude is typical of the arrogance with which a self-appointed wit might treat those less fortunate than or not so verbally gifted as himself. Although the monologue is a formal set piece with no real connection to the dramatic content of the play, there is an energy here that derives from the audience confrontation and which might be most effectively unleashed by keeping physicalization minimal (in conscious contrast to "insipid rogues" and "strutting heroes") while building deliberately to a rousing final couplet.

William Wycherley appears early in the Restoration canon. His sympathies are clearly with a previous age, and so his wit tends to sound more caustic and less flowery than that of most other writers of his day. Hence Manly, railing—or complaining—in *The Plain Dealer* in a manner reminiscent of certain Jacobean writers, sets forth and eloquently defends an exceptionally high standard for social behavior and personal integrity. As is very often the case among Restoration characters, Manly's name is the primary key to his general attitude and demeanor. Lord Foppington of *The Relapse*, by contrast, is so much a slave to fashion that even his name is likely to change at a moment's notice. His catalogue of hours, although satirical, is probably a fairly accurate description of a dandy's day. The frequent substitution of "a" for "o" marks an affectation of speech, and the actor should experiment with a range of pronunciation until he comes up with a vowel sound that is comfortable for him to sustain, believable, and appropriate to his image of Foppington.

The romance of Millamant and Mirabell in *The Way of the World* epitomizes the dazzling repartee of the well bred and exquisitely mannered. As marriage is obviously considered unfashionable by such persons, each partner must name those provisions that might render the state of matrimony bearable. Mirabell, having agreed to Millamant's stipulations, sets conditions of his own. The actor must speak well and nimbly, and if not naturally graceful he should stand still. A bit of warmth may be allowed—these two really do care for one another—but it should be kept mostly under cover.

In *The Relapse*, Berinthia's advice to the lovelorn (and supposedly betrayed) Amanda is part of a complex plot to render Amanda, who is married to Loveless, susceptible to another man's advances. Berinthia hopes to make Loveless available to her own amorous ends, so her designs on him are the subtext here, and her cunning is crucial to the life of a scene. She is worldly-wise, amoral, and something of a vicious meddler, but nevertheless attractive.

Life out of the City, except when idealized in pastoral verse, was considered anathema to polite society—a sort of living death, away from the playhouses, parties, and other social attractions of the London season. In *The Beaux' Stratagem*, Mrs. Sullen affects the manner and tastes of the genteel and becomes a veritable fountain of disapproval when faced with anything that might be considered déclassé, including her husband (who appears in the scene, out of earshort) and the very institution of marriage. Beneath all the wit, the fun, and the easy sophistication, Millamant's conditions for marriage may be interpreted as a powerful plea for independence—or at least the appearance of independence. In this companion piece to Mirabell's speech, Millamant uses each article to further test the limits of her lover's liberality and affection. Approached in this manner, the scene can be poignant and intensely active. Millamant must be a woman of presence and power, and a strong physical image may help. Her own description of herself as "sole empress of my tea-table," offers a wealth of delicious possibilities, suggesting restraint, focus, and painstaking attention to detail.

Cat's monologue in *The Author's Farce* is something of a curiosity, and I include it mainly because it presents a wealth of character opportunities rare among women's classical monologues: slyness, arch sexuality, direct audience confrontation, and a defined animal language. The references are obscure and the language convoluted, so this won't be an easy speech to master, but the payoff is worth it.

The Rehearsal
by George Villiers, Duke of Buckingham
(Prologue)

JOHN LACY

We might well call this short mock-play of ours
A posy made of weeds instead of flowers;

Yet such have been presented to your noses,
And there are such, I fear, who thought 'em roses.
Would some of 'em were here, to see, this night,
What stuff it is in which they took delight.

Here, brisk, insipid rogues, for wit, let fall
Sometimes dull sense; but oft'ner, none at all:
There, strutting heroes, with a grim-fac'd train,
Shall brave the gods, in King Cambyses's vein.   10
For (changing rules, of late, as if men writ
In spite of reason, nature, art, and wit)
Our poets make us laugh at tragedy,
And with their comedies they make us cry.

Now, critics, do your worst, that here are met;
For, like a rook, I have hedg'd in my bet.
If you approve, I shall assume the state
Of those high-flyers whom I imitate:
and justly too, for I will teach you more
Than ever they would let you know before: 20
I will not only show the feats they do,
But give you all their reasons for 'em too.
Some honour may to me from hence arise.

But if, by my endeavours, you grow wise,
And what you once so prais'd shall now despise,

Then I'll cry out, swell'd with poetic rage,
'Tis I, John Lacy, have reform'd your stage.

10. King Cambyses: ancient Persian ruler and a Restoration model for bombast.
16. rook: a sharper at cards or dice; swindler.

The Plain Dealer
by William Wycherley
(Act I, Scene 1)

MANLY

I, that am an unmannerly sea-fellow, if I ever speak well
of people, which is very seldom indeed, it would be sure
to be behind their backs; and if I would say or do ill to
any, it should be to their faces.

                      I would jostle a proud,
strutting, overlooking coxcomb, at the head of his sy-
cophants, rather than put out my tongue at him when
he were past me; would frown in the arrogant, big, dull
face of an overgrown knave of business, rather than vent
my spleen against him when his back were turned; would
give fawning slaves the lie whilst they embrace or com-   10
mend me; cowards whilst they brag; call a rascal by no
other title, though his father had left him a duke's; laugh
at fools aloud before their mistresses; and must desire
people to leave me, when their visits grow at last as
troublesome as they were at first impertinent. A pox!
why should any one, because he has nothing to do, go
and disturb another man's business?

I know that generally no man can be a great enemy but
under the name of friend; and if you are a cuckold, it is
your friend only that makes you so, for your enemy is   20
not admitted to your house: if you are cheated in your
fortune, 'tis your friend that does it, for your enemy is
not made your trustee: if your honour or good name be

injured, 'tis your friend that does it still, because your
enemy is not believed against you.

    Therefore, I rather
choose to go where honest, downright barbarity is pro-
fessed, where men devour one another like generous
hungry lions and tigers, not like crocodiles; where they
think the devil white, of our complexion; and I am already
so far an Indian.

    But if your weak faith doubts this miracle 30
of a woman, come along with me, and believe; and thou
wilt find her so handsome, that thou, who art so much
my friend, wilt have a mind to lie with her, and so wilt
not fail to discover what her faith and thine is to me.

 When we're in love, the great adversity,
 Our friends and mistresses at once we try.

5. coxcomb: fool; reference is to a traditional fool's cap like a cock's comb.
8. knave of business: an unprincipled businessman.
8–9. vent my spleen: curse.
30. Indian: general term for savage.

The Relapse
by Sir John Vanbrugh
(Act II)

LORD FOPPINGTON
To mind the inside of a book is to entertain one's self
with the forced product of another man's brain.

    Naw I
think a man of quality and breeding may be much better
diverted with the natural sprauts of his own. But to say
the truth, Madam, let a man love reading never so well,
when once he comes to know this tawn he finds so many
better ways of passing the four-and-twenty hours that
'twere ten thousand pities he should consume his time

in that.

Far example, Madam, my life;

my life, Madam,
is a perpetual stream of pleasure, that glides through   10
such a variety of entertainments I believe the wisest of
our ancestors never had the least conception of any of
'em.

I rise, Madam, about ten a'clack.

I don't rise sooner,
because 'tis the worst thing in the world for the complexion; nat that I pretend to be a beau, but a man must
endeavour to look wholesome, lest he make so nauseous
a figure in the side-bax, the ladies should be compelled
to turn their eyes upon the play. So at ten a'clack, I say,
I rise.

Naw, if I find 'tis a good day, I resalve to take a
turn in the park, and see the fine women; so huddle on   20
my clothes, and get dressed by one. If it be nasty weather,
I take a turn in the chocolate-hause, where, as you walk,
Madam, you have the prettiest prospect in the world;
you have looking-glasses all round you.

But I'm afraid I
tire the company?

Why then, ladies, from thence I go to
dinner at Lacket's, where you are so nicely and delicately
served that, stap my vitals, they shall compose you a dish
no bigger than a saucer, shall come to fifty shillings.
Between eating my dinner, and washing my mauth, ladies, I spend my time till I go to the play, where, till   30
nine a'clack, I entertain myself with looking upon the
company; and usually dispose of one hour more in leading
'em aut.

So there's twelve of the four-and-twenty pretty
well over.

The other twelve, Madam, are disposed of in
two articles: in the first four I toast myself drunk, and in

t'other eight I sleep myself sober again.

Thus, ladies,
you see my life is an eternal raund O of delights.

17 side-bax: side-box; accommodation at the theatre; Restoration audiences
    were notorious for their rowdiness and their disregard of the play being per-
    formed.
22. chocolate-hause: chocolate-house; social gathering place, like a coffeehouse.
24–25. But . . . company: Foppington responds perhaps to a yawn among his
    listeners, or else is simply seeking tangible encouragement.
27. stap my vitals: stop my vitals; a mild expletive.

The Way of the World
by William Congreve
(Act IV)

MIRABELL

Well, have I liberty to offer conditions—that when you
are dwindled into a wife, I may not be beyond measure
enlarged into a husband?

I thank you. *Imprimis* then, I covenant that your acquaintance be general; that you admit no sworn confi-
dante, or intimate of your own sex; no she-friend to screen
her affairs under your countenance, and tempt you to
make trial of a mutual secrecy. No decoy-duck to wheedle
you a "fop-scrambling" to the play in a mask—then bring
you home in a pretended fright, when you think you   10
shall be found out—and rail at me for missing the play,
and disappointing the frolic which you had, to pick me
up and prove my constancy.

Item, I article that you continue to like your own face as
long as I shall; and while it passes current with me, that
you endeavour not to new-coin it. To which end, together
with all vizards for the day, I prohibit all masks for the

night, made of oiled-skins and I know not what—hog's
bones, hare's gall, pig-water, and the marrow of a roasted
cat. In short, I forbid all commerce with the gentle woman   20
in What-d'ye-call-it Court.

Item, I shut my doors against all bawds with baskets, and
pennyworths of muslin, china, fans, atlases, etc.

Item, when you shall be breeding—which may be presumed, with a blessing on our endeavours—I denounce
against all strait lacing, squeezing for a shape, till you
mould my boy's head like a sugar-loaf, and instead of a
man-child, make me the father to a crooked billet.

Lastly, to the dominion of the tea-table I submit, but
with *proviso* that you exceed not in your province, but   30
restrain yourself to native and simple tea-table drinks,
as tea, chocolate, and coffee, as likewise to genuine and
authorized tea-table talk—such as mending of fashions,
spoiling reputations, railing at absent friends, and so
forth—but that on no account you encroach upon the
men's prerogative, and presume to drink healths, or toast
fellows; for prevention of which I banish all foreign forces,
all auxiliaries to the tea-table, as orange-brandy, all aniseed, cinnamon, citron, and Barbadoes waters, together
with ratafia and the most noble spirit of clary, but for   40
cowslip-wine, poppy water, and all dormitives, those I
allow.

These *provisos* admitted, in other things I may prove a
tractable and complying husband.

9. fop-scrambling: act of contending with fops or fools.
15. passes current: is acceptable; pun on currency refers to Millamant's face as
   legal tender.
17. vizards: masks; it was customary for ladies to go about masked, especially to
   the theatre. masks: beauty aids, different from the masks referred to as
   vizards.

21. What-d'ye-call-it Court: he won't even mention the name of the street where such transactions occur.
22. bawds: procuresses.
26. strait lacing: use of tight corsets.
28. crooked billet: bent stick, cripple.
29. dominion of the tea-table: refers to a specific condition of Millamant's; page 38, line 249.
38–39. aniseed, cinnamon, citron: all beverages derived from these ingredients; anisette, cinnamon cordial, citron-water (a lemon-flavored brandy). Barbadoes waters: rum.
40. ratafia: a fruit-flavored liqueur. clary: claret, Bordeaux wine.
41. dormitives: soporifics, opiates.

The Relapse
by Sir John Vanbrugh
(Act V, Scene 2)

BERINTHIA

Why, there's the mystery: you have been so bountiful you have cloyed him.

Fond wives do by their husbands as barren wives do by their lap-dogs: cram 'em with sweetmeats till they spoil their stomachs. You should consider that in matters of love men's eyes are always bigger than their bellies. They have violent appetites, 'tis true, but they have soon dined.

Consider what they and we are composed of. For nature has made them children, and us babies. Now, Amanda, how we used our babies, you may remember. We were mad to have 'em as soon as we saw 'em; kissed 'em to pieces as soon as we got 'em; then pulled off their clothes, saw 'em naked, and so threw 'em away.

You must know after all, Amanda, the inconstancy we commonly see in men of brains does not so much proceed from the uncertainty of their temper as from the misfortunes of their love.

A man sees perhaps a hundred women he likes well enough for an intrigue and away, but possibly, through the whole course of his life, does not find above one who is exactly what he could wish her: now her, 'tis a thousand to one, he never gets. Either she is not to be had at all (though that seldom happens, you'll say) or he wants those opportunities that are necessary to gain her. Either she likes somebody else much better than him or uses him like a dog because he likes nobody so well as her. Still

something or other fate claps in the way between them
and the woman they are capable of being fond of:
                                    and this
makes them wander about from mistress to mistress, like
a pilgrim from town to town, who every night must have
a fresh lodging, and 's in hast to be gone in the morning.   30

The Beaux' Stratagem
by George Farquhar
(Act II, Scene 1)

MRS. SULLEN

Country pleasures! Racks and torments!
                                    Dost think, child,
that my limbs were made for leaping of ditches, and
clambering over stiles? or that my parents, wisely fore-
seeing my future happiness in country pleasures, had
early instructed me in the rural accomplishments of
drinking fat ale, playing at whisk, and smoking tobacco
with my husband? or of spreading of plasters, brewing
of diet-drinks, and stilling rosemary-water, with the good
old gentlewoman, my mother-in-law?

Not that I disapprove rural pleasures, as the poets have   10
painted them; in their landscape, every Phyllis has her
Corydon, every murmuring stream, and every flow'ry
mead, gives fresh alarms to love. Besides, you'll find that
their couples were never married.

But yonder I see my Corydon, and a sweet swain it is,
heaven knows!
                    Come, Dorinda, don't be angry, he's my
husband, and your brother; and, between both, is he not
a sad brute?

O Sister, Sister! if ever you marry, beware of a sullen, silent sot, one that's always musing, but never thinks. There's some diversion in a talking blockhead; and since a woman must wear chains, I would have the pleasure of hearing 'em rattle a little.   20

                    Now you shall see, but take this by the way.

                    He came home this morning at his usual hour of four, wakened me out of a sweet dream of something else by tumbling over the tea-table, which he broke all to pieces; after his man and he had rolled about the room like sick passengers in a storm, he comes flounce into bed, dead as a salmon into a fishmonger's basket; his feet cold as ice, his breath hot as a furnace, and his hands and his face as greasy as his flannel night-cap. O matrimony! He tosses up the clothes with a barbarous swing over his shoulders, disorders the whole economy of my bed, leaves me half naked, and my whole night's comfort is the tuneable serenade of that wakeful nightingale, his nose!   30

                    Oh, the pleasure of counting the melancholy clock by a snoring husband!

But now, Sister, you shall see how handsomely, being a well-bred man, he will beg my pardon.

3. stiles: series of steps or rungs by which a person may climb over a wall or hedge.
6. whisk: earlier name for whist, a card game.
7. spreading of plasters: applying curative dressings.
11–12. Phyllis, Corydon: names common in pastoral literature; shepherdess and shepherd.
11–16. It should be noted that Mrs. Sullen waxes poetical here and uses the actual vocabulary of pastoral verse.
25–26. a sweet dream of something else: what was she dreaming about?
38–39. These last couple of lines are optional, but provide a good opportunity for irony; Sullen's attitude as he comes in is far from apologetic.

The Way of the World
by William Congreve
(Act IV)

MILLAMANT

Oh, I hate a lover that can dare to think he draws a moment's air independent on the bounty of his mistress.

There is not so impudent a thing in nature as the saucy look of an assured man, confident of success. The pedantic arrogance of a very husband has not so pragmatical an air. Ah!

I'll never marry unless I am first made sure of my will and pleasure.

—My dear liberty, shall I leave thee? My faithful solitude, my darling contemplation, must I bid you then adieu? Ay-h, adieu—my morning thoughts, agreeable wakings, indolent slumbers, all ye *douceurs*, ye *sommeils du matin*, adieu?

I can't do 't, 'tis more than impossible. Positively, Mirabell, I'll lie abed in a morning as long as I please.

And d'ee hear, I won't be called names after I'm married; postively I won't be called names. Ay, as wife, spouse, my dear, joy, jewel, love, sweetheart, and the rest of that nauseous cant in which men and their wives are so fulsomely familiar—I shall never bear that. Good Mirabell, don't let us be familiar or fond, nor kiss before folks, like my Lady Fadler and Sir Francis: nor go to Hyde Park together the first Sunday in a new chariot to provoke eyes and whispers, and then never to be seen there together again, as if we were proud of one another the first week, and ashamed of one another for ever after. Let us never visit together, nor go to a play together, but let us be very strange and well bred: let us be as strange as if we had been married a great while; and as well bred as if we were not married at all.

A few trifles more—as liberty to pay and receive visits to and from whom I please; to write and receive letters, without interrogatories or wry 30 faces on your part. To wear what I please; and choose conversation with regard only to my own taste; to have no obligation upon me to converse with wits that I don't like because they are your acquaintance; or to be intimate with fools, because they may be your relations. Come to dinner when I please, dine in my dressing-room when I'm out of humour, without giving a reason. To have my closet inviolate; to be sole empress of my tea-table, which you must never presume to approach without first asking leave.

And lastly, wherever I am, you shall always knock · 40 at the door before you come in.

These articles subscribed, if I continue to endure you a little longer, I may by degrees dwindle into a wife.

5. pragmatical: conceited, self-important.
9. Ay-h: an extended sigh of some sort.
11. *douceurs . . . matin:* sweetness, peacefulness; sleeps of morning; if the actress is not already comfortable with the language, these French references should be omitted.
13. d'ee: do ye.
19–20. Lady Fadler and Sir Francis: one should try to imagine the public billing and cooing of perhaps the least attractive possible couple.
24–26. Let us . . . well bred: the sentence structure may be deceptive here; the meaning is that whenever they are visiting or at a play together, they should act like strangers to each other.
38. closet: private room.

The Author's Farce
by Henry Fielding
(Epilogue)

CAT

I that am now a woman, lately was a cat.

Gallants, you seem to think this transformation
As strange as was the rabbit's procreation,
That 'tis as odd a cat should take the habit
Of breeding us as we should breed a rabbit.
I'll warrant eating one of them would be
As easy to a beau as—kissing me.
"I would not for the world that thing should catch us,"
Cries scar'd Sir Plume. "Fore gad, my lord, she'd scratch us."

Yet let not that deter you from your sport,   10
You'll find my nails are pared exceeding short.

But, ha, what murmurs through the benches roam!
The husbands cry, "We've cat enough at home."

This transformation can be strange to no man;
There's a great likeness 'twixt a cat and woman.

Chang'd by her lover's earnest prayer, we're told,
A cat was, to a beauteous maid of old.
Could modern husbands thus the gods prevail on,
Oh gemini! What wife would have no tail on?
Puss would be seen where madam lately sat,   20
And every Lady Townley be a cat.

Say, all of you, whose honeymoon is over,
What would you give such changes to discover,

And waking in the morn, instead of bride,
To find poor pussy purring by your side?
Say, gentle husbands, which of you would curse,
And cry, "My wife is alter'd for the worse?"

Should to our sex the gods like justice show,
And at our prayers transform our husbands too,
Many a lord who now his fellows scorns   30
Would then exceed a cat by nothing—but his horns.

So plenty then would be those foes to rats,
Henley might prove that all mankind are cats.

1. There is some silly business preceding this speech during which the Cat appears, is cursed, and leaves.
3. rabbit's procreation: reference to a practical joke of the time, in which a Mary Toft of Godalming in Surrey pretended to give birth to a litter of rabbits.
9. Sir Plume: a term of derision; Lady Townley is another such.
16–17. Chang'd . . . of old: reference to a traditional fable in which such a transformation occurred.
31. horns: emblem of the cuckold.
33. Henley: John Henley (1692–1756) was a well-known religious orator often ridiculed by the wits.

COMEDY OF CHARACTER
AND SITUATION

Amanda's husband, Loveless, is being chased by Berinthia, who, to further her designs on him, has struck up a close companionship with Amanda. As with most other adult situation comedies, there is nothing inherently funny about this situation in *The Relapse*. The apparently honest naïveté with which Loveless tries to solve a serious moral dilemma is what gives the speech its charm, and so it really should not be played for laughs. The relative looseness of the meter makes the speech a curious hybrid of verse and prose that seems particularly well suited to trying desperately to maintain a formal, organized, rational approach to a problem not really susceptible to reason.

The Beggar's Opera is about lowlifes—criminals, beggars, whores, etc.—aping the social forms and graces of the upper classes. Macheath became the inspiration for Mack the Knife of Bertolt Brecht's 1928 adaptation, *The Threepenny Opera*, but here he is still mostly heroic and not yet running to bourgeois fat. When not leading the most feared gang of cutthroats in London, he loves his pleasures, and not least among these is his bevy of bawdy beauties who present themselves to him almost as if for military inspection. The actor's key problem is to decide what each lady does to him as she passes—avoiding all grossness, of course. After all, Macheath does have aristocratic pretensions. Peachum is the businessman of the same play, head of a massive company of beggars, and so finds it natural to translate his daughter's marriage into terms of "property," "power," and business advantage. Although brief, this speech has an uncommon emotional and verbal range.

Each of the next three short speeches is a character actor's dream, and offers the germ of a full and fascinating personality. Antonio's vegetarian attempt at speech writing in *Venice Preserved* serves as both a parody of speechifying and a satire on politicians in general. The monologue is written to make him come off lovable no matter what the actor does, so for best results he should work against this and concentrate instead on achieving a believable public presence. Antonio is, after all, a lord and a senator. In attacking his son's "violence" and "passion," Sir Anthony Absolute of *The Rivals* falls prey to his own excess, uncontrollable anger. The central joke of the speech is "Can't you be cool, like me?" as he raves onward to the brilliantly fashioned punch line. In a much quieter mode, Sir Peter Teazle of *The School for Scandal* reflects on the good and ill fortunes attending marriage with a younger woman. He is absolutely reasonable, fully aware of his condition, and in sufficiently good humor that a wink on the last line would not be out of place.

Although the paradigm of social sloth, Sir Charles Easy, the "careless husband," lacks the sort of comic exaggeration common among other Restoration characters of his kind, and manages to emerge curiously believable. I can image a senior senator or semiretired bank president sharing his sentiments, if not always expressing them with such candor. There is a broken rhythm to Sir Charles's speech that supports the heavy breathing pattern typical of overweight men of advancing years. Time must be taken at the beats, for it is in the pauses that the character detail may be most fully explored, and all unnecessary movement should be avoided. The man enjoys deliberation and wears his laziness like a comfortable old silk dressing gown. The woman to whom he speaks should be thought of as an intimate and perhaps longtime acquaintance.

Margery Pinchwife, the "country wife," is the innocent who, in spite of being locked out of circulation by her jealous husband, meets and is attracted to the rake Horner. The degree of Margery's innocence is subject to a wide range of interpretation, but, in the context of Wycherley's antisocial morality— odd for his time—all guilt and blame must fall on her husband's head for his intractability and unreason. That she be naive, rather than arch or cunning, is essential. As to the letter, the "so"s and other expletives are an excellent aid to the actor, providing pivot points for transitions from writing to speech and back.

In an age that placed such great emphasis on social form and manner, it seems appropriate that considerable effort and imagination should have gone into preparing for any exciting social event. For each of the next three women, the excitement lies in the anticipated appearance of a lover or suitor. Least active of the three, Prue's monologue from *The Gentleman Dancing Master* is a detailed catalogue of her efforts to capture the attention of her chosen beau. Her relationship to her audience is most important. This could be a plea for help from an older, more experienced woman or perhaps schoolgirl confidences; or, if addressed to a man, her remarks suddenly achieve the most arch sort of coquetry. Choosing a place will also help; are we in a park, a drawing room, a bedchamber? *The Way of the World*'s Lady Wishfort is in complete command of her environment, whatever the specifics chosen. It might even be useful to imagine dozens of servants scurrying about to fulfill her every wish, instead of the single servant, Foible, actually in the text. Sir Rowland's imminent arrival provides special urgency. Melantha's location in the scene from *Marriage à la Mode* is only important to the extent that it is a projection of her nearly autoerotic fantasy, as she imagines in wide-screen living color her anticipated tryst with Rhodophil. The scene may be played very physically or cerebrally, in contrast to the violently passionate language; but in either case, Melantha's involvement must be so total that the interruption of the court's entrance can work dramatically.

In *The Beggar's Opera*, Polly's focus is also on what she anticipates rather than on the present; but here it is her husband Macheath's execution that she looks toward. She conjures up images of the hanging her parents have planned, and finally decides to help him escape—but not until she has derived a great deal of pleasure from the thought of his demise. Each detail should be carefully visualized and allowed time to sink in. Polly may be an ingenue, but she is a shrewd one and should not be played as if she were dull-witted. In a less romantic mood, there is Margaret, a militant version of Shakespeare's Kate in *Sauny the Scot,* an adaptation of *The Taming of the Shrew,* who not only plans an uprising against her husband, Petruchio, but also urges universal female rebellion, enlisting her sister, Biancha, as an ally. Barely controlled fury is about the right tone, with a clear image of an appropriately despicable Petruchio-substitute in mind.

Mrs. Candour of *The School for Scandal* embodies gossip raised to an art form, and her monologue should be performed with as few pauses as possible. No collection of characters from the age, however, could be considered representative without a sample of Mrs. Malaprop's unique style from *The Rivals.* She is a woman who has assembled a full vocabulary without much attention paid to meaning. Her habit of confusing words that sound alike is unconscious, and her diction and deportment ought to be as perfect as possible because she is, to herself of course, a very pineapple of politeness and verbal achievement.

The Relapse
by Sir John Vanbrugh
(Act III, Scene 2)

LOVELESS

Sure, fate has yet some business to be done,
Before Amanda's heart and mine must rest;

Else why, amongst those legions of her sex,
Which throng the world,
Should she pick out for her companion
The only one on earth
Whom nature has endow'd for her undoing?

"Undoing" was't I said?—Who shall undo her?
Is not her empire fix'd? Am I not hers?
Did she not rescue me, a grov'ling slave?   10
When, chain'd and bound by that black tyrant, Vice,
I labour'd in his vilest drudgery,

Did she not ransom me, and set me free?

Nay, more;
When by my follies sunk
To a poor tatter'd, despicable beggar,
Did she not lift me up to envy'd fortune?
Give me herself, and all that she possess'd?
Without a thought of more return,
Than what a poor repenting heart might make her.   20

Han't she done this?
                    And if she has,
Am I not strongly bound to love her for it?

To love her!
          —Why, do I not love her then?

By earth and heaven, I do!
Nay, I have demonstration that I do:
For I would sacrifice my life to serve her.

Yet hold:
               —if laying down my life
Be demonstration of my love,
What is't I feel in favour of Berinthia?
For should she be in danger, methinks, I could incline   30
To risk it for her service too; and yet I do not love her.

How then subsists my proof?—

—Oh, I have found it out.
What I would do for one is demonstration of my love;
And if I'd do as much for t'other,
If there is demonstration of my friendship—
Ay—It must be so.
I find I'm very much her friend.

—Yet let me ask myself one puzzling question more:
Whence springs this mighty friendship all at once?   40
For our acquaintance is of later date.
Now friendship's said to be a plant of tedious growth,
Its root compos'd of tender fibres,
Nice in their taste, cautious in spreading,
Check'd with the least corruption in the soil;
Long ere it take, and longer still ere it appear to do so.
Whilst mine is in a moment shot so high,
And fix'd so fast, it seems beyond the power
Of storms to shake it.
                    I doubt it thrives too fast. (*Musing*)
     (*Enter* BERINTHIA)

Ha! she here!

Nay, then,   50

Take heed, my heart, for there are dangers towards.

24. heaven: although the meter seems to indicate *heav'n*, I have left the additional
    syllable as a sign of emotion.
44. Nice: discriminating, delicate.
49. I doubt: I'm afraid.

The Beggar's Opera
by John Gay
(Act II, Scenes 3 and 4)

MACHEATH

I must have women. There is nothing unbends the mind
like them.

Dear Mrs. Coaxer, you are welcome. You look charm-
ingly today. I hope you don't want the repairs of quality,
and lay on paint.

Dolly Trull! kiss me, you slut; are you as amorous as
ever, hussy? You are always so taken up with stealing
hearts, that you don't allow yourself time to steal anything else. —Ah Dolly, thou wilt ever be a coquette.

Mrs. Vixen, I'm yours; I always loved a woman of wit   10
and spirit; they make charming mistresses, but plaguy
wives.

Betty Doxy! Come hither, hussy. Do you drink as hard
as ever? You had better stick to good wholesome beer;
for in troth, Betty, strong waters will in time ruin your
constitution. You should leave those to your betters.

What! and my pretty Jenny Diver too! As prim and de-
mure as ever! There is not any prude, though ever so

high bred, hath a more sanctified look, with a more mischievous heart. Ah! thou art a dear artful hypocrite.   20

Mrs. Slammekin! as careless and genteel as ever! all you
fine ladies, who know your own beauty, affect an undress.

But see, here's Suky Tawdry come to contradict what I
was saying. Everything she gets one way, she lays out
upon her back. Why, Suky, you must keep at least a
dozen tally-men.

Molly Brazen!
          (*She kisses him*)
                              That's well done, I love a
free-hearted wench. Thou hast a most agreeable assurance, girls, and art as willing as a turtle.

But hark! I hear music. The harper is at the door. "If   30
music be the food of love, play on." Ere you seat yourselves, ladies, what think you of a dance?

3. Mrs. Coaxer: each lady's name suggests some element of feminine allure and
   is a good place to begin the task of making each different.
4. want: require.
22. undress: informal attire.
26. tally-men: a pun suggesting that Suky does enough business to keep a dozen
   accountants busy while referring to "tally-husband," a man who pays for
   favors.
27. *She kisses him*: this is the only explicit stage direction in the speech.
29. turtle: turtledove.

The Beggar's Opera
by John Gay
(Act I, Scene 4)

PEACHUM

Look ye, wife.
          A handsome wench in our way of business

is as profitable as at the bar of a Temple coffee-house, who looks upon it as her livelihood to grant every liberty but one.

You see I would indulge the girl as far as prudently we can. In anything but marriage!

After that, my dear, how shall we be safe? Are we not then in her husband's power? For a husband hath the absolute power over all a wife's secrets but her own.

If the girl had the discretion of a court lady, who can have a dozen young fellows at her ear without complying with one, I should not matter it; but Polly is tinder, and a spark will at once set her on a flame.   10

Married! If the wench does not know her own profit, sure she knows her own pleasure better than to make herself a property!

My daughter to me should be, like a court lady to a minister of state, a key to the whole gang.

(POLLY *enters*)

Married! Do you think your mother and I should have lived comfortably so long together, if ever we had been married? Baggage!

2. Temple coffee-house: a coffeehouse at the Inns of Court in London, an example of ultimate respectability.

5. In anything but marriage: marriage, not sex, is the unforgivable sin.

10–11. I should not matter it: it would not matter to me.

Venice Preserved
by Thomas Otway
(Act V, Scene 1)

ANTONIO

Hum, hum, hah. Signior Priuli, my lord Priuli, my lord,

my lord, my lord. How we lords love to call one another by our titles.

My lord, my lord, my lord.—Pox on him, I am a lord as well as he. And so let him fiddle.—I'll warrant him he's gone to the Senate-house, and I'll be there too, soon enough for somebody.

Odd!—here's a tickling speech about the plot. I'll prove there's a plot with a vengeance—would I had it without book. Let me see—

"Most reverend senators, that there is a plot, surely by this time, no man that hath eyes or understanding in his head will presume to doubt; 'tis as plain as the light in the cowcumber"—   10

no—hold there—cowcumber does not come in yet—

" 'tis as plain as the light in the sun, or as the man in the moon, even at noonday. It is, indeed, a pumpkin-plot, which, just as it was mellow, we have gathered; and now we have gathered it, prepared and dressed it, shall we throw it like a pickled cowcumber out at the window? No! That it is not only a bloody, horrid, excrable, damnable, and audacious plot, but it is, as I may so say, a saucy plot; and we all know, most   20 reverend fathers, that what is sauce for a goose is sauce for a gander: therefore, I say, as those blood-thirsty ganders of the conspiracy would have destroyed us geese of the Senate, let us make haste to destroy them. So I humbly move for hanging"—

Hah, hurry durry, I think this will do, though I was something out, at first, about the sun and the cowcumber.

The Rivals
Richard Brinsley Sheridan
(Act II, Scene 1)

SIR ANTHONY ABSOLUTE

None of your passion, Sir! none of your violence! if you
please. It won't do with me, I promise you.

So you will fly out!
                    Can't you be cool, like me?
                                        What the
devil good can passion do! Passion is of no service, you
impudent, insolent, overbearing reprobate!
                                        —There you
sneer again! don't provoke me! But you rely upon the
mildness of my temper—you do, you dog! you play upon
the meekness of my disposition! Yet take care—the patience of a saint may be overcome at last!
                                        —but mark! I
give you six hours and a half to consider of this: if you   10
then agree, without any condition, to do everything on
earth that I choose, why—confound you! I may in time
forgive you.
                    If not, z——ds! don't enter the same hemi-
sphere with me! don't dare to breathe the same air, or
use the same light with me; but get an atmosphere and
a sun of your own! I'll strip you of your commission; I'll
lodge a five-and-threepence in the hands of trustees, and
you shall live on the interest. I'll disown you, I'll dis-
inherit you, I'll unget you! and—d—n me, if ever I call
you Jack again!   20

---

13. z——ds: zounds; his (Christ's) wounds; an epithet perhaps not as mild to Sir
   Anthony or Sheridan as it might seem.
16–17. I'll . . . trustees: refers to his son's, Captain Absolute's, allowance.
19. unget: opposite of beget.

The School for Scandal
by Richard Brinsley Sheridan
(Act I, Scene 2)

SIR PETER TEAZLE

When an old bachelor takes a young wife, what is he to expect?

'Tis now six months since Lady Teazle made me the happiest of men—and I have been the miserablest dog ever since that ever committed wedlock!

We tift a little going to church, and came to a quarrel before the bells were done ringing. I was more than once nearly choked with gall during the honeymoon, and had lost all comfort in life before my friends had done wishing me joy!

Yet I chose with caution—a girl bred wholly in the country, who never knew luxury beyond one silk gown, nor dissipation above the annual gala of a race ball.

Yet now she plays her part in all the extravagant fopperies of the fashion and the town, with as ready a grace as if she had never seen a bush nor a grass-plat out of Grosvenor Square!

'I am sneered at by my old acquaintance—paragraphed in the newspapers. She dissipates my fortune, and contradicts all my humors;

yet the worst of it is, I doubt I love her, or I should never bear all this.

However, I'll never be weak enough to own it.

10

4. tift: engaged in a petty disagreement.
14–15. Grosvenor Square: GROVEner; small park in the center of London.
18. I doubt: I'm afraid.
19. own: admit.

The Careless Husband
by Colley Cibber
(Act I, Scene 1, and Act III)

SIR CHARLES EASY

So!

the Day is come again—

Life but rises to another Stage,
and the same dull Journey is before us—How like Children do we judge of Happiness!

When I was stinted in
my Fortune, almost every thing was a Pleasure to me,
because most things then being out of my Reach, I had
always the Pleasure of hoping for 'em;

now Fortune's in
my hand, she's as insipid as an old Acquaintance—It's
mighty silly, Faith—

Just the same thing by my Wife
too;

I am told she's extremely handsome—nay, and I have
heard a great many People say she is certainly the best   10
Woman in the World—

why, I don't know but she may:
yet I could never find that her Person, or good Qualities,
gave me any concern—In my Eye the Woman has no
more Charms than my Mother.

Then seriously, I say, I am of late grown so very lazy in
my Pleasures, that I had rather lose a Woman, than go
through the Plague and Trouble of having or keeping
her;

and to be free, I have found so much, even in my
Acquaintance with you, whom I confess to be a Mistress
in the Art of Pleasing, that I am from henceforth resolved   20
to follow no Pleasure that rises above the Degree of

Amusement—

and that Woman that expects I should make her my Business; why—like my Business, is then in a fair way of being forgot:

When once she comes to reproach me with Vows, and Usage, and Stuff,—I had as lief hear her talk of Bills, Bonds, and Ejectments; her Passion becomes as troublesome as a Law-suit, and I would as soon converse with my Solicitor—

In short, I shall never care Sixpence for any Women that won't be obedient!

1. Day, Life, Stage, etc.: I have retained Cibber's capitalization of nouns because it seems, in this case, to reinforce Sir Charles's attitude to the world around him.

25–26. Vows . . . Ejectments: in rough parallels Sir Charles equates the intimate world of promises of fidelity (Vows), domestic habits (Usage), and personal accoutrements (Stuff) with the business world of legal petitions (Bills), obligations and deeds (Bonds), and legal proceedings that separate persons from their property and holdings (Ejectments). Not so very strangely, the first three words also have a place in law and business parlance. "Usage," in particular, may also mean interest on money borrowed.

28. Solicitor: lawyer.

The Country Wife
by William Wycherley
(Act IV, Scene 2)

MRS. PINCHWIFE

"For Mr. Horner."
       —So, I am glad he has told me his
name. Dear Mr. Horner! But why should I send thee
such a letter that will vex thee, and make thee angry
with me?
       Well, I will not send it.
                     —Ay, but then my
husband will kill me—for I see plainly he won't let me
love Mr. Horner—
           but what care I for my husband? I
won't, so I won't, send poor Mr. Horner such a letter—
But then my husband—
               but oh, what if I writ at bottom
my husband made me write it?
                     —Ay, but then my hus-
band would see't—Can one have no shift?
                       Ah, a London   10
woman would have had a hundred presently.
                         Stay—what
if I should write a letter, and wrap it up like this, and
write upon't too?
             Ay, but then my husband would see't—
I don't know what to do.—But yet evads I'll try, so I
will—for I will not send this letter to poor Mr. Horner,
come what will on't.

"Dear, sweet Mr. Horner"—(*She writes and repeats what
she hath writ.*)—so—"my husband would have me send
you a base, rude, unmannerly letter; but I won't"—so—
"and would have me forbid you loving me; but I won't"—   20

so—"and would have me say to you, I hate you, poor Mr. Horner; but I won't tell a lie for him"—there—"for I'm sure if you and I were in the country at cards together"—so—"I could not help treading on your toe under the table"—so—"or rubbing knees with you, and staring in your face, till you saw me"—very well—"and then looking down, and blushing for an hour together"— so—"but I must make haste before my husband come: and now he has taught me to write letters, you shall have longer ones from me, who am, dear, dear, poor, dear 30 Mr. Horner, your most humble friend, and servant to command till death,—Margery Pinchwife."

Stay, I must give him a hint at bottom—so—now wrap it up just like t'other—so—now write "For Mr. Horner"—

But oh now, what shall I do with it? for here comes my husband.

10. shift: available means or an ingenious device to implement a desired result.
27. together: altogether.

The Gentleman Dancing Master
by William Wycherley
(Act IV, Scene 1)

PRUE
All my hopes are in that coxcomb there:

I must take up with my mistress's leavings, though we chambermaids are wont to be beforehand with them.

But he is the dullest, modestest fool, for a frenchified fool, as ever I saw; for nobody could be more coming to him than I have

been, though I say it, and yet I am ne'er the nearer. I
have stolen away his handkerchief, and told him of it;
and yet he would never so much as struggle with me to
get it again: I have pulled off his peruke, untied his
ribbons, and have been very bold with him: yet he would   10
never be so with me: nay, I have pinched him, punched
him and tickled him; and yet he would never do the like
for me.

And to make my person more acceptable to him, I have
used art, as they say; for every night since he came, I
have worn the forehead-piece of bees-wax and hog's-
grease, and every morning washed with butter-milk and
wild tansy; and have put on every day for his only sake
my Sunday's bowdy stockings, and have new-chalked my
shoes, as constantly as the morning came: nay, I have   20
taken occasion to garter my stockings before him, as if
unawares of him; for a good leg and foot, with good shoes
and stockings, are very provoking, as they say; but the
devil a bit would he be provoked.

But I must think of a

way.

3. to be beforehand with: to have enough of.
4. frenchified: stylish.
9. peruke: wig; it was customary for gentleman of fashion to wear powdered
    wigs.
16. forehead-piece: a cloth covering worn on the forehead by ladies.
18. tansy: a garnish plant similar to parsley.
19. bowdy: scarlet; a new method of dyeing scarlet was brought to England in
    1643 by a German who established his dye house at Bow, near Stratford,
    and "Bow-dye" came to signify scarlet. new-chalked: whitened.

The Way of the World
by William Congreve
(Act IV, Scene 1)

LADY WISHFORT

Is Sir Rowland coming, say'st thou, Foible? and are things in order?

Have you pulvilled the coachman and postilion, that they may not stink of the stable when Sir Rowland comes by? And are the dancers and the music ready, that he may be entertained in all points with correspondence to his passion? And—

—well—and how do I look, Foible?

Well, and how shall I receive him? In what figure shall I give his heart the first impression? There is a great deal in the first impression. Shall I sit?

No, I won't sit—I'll walk—ay, I'll walk from the door upon his entrance; and then turn full upon him.

—No, that will be too sudden. I'll lie—ay, I'll lie down—I'll receive him in my little dressing-room; there's a couch—yes, yes, I'll give the first impression on a couch.—I won't lie neither, but loll and lean upon one elbow, with one foot a little dangling off, jogging in a thoughtful way—yes—and then as soon as he appears, start, ay, start and be surprised, and rise to meet him in a pretty disorder—yes—oh, nothing is more alluring than a levee from a couch in some confusion. It shows the foot to advantage, and furnishes with blushes, and recomposing airs beyond comparison.

Hark!

There's a coach.

2. pulvilled: perfumed. postilion: one who rides the horse on the left of the leading pair when four or more horses are used to draw a carriage.
19. levee: rising; from French.

Marriage à la Mode
by John Dryden
(Act III, Scene 1)

MELANTHA

(*Reading a letter*) "Beg the favour from you. —Gratify my passion—so far—assignation—in the grotto—behind the terrace—clock this evening—"

Well, for the *billets-doux* there is no man in Sicily must dispute with Rhodophil; they are so French, so *gallant*, and so *tendre*, that I cannot resist the temptation of the assignation.

Now, go you away, Philotis; it imports me to practise what to say to my servant when I meet him.
(*Exit* PHILOTIS)

Rhodophil, you'll wonder at my assurance to meet you here;—let me die, I am so out of breath with coming, that I can render you no reason of it.   10
                    —Then he will make this repartee; Madam, I have no reason to accuse you for that which is so great a favour to me.
                    —Then I reply, But why have you drawn me to this solitary place? Let me die, but I am apprehensive of some violence from you.
                    —Then says he, Solitude, madam, is most fit for lovers; but by this fair hand—
                    —Nay, now I vow you're rude, sir. Oh fie, fie, fie; I hope you'll be honourable?
                    —You'd laugh at me if I should, madam—
                    —What,

do you mean to throw me down thus? Ah me! ah! ah!   20
ah!

(*Enter* POLYDAMUS, LEONIDAS, *and* GUARDS)

Oh Venus! the king and court. Let me die, but I fear
they have found my foible, and will turn me into ridicule.

4. *billets-doux:* love letters, French; *gallant* and *tendre* are likewise French and
   should be spoken with an appropriate accent.
5. Rhodophil: if "Rhodophil" sounds to you, as it does to me, too much like a
   toothpaste ingredient, I suggest substituting some other classical-sounding
   romantic name used in this period, like Valentine (Congreve's *Love for Love*),
   Polydore (Otway's *The Orphan*), or Palamede (a courtier in *Marriage à la
   Mode*).

The Beggar's Opera
by John Gay
(Act I, Scene 12)

POLLY

Now I'm a wretch, indeed.
                            —Methinks I see him already
in the cart, sweeter and more lovely than the nosegay
in his hand!
            —I hear the crowd extolling his resolution
and intrepidity! —what volleys of sighs are sent from the
windows of Holborn, that so comely a youth should be
brought to disgrace! —I see him at the tree! The whole
circle are in tears! —even butchers weep! —Jack Ketch
himself hesitates to perform his duty, and would be glad
to lose his fee by a reprieve.
                            What then will become of
Polly?
        As yet I may inform him of their design, and aid   10
him in his escape. —It shall be so. —But then he flies,
absents himself, and I bar myself from his dear, dear
conversation! That too will distract me.
                            If he keep out of

the way, my papa and mama may in time relent, and we may be happy. If he stays, he is hanged, and then he is lost forever!

He intended to lie concealed in my room, till the dusk of the evening. If they are abroad, I'll this instant let him out, lest some accident should prevent him.

5. Holborn: district in London on the way to Tyburn, the place of execution.
7. Jack Ketch: traditional name for the public hangman.

Sauny the Scot
by John Lacy
(Act V)

MARGARET

Had I served him as bad as Eve did Adam, he could not have used me worse;

but I am resolved, now I'm got home again, I'll be revenged.

I'll muster up the spite of all the curs'd women since Noah's flood to do him mischief and add new vigour to my tongue. I have not pared my nails this fortnight; they are long enough to do him some execution, that's my comfort.

Thou art a fool, Biancha! come, learn of me: Thou art married to a man too; thou dost not know but thou mayest need my counsel, and make good use on't.

Thy husband bears thee fair yet;   10
but take heed of going home with him, for, when once he has thee within his verge, 'tis odds he'll have his freaks too—there's no trusting these men.

Thy temper is soft and easy; thou must learn to break him, or he'll break thy heart. Trust him and hang him; they're all alike.

Come,

thou shalt be my scholar;
                    learn to frown and cry out for
unkindness, but brave anger; thou hast a tongue, make
use on't—scold, fight, scratch, bite—anything. Still take
exceptions at all he does, if there be cause or not; if there
be reason for't, he'll laugh at thee. I'll make Petruchio   20
glad to wipe my shoes or walk my horse ere I have done
with him.

12. verge: range, sphere, power, control; also the male sexual organ. freaks:
    capricious whims, notions, vagaries.

The School for Scandal
by Richard Brinsley Sheridan
(Act I, Scene 1)

Mrs. Candour

My dear Lady Sneerwell, how have you been this
century?

—Mr. Surface, what news do you hear? —though indeed
it is no matter, for I think one hears nothing else but
scandal.

          Ah, Maria! child,—what, is the whole affair off
between you and Charles? His extravagance, I presume—the town talks of nothing else. I own I was hurt
to hear it, as indeed I was to learn, from the same quarter,
that your guardian, Sir Peter, and Lady Teazle have not
agreed lately so well as could be wished.   10

What's to be done? People will talk—there's no prevent-
ing it. —Why, it was but yesterday I was told that Miss
Gadabout had eloped with Sir Filigree Flirt. —But, Lord!
there's no minding what one hears—though, to be sure,
I had this from very good authority.

                    The world is so censorious, no character escapes.

      —Lord, now who would have suspected your friend, Miss Prim, of an indiscretion? Yet such is the ill-nature of people, that they say her uncle stopped her last week, just as she was stepping into the York Diligence with her dancing-master.

      But 20 what's to be done, as I said before? how will you prevent people from talking? To be sure, tale-bearers are as bad as the tale-makers. —Today, Mrs. Clackit assured me Mr. and Mrs. Honeymoon were at last become mere man and wife, like the rest of their acquaintances. — She likewise hinted that a certain widow, in the next street, had got rid of her dropsy and recovered her shape in a most surprising manner. And at the same time Miss Tattle, who was by, affirmed that Lord Buffalo had discovered his lady at a house of no extraordinary fame— 30 and that Sir Harry Bouquet and Tom Saunter were to measure swords on a similar provocation.

      But, Lord, do you think I would report these things! No, no! tale-bearers, as I said before, are just as bad as tale-makers. I confess, Mr. Surface, I cannot bear to hear people attacked behind their backs, and when ugly circumstances come out against one's acquaintance I own I always love to think the best.

      —By the bye, I hope it is not true that your brother is absolutely ruined?

      —But you must tell him to keep up his spirits—everybody almost is in the 40 same way! Lord Spindle, Sir Thomas Splint, Captain Quinze, and Mr. Nickit—all up, I hear, within this week; so, if Charles is undone, he'll find half his acquaintances ruined too—and that, you know, is a consolation.

20. York Diligence: a public coach bound for York.
26–28. a certain widow . . . manner: dropsy would have been the public excuse given for a case of pregnancy.

The Rivals
by Richard Brinsley Sheridan
(Act I, Scene 2)

MRS. MALAPROP

Observe me, Sir Anthony. I would by no means wish a daughter of mine to be a progeny of learning;
I don't think so much learning becomes a young woman; for instance—I would never let her meddle with Greek, or Hebrew, or Algebra, or Simony, or Fluxions, or Paradoxes, or such inflammatory branches of learning—neither would it be necessary for her to handle any of your mathematical, astronomical, diabolical instruments;—but, Sir Anthony, I would send her, at nine years old, to a boarding-school, in order to learn a little ingenuity and   10
artifice. Then, Sir, she should have a supercilious knowledge in accounts—and as she grew up, I would have her instructed in geometry, that she might know something of the contagious countries—but above all, Sir Anthony, she should be mistress of orthodoxy, that she might not misspell, and mispronounce words so shamefully as girls usually do; and likewise that she might reprehend the true meaning of what she is saying.
This, Sir Anthony, is what I would have a woman know—
—and I don't think there is a superstitious article in it.   20

5. Simony: the practice of buying or selling ecclesiastical preferments or other sacred things. Fluxions: effluvia; excesses of blood flowing to some part of the body.

TRAGEDY

Inspired by Shakespeare's *Antony and Cleopatra*, Dryden wrote *All for Love*, a scaled-down, almost domestic version of the story maintaining the dramatic unities and the measured imagery of Restoration verse. Dryden's characters, however, turn out to be great fun. Although a little reminiscent of *Hamlet*'s spooky battlement scenes, Serapion's doomsday tale is a more comfortable set piece; the events he describes, though horrible enough, are at some remove from the telling, and not an immediate, present threat. Consequently, the proper focus of the speech is the audience; it is they who must be made to appreciate, and perhaps fear, the danger. Antony's melancholy, although borrowed from several of Shakespeare's characters, settles quickly into grotesque overindulgence . . . but what a joy. No understatement here: in order to work, the scene must be played to the hilt, complete with throwing oneself to the ground. An acrobatic actor with good concentration and focus can have a great time working this up, and the result might be a refreshing change from overserious melodrama.

Demanding much more restraint is Pierre's enlistment of Jaffeir to the revolutionary cause, in *Venice Preserved*. This can be a rousing speech as it possesses all the required anti-oppressor sentiment, but any overacting must be avoided. The scene is intimate in scope, and should build in intensity slowly as Pierre subtly equates his own complaints with Jaffeir's, winning his trust . . . and sealing the bond with the final operatic oath. Shorter versions may begin with line 24 or 36, and end on line 69.

A perfect companion to Dryden's Antony, his Cleopatra is also given to melodrama and overstatement. What complicates her scene and makes it especially interesting is the very active presence of Ventidius and the rest of Antony's soldiers, making the speech a public presentation quite separate from the intimate parting scene that seems to be going on. Cleopatra, a daring tactician in her own right, skillfully and abruptly changes her mode of approach from rational defense to a plea for death to arrogant dismissal.

Although overplotted and operatic, *Venice Preserved* still provides a splendid array of characters, none of them more striking than Belvidera, daughter to the cruel senator Priuli and wife to the conspirator Jaffeir. Although a model of faithfulness, she manages to emerge a vivid and passionate individual brilliantly portrayed against the deadly politics of Renaissance Venice. In her first scene, Belvidera has discovered Jaffeir's complicity in a revolutionary plot that is to include her father's murder. To dissuade him from participating, she recounts the story of how she had been the victim of attempted rape at the hands of Renault, one of Jaffeir's associates. Her second speech has three parts: her farewell to Jaffeir as he is led to his execution, a private lament, and her complaint to her family and servants who come to take her home. The last two lines are stunning, a surrealistic touch of distraction anticipating a wasting madness to come.

All for Love
by John Dryden
(Act I)

SERAPION

Portents and prodigies are grown so frequent
That they have lost their name.
                              Our fruitful Nile
Flow'd ere the wonted season, with a torrent
So unexpected, and so wondrous fierce,
That the wild deluge overtook the haste
Ev'n of the hinds that watch'd it: men and beasts
Were borne above the tops of trees, that grew
On th'utmost margin of the water-mark.

Then, with so swift an ebb the flood drove backward,
It slipt from underneath the scaly herd: 10
Here monstrous phocae panted on the shore;
Forsaken dolphins there, with their broad tails,
Lay lashing the departing waves: hard by 'em,
Sea-horses flound'ring in the slimy mud,
Toss'd up their heads, and dash'd the ooze about 'em.

Last night, between the hours of twelve and one,
In a lone aisle o' th' temple while I walk'd,
A whirlwind rose, that, with a violent blast,
Shook all the dome: the doors around me clapt;
The iron wicket, that defends the vault,   20
Where the long race of Ptolemies is laid,
Burst open, and disclos'd the mighty dead.

From out each monument, in order plac'd,
An armed ghost start up:
                        the boy-king last

Rear'd his inglorious head.
                              A peal of groans
Then follow'd, and a lamentable voice
Cried, "Egypt is no more!"
                              My blood ran back,
My shaking knees against each other knock'd;
On the cold pavement down I fell entranc'd,
And so unfinish'd left the horrid scene.   30

10. scaly herd: fish.
11. phocae: seals or other members of the seal family or Phocidae.
21. Ptolemies: the dynasty of Egyptian rulers; including Tutankhamen, the "boy-king."
29. entranc'd: in a trance.

All for Love
by John Dryden
(Act I)

ANTONY

They tell me 'tis my birthday, and I'll keep it
With double pomp of sadness.
'Tis what the day deserves, which gave me breath.
Why was I rais'd the meteor of the world,
Hung in the skies, and blazing as I travell'd,
Till all my fires were spent; and then cast downward
To be trod out by Caesar?
                              Count thy gains

Now, Antony, wouldst thou be born for this?
Glutton of fortune, thy devouring youth
Has starv'd thy wanting age.   10
     (Having thrown himself down)
Lie there, thou shadow of an emperor;
The place thou pressest on thy mother earth
Is all thy empire now: now it contains thee;

Some few days hence, and then 'twill be too large,
When thou'rt contractd in thy narrow urn,
Shrunk to a few cold ashes;
                                    then Octavia
(For Cleopatra will not live to see it)
Octavia then will have thee all her own,
And bear thee in her widow'd hand to Caesar;
Caesar will weep, the crocodile will weep,   20
To see his rival of the universe
Lie still and peaceful there.
                                    I'll think no more on't.

Give me some music; look that it be sad:
I'll soothe my melancholy till I swell
And burst myself with sighing.
    (*Soft music*)
'Tis somewhat to my humour.
                                    Stay,
                        I fancy
I'm now turn'd wild, a commoner of nature,
Of all forsaken, and forsaking all;
Live in a shady forest's sylvan scene;
Stretch'd at my length beneath some blasted oak,   30
I lean my head upon the mossy bark,
And look just of a piece as I grew from it:
My uncomb'd locks, matted like mistletoe,
Hang o'er my hoary face; a murm'ring brook
Runs at my foot, the herd comes jumping by me,
And, fearless, quench their thirst, while I look on,
And take me for their fellow-citizen.

More of this image,
                more;
                        it lulls my thoughts.

Venice Preserved
by Thomas Otway
(Act I)

PIERRE

Curse on the common good that's so protected,
Where every slave that heaps up wealth enough
To do much wrong, becomes a lord of right!

I, who believ'd no ill could e'er come near me,
Found in the embraces of my Aquilina
A wretched, old, but itching senator;
A wealthy fool, that had bought out my title,
A rogue that uses beauty like a lambskin,
Barely to keep him warm. That filthy cuckoo, too,
Was in my absence crept into my nest,   10
And spoiling all my brood of noble pleasure.

I drove the rank old bearded Hirco stinking home.
The matter was complain'd of in the Senate;
I, summon'd to appear, and censur'd basely,
For violating something they call privilege—

This was the recompense of my service.
Would I'd been rather beaten by a coward!

A soldier's mistress, Jaffeir, 's his religion;
When that's profan'd, all other ties are broken;
That even dissolves all former bonds of service,   20
And from that hour I think myself as free
To be the foe as e're the friend of Venice—
Nay, dear Revenge, whene'er thou call'st I'm ready.

We have neither safety, unity, nor peace,
For the foundation's lost of common good;

Justice is lame as well as blind amongst us;
The laws (corrupted to their ends that make 'em)
Serve but for instruments of some new tyranny,
That every day starts up to enslave us deeper.

Now could this glorious cause but find out friends   30
To do it right! O Jaffeir! then mightst thou
Not wear these seals of woe upon thy face;
The proud Priuli should be taught humanity,
And learn to value such a son as thou art.

I dare not speak! But my heart bleeds this moment.

I pass'd this very moment by thy doors,
And found them guarded by a troop of villains;
The sons of public rapine were destroying;
They told me, by the sentence of the law,
They had commission to seize all thy fortune,   40
Nay, more,
            Priuli's cruel hand hath sign'd it.

Here stood a ruffian with a horrid face
Lording it o'er a pile of massy plate
Tumbled into a heap for public sale.
There was another making villainous jests
At thy undoing; he had ta'en possession
Of all thy ancient, most domestic ornaments,
Rich hangings intermix'd and wrought with gold;
The very bed which on thy wedding night
Receiv'd thee to the arms of Belvidera,   50
The scene of all thy joys, was violated
By the coarse hands of filthy dungeon villains,
And thrown amongst the common lumber.

Curse thy dull stars and the worse fate of Venice!
Where brothers, friends, and fathers, all are false;

Where there's no trust, no truth; where innocence
Stoops under vile oppression, and vice lords it.

Hadst thou but seen, as I did, how at last
Thy beauteous Belvidera, like a wretch
That's doom'd to banishment, came weeping forth,   60
Shining through tears, like April suns in shower
That labour to o'ercome the cloud that loads 'em;
Whilst two young virgins, on whose arms she lean'd,
Kindly look'd up, and at her grief grew sad,
As if they catch'd the sorrows that fell from her:

Even the lewd rabble that were gather'd round
To see the sight, stood mute when they beheld her,
Govern'd their roaring throats, and grumbled pity.
I could have hugg'd the greasy rogues; they pleas'd me

Rats die in holes and corners, dogs run mad;   70
Man knows a braver remedy for sorrow:

Revenge! the attribute of gods; they stamp'd it
With their great image on our natures.
                            Die?
Consider well the cause that calls upon thee,
And if thou art base enough, die then; remember
Thy Belvidera suffers.
                        Belvidera!

Die—damn first!
                 What! be decently interr'd
In a churchyard, and mingle thy brave dust
With stinking rogues that rot in dirty winding sheets—
Surfeit-slain fools, the common dung o' th' soil?   80

Burn!
First burn, and level Venice to thy ruin!
What! starve like beggar's brats in frosty weather

Under a hedge, and whine ourselves to death!
Thou, or thy cause, shall never want assistance
Whilst I have blood or fortune fit to serve thee;
Command my heart: thou art every way its master.

Swear a little—Swear!
By sea and air! by earth, by heaven and hell,
I will revenge my Belvidera's tears!   90

9. cuckoo: a common superstition held that cuckoos build no nest of their own,
   but leave their eggs to be hatched by other birds, which are then devoured
   by the young cuckoo they have reared.
33. Priuli: a powerful senator and Jaffeir's father-in-law.
73. Die?: Jaffeir makes a suicidal gesture.

All for Love
by John Dryden
(Act II)

CLEOPATRA

Yet may I speak?

How shall I plead my cause, when you, my judge,
Already have condemn'd me?
       Shall I bring
The love you bore me for my advocate?

That now is turn'd against me, that destroys me;
For love, once past, is, at the best forgotten;
but oft'ner sours to hate:
       'twill please my lord
To ruin me, and therefore I'll be guilty.
But, could I once have thought it would have pleas'd you,
That you would pry, with narrow searching eyes,   10
Into my faults, severe to my destruction,
And watching all advantages with care,
That serve to make me wretched?
        You seem griev'd
(And therein you are kind) that Caesar first
Enjoy'd my love, though you deserv'd it better;

I grieve for that, my lord, much more than you;
For, had I first been yours, it would have sav'd
My second choice: I never had been his,
And ne'er had been but yours. But Caesar first,
You say, possess'd my love. Not so, my lord: 20
He first possess'd my person, you, my love:
Caesar lov'd me; but I lov'd Antony.

———

If I endur'd him after, 'twas because
I judg'd it due to the first name of men;
And, half constrain'd, I gave, as to a tyrant,
What he would take by force.

How often have I wish'd some other Caesar,
Great as the first, and as the second young,
Would court my love, to be refus'd for you!

You leave me, Antony; and yet I love you,   30
Indeed I do: I have refus'd a kingdom—
That's a trifle:
For I could part with life, with anything,
But only you.
                   Oh, let me die but with you!
Is that a hard request?

No, you shall go; your int'rest calls you hence;
Yes, your dear int'rest pulls too strong, for these
Weak arms to hold you here.
                              Go; leave me, soldier
(For you're no more a lover); leave me dying:
Push me all pale and panting from your bosom,   40
And, when your march begins, let one run after,
Breathless almost for joy, and cry, "She's dead."

The soldiers shout; you then, perhaps, may sigh,
And muster all your Roman gravity:
Ventidius chides; and straight your brow clears up,
As I had never been.

Here let me breathe my last: envy me not
This minute in your arms: I'll die apace,
As fast as e'er I can, and end your trouble.

17–18. it would . . . choice: it would have saved me the trouble of choosing a
    second lover.
38. Weak arms . . . here: The original text includes the stage direction (*Takes
    his hand*), not a good move in a monologue, but indicating some action.

47–49. The last three lines are particularly difficult as she is supposed to be
      speaking them while clinging to Antony's bosom. If an imaginative so-
      lution is not forthcoming, simply omit "Here let . . . your arms." Inci-
      dentally, her argument succeeds.

Venice Preserved
by Thomas Otway
(Act III, Scene 2)

BELVIDERA

Do.
    strike thy sword into this bosom. Lay me
Dead on the earth, and then thou wilt be safe.

Murder my father!
            though his cruel nature
Has persecuted me to my undoing,
Driven me to basest wants, can I behold him
With smiles of vengeance, butcher'd in his age?
The sacred fountain of my life destroy'd?
And canst thou shed the blood that gave me being?

Nay, be a traitor too, and sell thy country?
Can thy great heart descend so vilely low,   10
Mix with hir'd slaves, bravoes, and common stabbers,
Nose-slitters, alley-lurking villains? Join
With such a crew, and take a ruffian's wages,
To cut the throats of wretches as they sleep?

What's he to whose curst hands last night thou gav'st me?

Was that well done?
            Oh! I could tell a story
Would rouse the lion heart out of its den,
And make it rage with terrifying fury.

Oh my love! if e'er
Thy Belvidera's peace deserv'd thy care,   20
Remove me from this place!
                    Last night, last night!

No sooner wert thou gone, and I alone,
Left in the pow'r of that old son of mischief;
No sooner was I lain on my sad bed,
But that vile wretch approach'd me; loose, unbutton'd,
Ready for violation.
                    Then my heart
Throbb'd with its fears. Oh, how I wept and sigh'd
And shrunk and trembled; wish'd in vain for him
That should protect me.
                    Thou, alas, wert gone!

He drew the hideous dagger forth thou gav'st him,   30
And with upbraiding smiles she said, "Behold, it;
This is the pledge of a false husband's love."
And in my arms then press'd, and would have clasp'd me;
But with my cries I scar'd his coward heart,
Till he withdrew and mutter'd vows to hell.

These are thy friends! with these thy life, thy honour,
Thy love—all's stak'd, and all will go to ruin.

11. bravoes: hired soldiers or assassins.

Venice Preserved
by Thomas Otway
(Act V, Scene 2)

BELVIDERA

Then hear me, too, just heaven!

Pour down your curses on this wretched head
With never-ceasing vengeance;
                                    let despair,
Danger, or infamy, nay all, surround me;
Starve me with wantings; let my eyes ne'er see
A sight of comfort, nor my heart know peace,
But dash my days with sorrow, nights with horrors
Wild as my own thoughts now, and let loose fury
To make me mad enough for what I lose,
If I must lose him.
                        If I must!
                                    —I will not.   10

Oh, turn, and hear me! Leave thy dagger with me;
Bequeath me something.
                                —Not one kiss at parting?

Oh my poor heart, when wilt thou break?
    (JAFFEIR *exits*)
All ill ones sure had charge of me this moment.
Curst be my days, and doubly curst my nights,
Which I must now mourn out in widow'd tears;
Blasted be every herb and fruit and tree;
Curst be the rain that falls upon the earth,
And may the general curse reach man and beast.
Oh, give me daggers, fire, or water!   20
How I could bleed, how burn, how drown, the waves
Huzzing and booming round my sinking head,
Till I descended to the peaceful bottom!

Oh, there's all quiet; here, all rage and fury:
The air's too thin, and pierces my weak brain:
I long for thick, substantial sleep.
                                Hell, hell,
Burst from the centre, rage and roar aloud
If though art half so hot, so mad as I am.

(*Enter* PRIULI *and* SERVANTS)
Who's there?

What?
          To my husband then conduct me quickly.   30
Are all things ready? Shall we die most gloriously?

Say not a word of this to my old father.

Murmuring streams, soft shades, and springing flowers,
Lutes, laurels, seas of milk, and ships of amber.

1. The speech begins abruptly and probably requires some preparation by the
   actress before speaking. Belvidera's words are in response to Jaffeir's blessings
   on her at parting—indicating that the situation really calls for curses.

ROMANCE

Sir Aston Cokain deserves a special section in this volume because he wrote excellent monologues, well-structured speeches for men and women marked by relative simplicity of language, complexity of nuance, and a wide range of emotional possibilities. Also, his works are virtually unknown today. Cokain was described by a critic of his day, Gerard Langbaine, as being "very much addicted to books and the study of poetry," and there can be little doubt that a year's travel through France and Italy helped place him firmly under the influence of continental styles and authors. His writing is sentimental and often languidly sensual, but always adheres—often self-consciously—to traditional classical forms and subjects. *A Masque*, for example, comprises songs, set dances, and formal arguments like the one included here in which the Satyr—a classical woodland figure—confronts the Lars Familiaris, a Roman household god who, a spokesman for home and hearth, has just finished an opening speech of welcome to the audience. The Satyr extols the "Golden Age" of antiquity, his own habitat, and the presumed time of pastoral innocence, and rejects the pressures and jealousies of modern society. It's a familiar theme, but one that subtly infuses much of Cokain's writing with genuine longing for a simpler world, a *Weltschmerz* more appropriate to nineteenth-century Romanticism than to the Restoration. The Satyr must be a convincing spokesman for his cause, and the actor has the option of mocking his captive, civilized audience, or adopting a gentler, sadder attitude, lamenting all poor mortals' lost freedom.

The Obstinate Lady is a romantic comedy packed with unrequited lovers, disguises, near suicides, and other conventional trappings common to the genre—each device developed in some uncommon direction or extended to some unexpected extreme of behavior. Antiphila's letter scene is unique for its deeply unabashed candor. As with most scenes of this type, the letter itself offers immense comic possibilities. The last sentence is addressed to the suitor Phylander, who is about to embark on a spoken equivalent to the poem Antiphila has just read. Carionil, whose self-pity is similar in style to Antony's in the previous section, refuses to be satisfied with theatrical gestures and actually tries to commit suicide. Fortunately, he turns out to be incompetent and fails miserably, managing only to faint at the sight of his own blood. The flood of classical allusions (lines 35 through 49) may be omitted for a shorter version of the speech, but I must caution the actor that verbal pyrotechnics are about the only thing Carionil really does well. Cleanthe is Lucora's sister, here disguised as a boy (Anclethe), and in love with Carionil. She is witness to Carionil's "suicide," thinks he has succeeded, and takes her cue from him—only she is clever enough to be interrupted before she stabs herself. Her performance is entirely controlled, self-conscious, and theatrical.

Horatio's monologue in *Trappolin Supposed a Prince* is, quite simply, a circus act, a tour de force that may be compared with Ira Gershwin's "Tchaikovsky" number in *Lady in the Dark*. While that song is a biographical index of Russian composers, this is a catalogue of Italian cities with an epithet attached to each, with only a blatantly superficial attempt (the first two lines and the closing couplet) to tie it in to the play. The speech has a strong inner rhythm, building to Capua (line 22) and then relaxing to a more leisurely pace, and its success depends on the actor's sensitivity to that rhythm and the variety of attitudes he can command. Paris's discourse on the pleasures of classical death in *The Tragedy of Ovid* appears in a masque within the play, and suggests an alternative to the Puritan hellfire that dominated the period's religious sensibilities. The monologue could be played as a kind of seduction, mildly vampirish perhaps, allowing the actor to present a calm, almost inhuman exterior while conjuring up a clear and active subtext. Clorina, accused of infidelity by her husband Bassanes, protests her innocence in what would be a fairly conventional manner, were it not for one quite macabre

physical detail: Bassanes has instructed the servants to tie fast
Clorina's arms and to fasten her dead alleged lover's heart in
her hands.

> Thus—that she may not close them or remove them;
> And put her paramour's heart into them—so.
> Now, foul adultress! thou may'st contemplate
> Of the affection it did bear thee once—
> Reflect upon the mountain of thy sins,
> Which hath overwhelmed the false Pyrontus! Look!
> Thou most libidinous woman, what a ruin
> Thy lust hath brought upon him and thyself!

Although I would not recommend the use of props here, the
physical circumstances of the scene are among the most
powerful ever created—and are as powerfully overcome by
Clorina, with dignity and passion.

A Masque
by Sir Aston Cokain
SATYR

Friend, forbear!

Thou liv'st among all fears, all noise, all cares,
While I walk merry under heaven's bright eye

We in the fields are free from any sin
Against th' almighty deities of heaven;
We know no law but nature's, do not tremble
At princes' frowns, have neither fear nor hope,
And are content,—a state the gods exceed not.

You languish in a perpetuity
Of thoughts, as unconfin'd as are your ends;   10
You truly lavish all your faculties
In getting covetous wealth, which we contemn.
Your sleeps are starting, full of dreams and fears,
And ours as quiet as the barques in calms.
The youthful spring makes us our beds of flowers,
And heaven-bright summer washeth us in springs
As clear as any of your mistress' eyes.
The plenteous autumn doth enrich our banquets
With earth's most curious fruits, and they unbought.
The healthful winter doth not pain our bones,   20
For we are arm'd for cold and heat in nature.

We have no unkind loves in meads or fields
That scorn our tears, or slight our amorous sighs;
Nor are we frantic with fond jealousy,
The greatest curse Jove could inflict on's Queen
For all her curious search into his life.
We in the woods esteem that beast the stateliest
That hath his head the richliest spread with horns.

The Golden Age remains with us, so fam'd
By your Athenian and Roman poets.   30
Thus we enjoy what all you strive to get
With all the boundless riches of your wit.

12. contemn: despise, disdain, scorn.
14. barques: pleasure boats.
25–28. Jove, chief of the gods in Roman mythology, regularly cheats on his queen,
     Juno, thereby setting horns on her head, the traditional symbol of the
     one being cheated on (though horns on the woman are uncommon). In
     the woods, says the Satyr, there is no jealousy and horns are a mark of
     distinction, presumably to stags.

The Obstinate Lady
by Sir Aston Cokain
(Act I, Scene 3)

ANTIPHILA

(Enter, reading)
"Fair Antiphila hath hair
Would grace the Paphian queen to wear;
Fit to tune heaven's lute withal,
When the gods for music call;
Fit to make a veil to hide
Aurora's blush each morning tide;
Fit to compose a crafty gin
To take the hearts of lookers in;
Able to make the stubborn kin,
And, who dislike it, to be judged blind.   10
Though it is soft and fine, it ties
My heart that it in fetters lies."

It is a neat I know not what—I have not poetry enough
in me to give it a name.
                         These lovers are the prettiest

fools, I think, in the world; and 'twere not for them, I
cannot tell what we women should do. We desire nothing
more than to be praised, and their love to us will do it
beyond our wishes.

        I gave Phylander, upon his long im-
portunity, a lock of hair and see into what a vein it has
put him! I'm sorry he had it not a week sooner; I should   20
then, perhaps, had a sonnet-book ere this.

                  'Tis pity wit
should lie obscurely within any, that a lock will give it
vent. I love him not; I should rather choose his father,
who is as earnest a suitor to me as he. Yet I know, because
of his age, very few ladies would be of my mind;

                       but as
yet I care for neither of them.

        (*Enter* PHYLANDER)

                Now I
must expect an assault. 'Tis in his ear already. He's very
fine.

    You must pardon me now, sir; I must leave you.

2. Paphian queen: Aphrodite; Paphos being a city of Cyprus sacred to the goddess.
7. gin: trap or snare.

The Obstinate Lady
by Sir Aston Cokain
(*Act II, Scene 2*)

CARIONIL

(*Reading*)
"Sir,—I am sorry that, against my use, I cannot answer
you more civilly; but I am blameless, the fault being in
your foolish passion, and not my desire. If in fairer terms
you should receive my reply, I am sure you would think
it some beginning of love to you; according to your desire
I have none, and I wish your love was such as mine, so

we might be friends. Yet I love you as a gentleman of
my acquaintance; but if any more you trouble me with
letters or courting, I will hate you. So I end. —Her
own,
    Lucora."   10

"Her own Lucora!"
                       I cannot now conceive
This lady of a human nature. Sure,
A woman cannot have so harsh a mind.

"So I end!"
               What! Will she end so always?
O, then, that I might end even now! that all
The sorrow that possesseth my whole body
In every member would mutiny against
My heart, that so I might die speedily!

Is it not miraculously strange that this
Poor microcosm, this little body, should   20
Contain all the sorrow this great world can
Inflict upon it, and not sink beneath
So huge a burden? One hill does overcome
The struggling of Enceladus, a giant;
And yet I stand, I live! What! am I of
Lucora's temper—impregnable? Oh-oh-oh!

I'm manly, boy! for women cannot tell
What thing affliction is, their stony hearts
Relent so little at it in their lovers.
O!
   I shall never have her!
                       Now I give   30
Liberty to a just despair to rack me;
And it must ever do so.
                     What a chaos
Of misery is an unfortunate lover!

Would she would love me after I am dead for her!
It were some happiness to think that, Anclethe!
Thou art a good boy; but this lady—O my heart!

Could sitting down in Cassiopeia's chair,
And kicking proud Arctophylax from the sky;
Could stopping the Septentrian sevenfold team,
And putting out the starry eagle's eyes;   40
Could swimming violently up those rocks
From which the Memphian Nilus tumbles down;
Could the compelling of rash Phaeton's sire
To change his course, and run from north to south;
Could the adventuring to undertake
A journey through Africa's dread'st wilderness
When the Aeolians do loudest breathe,
And veil the sun with sandy mountains' height,
Enforce her to repent the tragedy—

By these attempts drawn on me she should find   50
What truth of love was in her servant's mind.

I have prattled too much, but I have done.
No longer shall my happiness be delayed,
Nor the displeased destinies any more
Jeer the sad depth of wretchedness I live in.
Thus—Here I fall, her cruel sacrifice!
    (*Stabs himself*)
Patience, Anclethe! Commend me to Lucora,
That angel beauty without angel pity!
Tell her my woeful story,—how e'er since
Thou knew'st me, I have languished for her;   60
That I have spent whole nights in tears and sighs,
Whole days in solitude, to think of her;
That I did suffer her unkindness, while
I had a dram of patience left with me!

Tell her how her most cruel letter rais'd
A despair higher than my strength, and that
Under her strange unkindness I am fall'n.

Weep not, Anclethe!
                I am faint—struck dumb!

Fly, passionate soul, into Elysium!
  (*He faints*)

37–39. The references in this section are to monumental or cosmic tasks. Cassiopeia is of some importance mythologically as Andromeda's mother; her "chair" is the constellation named after her, and Arctophylax may be a reference to a brilliant new star that appeared in the constellation in 1572 only to disappear again. The Septentrian sevenfold team are the seven stars comprising the constellation of the Great Bear, and the starry eagle is the eagle-star, Altair. Memphian Nilus is the Egyptian Nile, whose source was said to have been hidden as a result of Phaeton's misguided attempt to steer the chariot of the sun, his sire. The Aeolians are the winds.

The Obstinate Lady
by Sir Aston Cokain
(Act II, Scene 2)

CLEANTHE

O, my dear lord!
              brave young Carionil!
I'll wash thy wound with tears, stop it with sighs!

Unkindest day that ever wore the sun!
Thou art accurst, for giving light unto
His hand to guide it to an act so much
Beneath manhood. O me!
              I am undone!
What now will my disguise avail me in,

Foolish sister Lucora?
                          O ye heavens!
Where lies our difference? Are we not the same
By birth on both sides —of one sex? Sure, nature   10
Degenerates against itself, or this
Untimely—O ye gods! I dare not name it,

Nor will I believe it. He is alive!
So suddenly the world cannot be ruin'd;
Which is if he be lost. All virtue gone—
All valour, piety, and everything
Morality can boast of.
                          My lord! noble
Carionil!
            He doth not hear me.
                          Alas!
I am forever most desolate of women.
Injurious heart-strings, break! Why do you tie   20
Me to a life millions of degrees more loathsome
Than the forgetful sepulchre of death?
Would, some commiserating benevolent star,
Which carries fate in't, would, in pity to
My misery, take me from it!
                          For love he
Lies here this bemoaned spectacle, and shall
My passion be undervalued? Tears, nor sighs,
Nor dirges sung by me eternally
Can parallel our loves at full.
                          It must be
The same way, and it shall;
                          the same blade   30
Shall be the instrument, and I receive it
Tragediously here on my knees.
                          Would some
Kind body would inter us in one tomb!
Be firm, my hand, and bold!

Trappolin Supposed a Prince
by Sir Aston Cokain
(Act II, Scene 3)

HORATIO

Let others travel Italy all over,
To talk of such a city, such a place,—

Go to magnificent and holy Rome,
Once the sole empress of the conquer'd world;
To Venice rich, commanding, politic;
Unto sweet Naples, plenteous in ability;
Unto great Milan; unto fat Bologna;
Civil Ferrara, Ariosto's town;
Strong-walled Padua, which Antenor built
The Trojan prince, and Titus Livius fames   10
For his nativity and sepulchre;
To subtle Bergamo, most highly honoured
For near relation to Torquato Tasso;
To proud and stately Genoa, renown'd
By her seafaring citizen Colombo;
Worthy Verona, old Catullus' city;
Bloody Peruggia, warlike Bessia;
Glorious Mantua, Virgilius Maro's birth-place;
Good Rimini, iron Pistoya;
Fine-languag'd Sienna, and industrious Lucca;   20
Odd-humour'd Forly, honest old Ravenna;
Ill-aired Simegallia; Capua,
Effeminate and amorous, wherein
The Carthaginian captain's soldiers were
Spoil'd and debauch'd with pleasures; Pisa hanging;
Pesaro, a garden of best fruits; Ancona
Prais'd for the Port Loyal; and true Urbino,
Round Ascoli, long Recanati, built
Upon a steep hill's ridge; Foligno, full

Of sugry streets, among the Apennine;   30
Faro, for handsome women most extoll'd;
And Modena, happiest of them all,—

From beauteous, comely Florence, when I part
Without Prudentia, thunder strike my heart!

The Tradgedy of Ovid
by Sir Aston Cokain
(Act I, Scene 3)

PARIS
You need not, Maia's son, for I am here.

I had not made such a stay, but was in talk
With my fair Queen in a delicious walk,
Where Agamemnon and the Spartan king,
And all those many Princes they did bring
To fight for the revenge of that fam'd rape,
Did laugh at our discourse, not envy at.

Thrice happy are those shades, where none do hear
Those passions that so tyrannize it here.

The Grecian chieftains have a thousand times   10
Curs'd their own rage that cross'd us in our crimes;
For when their wiser souls were loosen'd from
Their bodies, forc'd unto Elysium
By violent deaths, and clearly understood
Those follies they had sealed with their blood,
Amazement seiz'd upon them all.
                            Our Troy,
Which that so fatal quarrel did destroy,
Had flourish'd still in pomp—all they and we

Had liv'd in peace and in felicity,
And died in our own beds, had they been bless'd   20
T'have had those thoughts wherewith th'are now possess'd.
We are not jealous in those plains of bliss:
They for fruition care not, there, that kiss.

Helen of Greece and I, without despite
To Menelaus' self, take what delight
Pleaseth us there the most.
                              Every one there
Slights those things most they doted upon here.

Our bodies being compos'd of elements,
Incline mankind to seek to please the sense;
But there our spirits, being unconfin'd,   30
Strive at the satisfaction of the mind.
Though souls embrace, they organs want and places
To raise a jealousy at their embraces;

We at our old amours do often laugh.

The Tragedy of Ovid
by Sir Aston Cokain
(Act IV, Scene 2)

CLORINA
I have at large, calling the gods to witness
That what I have told swerv'd not a jot from truth,
Related to you all the particulars
Of his unruly love,
                    —that he surpris'd me—
Came in at my window whilst I was asleep:

With what an horror I was stricken at it
When I perceiv'd 'twas he; how I rail'd at him,

Call'd him by the worst names that I could think on,
Bade him begone for ever from my sight;

That I look'd on him like a basilisk,   10
The ruin of his honour and mine own;

That I would tell you of him, my Bassanes—
Inform you what a devil's company
You kept i' th' likeness of a friend!
                                        Just gods!
Protect my innocence, and by some means
Divine inspire these truths into his heart!

Thrice happy are those souls that from the cares
And slanders of this wicked age are free,
Walk up and down Elysium in their thin
And airy substances, and have them so   20
Transparent that their thoughts may all be seen!
Would mine were such!
                            O that the deities
Would lend their eyes a while to you, that you
Might search, Bassanes, every cranny of
My heart! I do not know a thought I have
I would conceal from you.

PARODIES

In *The Rehearsal*, George Villiers's critique of heroic writing is principally expressed in a play within a play, in which the superhero Volscius meets Parthenope, falls in love, and is tragically spurned, all in about eleven lines. The extended "boot" metaphor provides a wealth of comic business.

Fielding's Grizzle is Princess Huncamunca's suitor, whom she rejects for Tom Thumb; the Ghost is that of Gaffer Thumb, Tom's father and old friend to the king, before whom he appears; Noodle is the tragic messenger, all in *The Tragedy of Tragedies*. Grizzle's two speeches may easily be combined into a single scene, with a turn or some other movement indicating his exit and quick return with the marriage license. The actor playing the Ghost might imagine himself actually surrounded by all the gothic furnishings the scene implies. In Noodle's scene, I have taken the liberty of including some of the king's lines (17–22) in order to make the speech longer. The whole thing is weird enough that it should be possible for the actor either to justify Noodle's saying those lines—or to simply switch roles and become the king for a bit. This is probably the wackiest play ever written, and almost anything should work, provided it is done fully and played straight. The last scene, from *The Historical Register for the Year 1736*, is an auction and Hen is the auctioneer. That the commodities up for sale are intangibles such as "political honesty," "patriotism," and the like affords the actor a multitude of gestural possibilities. Otherwise, the decorum and form of an auction (whether a hushed estate sale at Sotheby's or a Texas hog market) should be observed.

The Rehearsal
by George Villiers, Duke of Buckingham
(Act III, Scene 5)

VOLSCIUS

Bless me! how frail are all my best resolves!

How, in a moment, is my purpose chang'd!
Too soon I thought myself secure from love.

Fair Madam, give me leave to ask her name
Who does so gently rob me of my fame:
For I should meet the army out of town,
And, if I fail, must hazard my renown.
   (PARTHENOPE *gives him her name, then leaves*)
Oh inauspicious stars! that I was born
To sudden love and to more sudden scorn!
   (VOLSCIUS *sits down to pull on his boots*)
How has my passion made me Cupid's scoff!   10
This hasty boot is on, the other off,
And sullen lies, with amorous design
To quit loud fame and make that beauty mine.

My legs, the emblem of my various thought,
Show to what sad distraction I am brought.

Sometimes with stubborn honour, like this boot,
My mind is guarded, and resolv'd to do't:

Sometimes, again, that very mind, by love
Disarmed, like this other leg does prove.

Shall I to Honour or to Love give way?   20

THE TRAGEDY OF TRAGEDIES

"Go on," cries Honour; tender Love says, "Nay!"
Honour aloud commands, "Pluck both boots on";
But softer Love does whisper, "Put on none."

What shall I do? What conduct shall I find
To lead me through this twilight of my mind?

For as bright day with black approach of night
Contending, makes a doubtful, puzzling light,
So does my honour and my love together
Puzzle me so, I can resolve for neither.
    (*Goes out hopping with one boot on, and the other off*)

The Tragedy of Tragedies
or The Life and Death
of Tom Thumb the Great
by Henry Fielding
(*Act II, Scene 5*)

GRIZZLE
Oh, Huncamunca, Huncamunca, oh!

Thy pouting breasts, like kettle-drums of brass,
Beat everlasting loud alarms of joy;
As bright as brass they are, and oh, as hard;
Oh! Huncamunca, Huncamunca, oh!

O Huncamunca, well I know that you
A princess are, and a king's daughter, too.
But love no meanness scorns, no grandeur fears,
Love often lords into the cellar bears,
And bids the sturdy porter come upstairs.   10
For what's too high for love, or what's too low?
Oh! Huncamunca, Huncamunca, oh!

And can my princess Tom Thumb truly wed,
One fitter for your pocket than your bed!

Advis'd by me, the worthless baby shun,
Or you will ne'er be brought to bed of one.

Oh! take me to thy arms, and never flinch,
Who am a man, by Jupiter! ev'ry inch.
Then, while in joys together lost we lie,
I'll press thy soul while gods stand wishing by.   20

Oh! let him seek some dwarf, some fairy miss,
Where no joint-stool must lift him to the kiss.
But, by the stars and glory you appear
Much fitter for a Prussian grenadier;

One globe alone on Atlas' shoulders rests,
Two globes are less than Huncamunca's breasts;
The milky way is not so white, that's flat,
And sure thy breasts are full as large as that.
    (HUNCAMUNCA *responds*)
Ah! speak that o'er again, and let the sound
From one pole to another pole rebound;   30
The earth and sky are each a battledore,
And keep the sound, that shuttlecock, up an hour;

To Doctors Commons for a license I,
Swift as an arrow from a bow, will fly.
My quick return shall to my charmer prove
I travel on the post-horses of love.

31. battledore: racket used in a game played with a shuttlecock similar to
    badminton.

The Tragedy of Tragedies
or The Life and Death
of Tom Thumb the Great
by Henry Fielding
(Act II, Scene 10)

GRIZZLE

Where has my Huncamunca been? See here
The license in my hand!

Tom Thumb, I'm on the rack, I'm in a flame,
Tom Thumb, Tom Thumb, Tom Thumb, you love the name;
So pleasing is that sound, that, were you dumb,
You still would find a voice to cry, "Tom Thumb."

Ha! dost thou own thy falsehood to my face?
Think'st thou that I will share thy husband's place?
Since to that office one cannot suffice,
And since you scorn to dine one single dish on,   10
Go, get your husband put into commission,
Commissioners to discharge (ye gods! it fine is)
The duty of a husband to your Highness.

Yet think not long I will my rival bear,
Or unreveng'd the slighted willow wear;

The gloomy, brooding tempest, now confin'd
Within the hollow caverns of my mind,
In dreadful whirl shall roll along the coasts,
Shall thin the land of all the men it boasts,
And cram up ev'ry chink of hell with ghosts.   20

So have I seen, in some dark winter's day,
A sudden storm rush down the sky's highway,

Sweep through the streets with terrible ding dong,
Gush through the spouts, and wash whole crowds along.
The crowded shops the thronging vermin screen,
Together cram the dirty and the clean,
And not one shoe-boy in the street is seen.

11–13. Grizzle is suggesting that Huncamunca authorize (commission) Thumb
to find others more capable (commissioners) to be entrusted with her
pleasure.
15. slighted willow: symbol of unrequited love, also associated with pliability.

The Tragedy of Tragedies
or The Life and Death
of Tom Thumb the Great
by Henry Fielding
(Act III, Scenes 1 and 2)

GHOST
Hail! ye black horrors of midnight's midnoon!

Ye fairies, goblins, bats, and sceech-owls, hail!

And, oh! ye mortal watchmen; whose hoarse throats
Th'immortal ghosts' dread croakings counterfeit,
All hail!
        Ye dancing phantoms, who, by day,
Are some condemn'd to fast, some feast in fire,
Now play in churchyards, skipping o'er the graves,
To the loud music of the silent bell,
All hail!
        I am a ghost;

Would I were something more, that we again   10
Might feel each other in the warm embrace,

Oh! Now prepare to hear—which but to hear
Is full enough to send thy spirit hence.

Thy subjects up in arms, by Grizzle led,
Will, ere thy rosy-finger'd morn shall ope
The shutters of the sky, before the gate
Of this thy royal palace, swarming spread.
So have I seen the bees in clusters swarm,
So have I seen the stars in frosty nights,
So have I seen the sand in windy days,   20
So have I seen the ghosts on Pluto's shore,
So have I seen the flowers in spring arise,
So have I seen the leaves in autumn fall,
So have I seen the fruits in summer smile,
So have I seen the snow in winter frown.

Arthur, beware! I must this moment hence,
Not frighted by your voice, but by the cocks!
Arthur beware, beware, beware, beware!
Strive to avert thy yet impending fate;
For, if thou'rt kill'd today,   30
Tomorrow all thy care will come too late.

27. Not frighted by your voice: the king has interrupted the Ghost's catalogue
of metaphors.

The Tragedy of Tragedies
or The Life and Death
of Tom Thumb the Great
by Henry Fielding
(Act III, Scene 10)

NOODLE
Oh! monstrous, dreadful, terrible. Oh! Oh!

Deaf be my ears, for ever blind my eyes!
Dumb be my tongue! feet lame! all senses lost!
Howl wolves, grunt bears, hiss snakes, shriek all ye ghosts!

I mean, my liege,
Only to grace my tale with decent horror.

Whilst from my garret, twice two stories high,
I look'd abroad into the streets below,
I saw Tom Thumb attended by the mob;
Twice twenty shoe-boys, twice two dozen links,   10
Chairmen and porters, hackney-coachmen, whores.

Aloft he bore the grizzly head of Grizzle;

When of a sudden thro' the streets there came
A cow, of larger than the usual size,
And in a moment—guess, oh! guess the rest!—
And in a moment swallow'd up Tom Thumb.

Shut up again the prisons, bid my treasurer
Not give three farthings out—hang all the culprits,
Guilty or not—no matter—ravish virgins;
Go bid the schoolmasters whip all their boys;   20
Let lawyers, parsons, and physicians loose
To rob, impose on, and to kill the world.

Her majesty the queen is in a swoon.

10. links: link-boys, torch carriers.

The Historical Register
for the Year 1736
by Henry Fielding
(Act I)

HEN

Madam, I am just mounting the pulpit. I hope you like the catalogue, ladies?

I dare swear, gentlemen and ladies, this auction will give general satisfaction. It is the first of its kind which I ever had the honor to exhibit, and I believe I may challenge the world to produce some of the curiosities which this choice cabinet contains: a catalogue of curiosities which were collected by the indefatigable pains of that celebrated virtuoso, Peter Humdrum, Esquire, which will be sold by auction, by Christopher Hen, on Monday the 21st day of March, beginning at Lot 1.

Gentlemen and ladies, this is Lot 1: a most curious remnant of political honesty.

Who puts it up, gentlemen? It will make you a very good cloak. You see it's both sides alike, so you may turn it as often as you will. Come—five pounds for this curious remnant. I assure you, several great men have made their birthday suits out of the same piece. It will wear forever and never be the worse for wearing. —Five pounds is bid. Nobody more than five pounds for this curious piece of political honesty? Five pound. No more? (Knocks) Lord Both-Sides.

—Lot 2. A most delicate piece of patriotism, gentlemen. Who bids? Ten pounds for this piece of patriotism?

Sir, I assure you several gentlemen at court have

worn the same. 'Tis a quite different thing within to what it is without. You take it for the old patriotism, whereas it is indeed like that in nothing but the cut, but, alas! sir, there is a great difference in the stuff. But, sir, I don't propose this for a town suit. This is only proper for the country. Consider, gentlemen, what a figure this will make at an election. Come—five pound? One   30 guinea?

     (Silence)

        Put patriotism by.

               Lot 3. Three grains of modesty. Come, ladies, consider how scarce this valuable commodity is. —Half a crown for all this modesty? —Is there not one lady in the room who wants any modesty? It serves mighty well to blush behind a fan with, or to wear under a lady's mask at a masquerade.

     (Silence)

        What? Nobody bid?

             Well, lay modesty aside.